# SPINNING HISTORY

# SPINNING HISTORY

Politics and Propaganda in
World War II

## NATHANIEL LANDE

Skyhorse Publishing

Skyhorse Publishing books may be purchased in bulk at special discounts for sales promotion, corporate gifts, fund-raising, or educational purposes. Special editions can also be created to specifications. For details, contact the Special Sales Department, Skyhorse Publishing, 307 West 36th Street, 11th Floor, New York, NY 10018 or info@skyhorsepublishing.com.

Skyhorse® and Skyhorse Publishing® are registered trademarks of Skyhorse Publishing, Inc.®, a Delaware corporation.

Visit our website at www.skyhorsepublishing.com.

10 9 8 7 6 5 4 3 2 1

Library of Congress Cataloging-in-Publication Data is available on file.

Cover design by Rain Saukas

Print ISBN: 978-1-5107-1586-8
Ebook ISBN: 978-1-5107-1587-5

Printed in the United States of America

# Contents

⎯⎯⎯∞∞∞⎯⎯⎯

# Prologue

If you lived through the 1930s and 1940s and had an interest in the world around you, you may have been aware that political, military, and media leaders used elements of drama and social psychology in the course of World War II. Many still remembered the devastating toll taken by World War I, and governments sought the most effective means of shaping emotions and opinions in this new conflict. Leaders orchestrated and shaped what was an ongoing, evolving history, creating a theatrical framework on both the home front and the front lines by applying elements of drama and new technologies that formed a consensual reality, a reality that fueled a media and entertainment industry that in turn—sometimes subtly, sometimes loudly—manipulated and maintained the illusions within and surrounding the war. All sides employed a variety of theatrical devices, each determined to ensure a hit. As in the theater, they competed with one another to make an impression, to secure and hold the audience's interest, to arouse desire, and to provoke a response.

From the National Socialist blueprint—the Hitler script that was *Mein Kampf* and the elaborate, extravagantly staged Nazi performances at the Nuremberg rallies—to stirring British oratory and radio propaganda, to Roosevelt's outmaneuvering of the isolationists on the home front, dramaturgy played a vital role in an event of global consequence.

In their influential work on symbolic interaction, Michael Overington and Iain Mangham document that the parallels between theater and warfare are unmistakable and of vital importance, so that under the direction of political leaders, the rigorous application of theatrical devices created a war-entertainment machine in America and Europe that took on a life of its own.

The broader notion that life and theater resemble one another is by no means just a twentieth- or twenty-first century one; it can be traced back to the dramatic unities of Aristotle and Shakespeare. But in WWII, this dramatic perspective took a new form, and leaders elevated spin to achieve their ends. Media was integrated with politics, spinning a tapestry the world had not yet seen.

In terms of history, drama was used to service this spin, to build a workers' or citizens' army, to obtain arms, to inspire fighting courage, for land and ideals, for a new society; for a Motherland forged in the Great Patriotic War; a Fatherland built on a utopian platform of world domination.

The freedoms built into America's arsenal for democracy, the spirit of Avalon carried by the Commonwealth, the collective reforms in the USSR, the National Socialist German Workers Party, were led by master dramatists.

Winston Churchill, Franklin Roosevelt, Adolf Hitler, and Joseph Stalin functioned, as it were, as theatrical entrepreneurs, writer-directors who wrote, enacted, and implemented their own script. Hitler's grand drama for his Third Reich began in the early 1930s. His intuitive understanding of staging and theatrics helped capture an entire nation. For the British, a meticulously realized theatrical structure was used to convince a country, alone against Hitler, of the need and, crucially, of their ability to fight and win an ultimate struggle. In the United States, where both cultural tradition and political pressure were urging Americans to remain firmly backstage, the act of engagement was a high priority for those who needed, by chance or circumstance, to be on the marquee.

Stalin's rise was more brutal and less dramatic. He had to apply propaganda to establish his image in the eyes of the public. He had cities named after him; history books were rewritten presenting him as a leader playing a prominent role in the revolution of the Soviet Union and building him to the status of a mythological legend. Controlling media, he had his name included in the Soviet national anthem. Propaganda could build his revolution, but only if the masses rallied behind one another, transforming the message produced by his media machine into reality.

• • •

Erwin Goffman, a pioneer of impression management, argued that war, viewed in terms of a theatrical production, demonstrates that reality is or at least can be a reflection of dramatic intrusion. In other words, during wartime, life imitates art in dramatic ways. On all sides at all times during the war, strenuous efforts were made to provoke an emotional response and reaction from the audience. It was a time of costume and conflict, set and soliloquy, music and march, all this underscoring that war, while horribly real, could also be seen as a vast, epic drama, one created to enable populations to accept and cope with a terrifying reality.

As in a wartime film about adventurous aviators or a heroic king on the fields of Agincourt, a theatrical framework allowed political and military leaders to be supported by the entertainment and communications media, to structure the events of the war within accepted and understood dramatic conventions. Each sought to harness their own and the collective national energy to uplift and sustain the morale of their people—and also to chasten, even silence, critics.

• • •

In this war, had you been a general, part of your training would have been to learn to master both tactical skills and, more importantly, strategic ones, to manipulate and guide the behavior of your cast members, soldiers and civilians, in a manner that undermined or rewrote the enemy's script, that enacted their own and used it to advance their cause.

If you had been a foot soldier on the front lines, you would have performed in uniform and played a highly risky but decisive role in a drama that demanded an emotional response from its audience back home.

If you were trapped with the British Expeditionary Force on the Western Front in France, you may have been dramatically rescued by the *Royal Daffodil* or the *Bluebird of Chelsea*, part of a courageous armada of small fishing craft, steamers, and ferries that took you back to England during the evacuation of Dunkirk and been one of the men who made it back home. You would have participated in what is often celebrated by the Brits, and called the Miracle of Dunkirk, with incalculable misfortune for the German forces.

In one of the stranger twists of World War II, Hitler's armored units, seemingly on the verge of a stunning victory, suddenly halted their advance on Dunkirk. According to some accounts, Hermann Göring wanted to take a share of the spotlight and impress Hitler and boasted that his Luftwaffe alone could destroy the trapped troops by attacking from the air. But weather interceded.

The British could hardly believe their luck.

• • •

Göring's planes were hampered by cloudy weather and then struck by British pilots flying their new Spitfires, buying time for the troops waiting on the beach and at Dunkirk harbor. After a two-day wait, realizing that Göring couldn't live up to his plan so easily, Hitler ordered his armored columns to move on Dunkirk, but by this time, nearly the entire British Expeditionary Force had escaped by sea, knowing that someday, somewhere, they would fight Hitler again.

Had you been part of Operation Fortitude, a crucial misdirection strategy staged in parallel with the 1944 D-Day invasion, you would have been an actor taking part in an elaborate deception, complete with sets that were constructed with make-believe equipment. Thousands of inflated rubber tanks and landing craft, dummy airfields, and a mass of decoy lighting were placed at diversionary departure points. This was pure theater. Perhaps you would have added a public presence as you and General George S. Patton made appearances for bogus daily inspections. The Allies depended on Berlin to conduct aerial surveillance, and Hitler was convinced the plan was authentic, that Patton would indeed lead the invasion, landing at Calais. The deception worked. The invasion was in fact directed by Dwight Eisenhower and the landings were staged over two hundred miles away.

If you had crossed the English Channel and fought on the beaches of Normandy, you would have been part of a mighty road company with a cast of thousands. Thirty-eight convoys of 745 ships, with four thousand craft, landed 185,000 of your fellow soldiers and twenty thousand vehicles in three days. One thousand aircraft dropped another eighteen thousand paratroopers. Thousands of trucks and tanks with tons of supplies landed on the bloodstained beaches of Omaha, Utah, Juno, Sword, and Gold. This was an impersonal striking assault of force, and in the havoc of man and machine, a correspondent named Ernie Pyle wrote about horror, bravery, and sadness, impacting readers in a different way. Far more intimate than patriotic victories. If you had been along with Ernie on those beaches, you would have been witness to a personal and heartbreaking commentary that you might never forget: "It was a lovely day for a stroll."

If you had been Jewish and lived in Europe, in all probability you would have gone to a concentration camp. If you were among the "lucky" ones, you might have ended up in Terezín, a place promoted as "Hitler's gift to the Jews," where you would unwittingly perform a part in an international performance. In return for your safety, you, along with the chosen few of Europe's Jewry—among them artists and musicians, veterans of WWI, aristocrats and statesmen, and those who had distinguished themselves as lawyers, professors, and doctors—would have turned over your home, any works of art, and other assets in your possession. For this you would have found for yourself and your family a home, a safe haven in which to sit out the war. Arriving in your finest livery, with the expectation of comfortable, not to say luxurious, living standards, complete with a spa, you were confronted with the shocking reality. Conditions were appalling and you had merely secured for yourself a temporary stay at a transition camp from which you would, in all likelihood, eventually be transported to a work and extermination camp in the east: Auschwitz-Birkenau. If you had not already been shipped out by this stage, you would have witnessed an international inspection, conducted by the International Red Cross, to promote world opinion that the German soul was indeed deeply compassionate. In the course of the preceding days and weeks the camp had been carefully refurbished and beautified, becoming a Potemkin village where the Nazis staged a spin scam of spectacular proportions and temporary success.

If you were a music-loving child at Terezín at this time, you might have been chosen to take part in a children's opera, one that was joyfully performed for the occasion. But afterward you would have been sent on a transport on the railway line extended for this purpose, freighted without hope, to the gas chambers of Auschwitz.

If you were a patriotic German living in the Fatherland, you may have been awestruck by the cathedral of lights at the Nuremberg rallies, at the torchlight parades and Thingplätze, capacious arenas constructed to stage events that embodied Teutonic culture, productions that climaxed with a representation of the führer descending as your god on a dramatic device, an Aryan deus ex machina. Had you been at a particular Munich performance, you might have been so engaged as to be one of the three hundred thousand inspired to join the Nazi Party the next day.

Had you been a general or German statesman at Wannsee, a stunning lakeside setting near Berlin, you would have watched Reich Protector Reinhard Heydrich, architect of the Holocaust, inaugurating the plans for the Final Solution, and then afterward you might have refreshed yourself without a care, enjoying the leisurely activities of the weekend.

There again, you may have been in Washington, and enlisted in Roosevelt's platoon of poets, headed by laureate Archibald MacLeish, joining one of the alphabet of organizations that helped to script the war effort.

In the Soviet Union, you may have fought along with General Georgy Zhukov, who reached heroic status culminating in the Battle of Berlin.

Or back in London, you might have participated in one of Churchill's brilliant "black" propaganda productions at Electra House where bogus radio stations transmitted broadcasts to Germany in perfect German, soap operas and concerts, while disseminating news, real and invented.

On the bombed-out home front in London, you would have heard Vera Lynn trilling "A Nightingale Sang in Berkeley Square" and "I'll Be Seeing You," or Gracie Fields belting out "There'll Always Be an England," as you waited for the lights to go on again all over the world. You would have heard music in the background taking you to another place, a hopeful time. You may have wondered, *Is this not the stuff of drama?*

As a witness to history unfolding before your eyes, you would have seen the shaping of World War II in dramatic terms to fit your country's needs for national survival and military dominance.

You might also have taken a part as a narrator. If you had been a correspondent embedded in World War II, for instance, you would have used radio, newsreels, and print to report from up close and personal an evolving drama to a distant audience back home. You would have been part of a company of correspondents, an interpreter of a war, a player in a theatrical event that was controlled partly by the producers of the play. In the theater of national and international politics, sociologist Peter Hall writes, "No issue really develops without some staging around a dramatic event."

• • •

Governments used oratory and entertainment to establish a framework that would support their respective wartime finales both in the theater of warfare and the theater surrounding and supporting this war, to inspire the home front audience. All sides needed this painstakingly constructed framework for the war.

Politics and propaganda are well-suited—in fact, intimate—companions. "In Wartime," Winston Churchill told Franklin Roosevelt, "truth is so precious that she should always be attended by a bodyguard of lies." This particular war involved "tangle within tangle, conflict within conflict, plot and counter plot, ruse and treachery, cross and double cross, true agent, false agent, double agent, gold and steel, the bomb, the dagger, costume and deception, and the firing party interwoven in many a texture so intricate as to be incredible and yet true."

It cannot be denied that war resembles theater. It cannot be denied that propaganda, in the various strands of the media, influences and shapes actual events and real conflicts. Each member of the audience must come to see that any given war can be better understood by considering the theatricality, the artifice, and the underlying truths as the drama unfolds.

One politician who discussed the connection between propaganda, politics, and theater was Edmund Burke, the eighteenth-century Irish statesman and political theorist. Born in Dublin, after moving to London he served as a member of Parliament, and came to see the stage as a powerful medium for interaction between manners and attitudes, and as a mirror of contemporary society. The stage was not only a reflection of life, but also a performance of life itself. Burke believed that drama was an education for the political statesman: politicians should analyze and treat men in much the same way as a dramatist does.

Central to this belief was the idea that the stage provided an insight into the motives of human beings in political situations. The stage could actually teach political actors how to make use of men and situations imaginatively. Great statesmen often knew the history of the stage and were well versed in all its techniques.

The war had many inherently theatrical aspects, including masterful mise en scène by the leaders, and propaganda was only one aspect of the production. The huge audiences for radio, motion pictures, and print media, as well as radical innovations in applicable technology, made this a very different war on the home front and the front lines.

The connection between theater and war is immediately evident in what is often a shared vocabulary: the war took place in the European theater and the Pacific theater; etymologically, "troupe" and "troops" are the same word; a successful show is a hit. But of course the parallels run much deeper, including seven fundamental categories:

1. Theater is a structure for ideas. War is a structure for ideology.
2. In theater, actors play characters. In war, people "play" soldiers.
3. Theater is performance. War is performance.
4. Theater is live. War is live.
5. Theater involves a scripted play. War follows a staging plan.
6. Theater uses props and costumes. War uses weapons and uniforms.
7. Theater has a director, a play with conflict, and an audience. War has a general, a script with conflict, and an audience.

• • •

Four leaders scripted the production in the European Theater of War. Each had his distinctive personality and little tolerance for interference. Franklin Roosevelt, hiding his steel leg braces worn since childhood, cloaked his masterful temperament in an amicable manner. Winston Churchill was much more tenacious, short, round, rosy, a mighty man in the trenches, a mighty talker, whose eloquent speech lisped in private conversation but knew no hesitation before a public or parliament in the ringing rhythms of Milton and the King James Bible. Adolf Hitler, dogmatic, ruthless, his character etched by ambition, feeling anchored in stone, and a persona framed by pose and posture, had little appeal except a rare jig, or a fondness for pretty ladies and well-behaved children, yet he proved an electrifyingly charismatic orator. And Joseph Stalin, the man of steel from Georgia, shrewd and silent, a master of secret service and intelligence, often quiet, but an expert manipulator achieving his grand ambition for Soviet society.

Such differences were not strange for leaders who did not come to power by accident. They had forced their way to the top because they were rulers by will and temperament, reaching their eminence, truly foreboding in responsibility, from such different backgrounds and such different processes. Two of the representatives of democracies had aristocratic heritage. Churchill liked to think of himself as half American, but he was English in every fiber of this being and every turn of thought. Hitler, while aspiring to some artistic appreciation, fell short from the canvas, born in modest surroundings, a failed artist and hollow bohemian who became a ruthless street fighter led by fanatical instinct. His intellect had no scholarly timbre.

In their lives and thought and view of government there was no common ground between Roosevelt and Churchill, Hitler and Stalin, except that they were adept politicians, gaining control of their respective governments, the president by free election, the prime minister by circumstance, the German leader by treachery, and Stalin by cunning manipulation.

Here the commonality ends. Roosevelt typified the oldest America. His Groton-Harvard-Hyde Park background was as remote from Hitler's as the White House was from Berchtesgaden. Churchill's childhood landscape was the estate at Blenheim Palace. His Marlborough heritage, his education at Harrow, were fitting for a man of honor. Stalin's early years were spent in a seminary, until his cunning and determination led him on the path to power. Hitler was the son of an illegitimate father, a product of a state public school, a *Volksschule* rooted in discipline and Austrian/German nationalism, and ultimately a product of his manifesto, *Mein Kampf*.

Neither Churchill, nor Roosevelt, nor Stalin could imagine such a focused fanatic, a conspirator who in singular focus, organized revolt, and revolution had taken control of a land that had produced some of the most respected scientists and composers, artists, and writers. He would go on to write a masterful if deranged script for its destiny, its future history.

Historical drama does not stand still, however. Sooner or later, even for each of the conquerors with whom Hitler not unreasonably classified himself—Caesar, Alexander, Napoleon—the curtain must fall. For him as for them, it would fall on a tragedy.

# Behind the Scenes in a Sundered Country: The Nazis Set the Stage in the European Theater

In war, the boundary between actor and audience is more ambiguous than it seems. The roles in a live performance continually change. While a government and its leaders frame scenes to which the public will respond, the public's response gives the event its validity.

—Conor Cruise O'Brien

*Without any acknowledgement of their contribution to Germany, the Jewish population is presented as an enemy of the people, a useful concept Hitler advances to gain stage presence. He identifies them vividly, with a yellow star, dehumanizing, degrading, and adding a flourish of visual potency.*

*The People's Choric Theater is established as a highlight of prewar National Socialism. Taking its lessons from the Germans Piscator and Brecht, who reimagined "epic theater" with its use of the Greek chorus, the People's Choric Theater takes over stages nationwide as Goebbels produces a play called* The Road to the Third Reich, *with its inspiring tale of a Teutonic knight who returns from war abroad to find his Fatherland taken over by political opportunists.*

*Joseph Goebbels, heading the Ministry of Public Enlightenment and Propaganda, meets with Hitler every day. The minister is a small man, but when standing always reaches to be taller. His shifting, darting eyes blink incessantly, so much so he is called "der blink" in inner circles. He is fond of his uniform, and his actions are well defined. The ministry grows steadily and Joseph Goebbels directs all media. Radio is exploited to its full potential with radio companies receiving grants from the government to build cheaper receivers.*

*Lighting, posters, drums, patriotic songs, precision-marching troops dressed in a wardrobe of brown shirts, black boots, gray tunics, medals, and ribbons, are part of the stagecraft that reinforces the message.*

*Then, the collaborators stage their most dramatic event—Nuremberg— with a highly effective, stirring drama to inspire the masses. Theirs is a political movement in a great hurry, losing no time in establishing its own glittering mythology with a calendar of feast days. All the swastika-draped occasions are planned to coincide with the Reich's favorite holidays, a congeries of Christian, pagan, and traditional German celebration. Recast as the Holy Spirit, Hitler joins the Holy Trinity, and from "The Night of the Long Knives" to "Kristallnacht," from the grotesque artifice of Theresienstadt to the horrors coolly calculated at Wannsee, the stage for the globally devastating drama is set.*

• • •

When writing about any other country, a military historian might begin with its history and people, the architecture, the atmosphere; but in Germany, one would have to begin and end with politics. Its political landscape is as fascinating as anything nature has created, the formidable mountain fortresses of the Alps notwithstanding.

In Berlin, above the treetops of the Tiergarten, gleamed the golden figure of an immense Winged Victory celebrating a series of Prussian triumphs over the French, Danes, Austrians, and Bavarians. The statue's sandstone blocks supported a two-hundred-foot column, ringed with the barrels of French cannons captured in the Danish-Prussian War. It has been a Victory Column looking over Berlin, its subsequent wars, its politics, and a symbol of a cultural capital.

During the 1920s, the whole world camped out on the doorstep of the city, attending theater, arguing about art in Kurfürstendamm cafés, and listening to music. Summing up the charm of Berlin, the phrase *Berliner Luft*, the "air of Berlin," comes to mind. The meaning is also a matter of intangibles—the singing in beer gardens, the citizens' incessant joke-telling, and the spirit of the time. All of these had a heady effect on the quality of life.

But before the Nazis rose to power in 1933, Berlin under the Weimar Republic was a city of social contrast, and theater. In Berlin, the English and Americans came and went in droves. Playwright Christopher Isherwood, author of *Goodbye to Berlin*, gave English lessons and in return received life lessons. Paul Whiteman and his orchestra received ovations at the Philharmonic; Josephine Baker, dressed only in a bunch of bananas, caused a sensation at the Nelson Revue. Shortly before, Albert Einstein and Max Planck had been teaching physics at the Kaiser Wilhelm Institute. Siemens Electrical Engineering Company was sparking, and Krupp was producing steel at the height of the golden age.

After the German defeat in World War I, with inflation wildly out of control, Germany's golden era was a heroic but threadbare age of the *Threepenny Opera* by Bertolt Brecht and Kurt Weill, of Josef von Sternberg's *The Blue Angel* with Marlene Dietrich. Theater was influenced by Max Reinhardt and Erwin Piscator, who specialized in the atmosphere of illusion. Their innovative techniques included revolving stages, treadmills, and the use of the theater as a vehicle for social reportage. Actors paraded around with placards and signs, newsreel footage was projected to complement the drama onstage, and on one occasion there was the sound of simulated heartbeats.

Visitor and Berliner alike could go to a different play or opera every night as well as attend notably different performances where tradition was challenged and mores became unbuttoned. There were beer gardens, plays and operas, vaudeville and cabarets where Marlene Dietrich displayed her incredible legs and in a smoky voice sang "Ich bin von Kopf bis Fuss auf Liebe eingestellt" to an enchanted and appreciative cabaret audience.

In the great parks, Berliners took Sunday strolls over bridle paths, past lakes with wild ducks and small winding streams that led to the Victory Mall, where Germany's conquering heroes, kings, princes, and generals stood in splendid array, dressed as cavalry gentlemen with tunic and sword.

Nearby, at its northernmost edge, stood the ornate, domed Reichstag, home of the German parliament, which withstood the ravages of time until it fell victim to a mysterious fire, which among other things ushered in the rise of a man from humble origins to formidable power, from struggling young Austrian artist to chancellor of Germany. He needed an excuse, he needed to assert an iron grip on the whole of Germany, and he needed more than a fire to fan the will of the German people.

Eventually, the marginalized people drawn to German nationalism found it impossible to adjust to a democratic Germany. The majority were nihilists, super-patriots, militarists, and thugs, forming the backbone of the Nazi Party who declared war on the avant-garde, the Jews, the Bolsheviks, anything that was not identifiably Teutonic.

With spin, the county would adopt a directed consciousness to influence perception of people and events, a confluence of professional communication, public relations, impression management, and propaganda, creating a unified public perception that would in time drive a war.

The German army took notice and rehearsed using costumes and props, playing war in backyard playgrounds and sand-boxes. Under the terms of the Treaty of Versailles, the German army was limited to one hundred thousand troops, and modern weapons were barred. The victorious Allies limited a defeated Germany to a skeletal self-defense force, one without offensive potential. Or so they thought.

There were some who did not want to follow the imposed restrictions, notably the highest-ranking officer in the Reichswehr, a defense force from 1918 until 1935, General Hans von Seeckt. Von Seeckt appeared as an "old-fashioned" Prussian military man with a monocle, his costume projecting a comforting if slightly ludicrous image. Beneath this exterior, however, was a man intent upon restoring Germany to its former military prowess. Indeed, he skillfully circumvented the Versailles Treaty's rules and created a well-schooled force of bright, physically rugged enlisted men who signed on for a twelve-year tour. It was all a deception. Von Seeckt was planning for the emergence of National Socialism.

With the equipment of modern warfare beyond his grasp, the general used props to choreograph his troops in conflict. His soldiers constructed ersatz tanks by housing automobiles in covers made of canvas, cardboard, and tin. Wooden anti-tank and anti-aircraft guns were hewn to perfectly resemble their authentic counterparts. Targets for gunners were built from Black Forest pine and balloons. To disguise his long-term plans, in newsreels projected in Germany and abroad, von Seeckt participated in publicity campaigns designed to show army personnel learning occupational skills as a prelude to re-entering the civilian workforce. While von Seeckt was nurturing the nucleus of the most powerful war machine the world had ever seen, the nations that had defeated Germany a decade before laughed at his army's efforts to free themselves from the shackles of Versailles.

Then, on February 27, 1933, a scene of expansive dramatic proportions was scripted with a fire set by an arsonist that raged through the Reichstag, and the fire inflamed support for Hitler's National Socialist Party in the subsequent elections. Following Chancellor Paul von Hindenburg's death on August 2, 1934, Hitler assumed the role of German head of state, consolidating Nazi power. In his first foreign policy statements, Hitler lodged a protest after Berlin's most prominent building was set alight: "Whoever lights the torch of war in Europe can wish for nothing but chaos." The plausibility of Hitler's pacific foreign policy melted when he repudiated the Versailles Treaty and jettisoned the ban on German rearmament. Von Seeckt's troops constituted the core of noncommissioned officers at the center of the German army, renamed the *Wehrmacht*.

Alarmed by this resurgence of German militarism, France, Britain, and America's President Roosevelt reprimanded the newly installed führer. Hitler used a device with which he had become familiar during his *Sturm und Drang* ("Storm and Stress") years while fighting the left: a bold lie. Promising each expansion of the German military would be the last, he constructed plans for a loud war machine, stronger than those of any potential adversary. Paradoxically, as Germany rearmed, diplomatic protests from the allies of World War I became a whisper. But it all soon became a shout coupled with pomp and circumstance reminiscent of Imperial Germany. Adolf Hitler, aggrandizer of the Reich, celebrated his birthday. Diplomats of "friendly" nations, including the US chargé d'affaires, signed the register at the grand new Chancellery.

His Majesty the King of England sent the führer the birthday greetings he customarily sent to all rulers. Church bells rang from swastika-decorated churches as the day began. Labor Front leader, Dr. Robert Ley, presented the führer with a Volkswagen, an inexpensive, German-manufactured car not yet available to the public. From the more military-minded came birthday gifts of pistols, hand grenades, an assortment of knives and daggers, and a live eagle, which the führer released into the Bavarian mountains.

Due attention was given to proper dress. One practiced in stagecraft knew the value of such things—costumes carry an impression. When Hitler came to power, Germany suddenly blossomed out into a wide variety of uniforms. Hitler preferred brown khaki. His generals: Herman Göring, a loose-fitting gray tunic; Reinhard Heydrich, a more slimming line with black stripes to show off his tall good looks. No matter the fabric, each uniform was highlighted with a red armband with a circle of white, with a black swastika at its center. No expense was spared. Heinrich Himmler demanded black and commissioned Hugo Boss in Bavaria to design and manufacture uniforms for the SS, the Schutzstaffel, a major paramilitary organization under Adolf Hitler.

Uniforms in the military, as on stage, were designed to command authority, to instill superiority, to create an impression, to instill fear, to project power.

There were Stormtroopers in brown, SS men in black, the Labor Corps in green, Hitler Youth in shorts, brown shirts, and Sam Browne belts, and the young ladies of the BDM (Bund Deutscher Mädel, the League of German Girls) in black skirts and white blouses; there even were the Pimpfe, the cub scouts of the Nazi movement, dressed in black as mini-SS men. They all thronged in crowds: "We want to see our Führer!"

Along with uniform, Hitler knew that a dramaturge must craft a script to express some aspect of reality, some measure of experience, some vision or conviction about the world. Like any artist, he shaped his personal vision of many experiences into an organized script that was more than words on a page: it was a blueprint of a special kind of experience created to appeal as much to the ear as to the eye. He spent much time practicing gestures before a mirror, to be effective, to give emphases, to dramatically persuade. He effected a technique that began before he ever took to the stage, usually using the rhythm of a battery of synchronized drums, beating slowly then building in tempo, and when the masses were ready, he came onstage, saying nothing at first, posing and looking over the thousands in attendance, and then speaking very quietly, as the crowd leaned forward to hear every word, and then in an almost hypnotized cadence, raised his voice to a feverish pitch, making every point emphatically, with the crowd chanting "Sieg Heil" in unison.

It was the proud, often mythical past that Hitler himself would turn to in creating his production—he had a paranoid and unremitting hatred for any cultural creation or movement more modern than that of the Wagner era. *Kulturpolitik* was high on his list of priorities.

Indeed, the destruction of Germany began in Berlin not with the first air raids of World War II, but with the burning of books in Berlin on May 10, 1933. On that notorious occasion, on the Opernplatz, next to the State Opera where Mendelssohn's music was born, great bonfires were lit and students in brown uniforms threw tons of books, countless works of great literature, into the flames. For the first time in modern history, the Nazi government chose to willfully loot, to burn books, and to destroy art treasures in its own museums, in an effort to destroy the past in place of the new.

Up the steps of every stage strode Joseph Goebbels, Hitler's propaganda minister, known for his deep and virulent anti-Semitism, which in time led him to support the extermination of the Jews through the Final Solution. After earning a PhD from Heidelberg University in 1921, he went on to work as a journalist and later a bank clerk, and in his spare time wrote novels and plays, all rejected by publishers. Then Goebbels was conscripted into Hitler's theater, becoming a leading performer in the National Socialist German Workers' Party.

He was on hand to address the crowd and newsreel cameras at Berlin's great editorial bonfire, and so, indeed, the destruction of Germany began on that notorious day in 1933 when Nazi loyalty rituals scripted the event. The Sturmabteilung (a paramilitary group under the Nazi Party), wearing their familiar brown shirts, threw the books into the flames. Goebbels addressed the crowd and the newsreel cameras: the burning of books, he said, was a symbolic action to "show the world that a new Germany will ascend from the flames in our own hearts." That evening, more than thirty thousand books were burned, part of a calculated effort to redefine German culture and world history.

Like many propaganda events, such as those at Nuremberg, the book burnings were designed as spectacle. The fires turned the work of great German thinkers and philosophers, who had been central to European literature and philosophy for centuries, to ash. Leibnitz, Kant, Hegel, Schopenhauer, Marx, Nietzsche, and Heidegger had to be dispensed with in place of Nazi ideology. Likewise the books of American writers Jack London, Ernest Hemingway, Theodore Dreiser, Sinclair Lewis, and Helen Keller. A century earlier, Heinrich Heine, the great German poet, wrote: "Where one burns books, one will, in the end, burn people."

During this time, Germany appeared as a country in a film running backward, with two ideologies, both profane, both about political doctrine and performance. One was the war against democracies and communism, the other, at its core—blatantly clear since Hitler's *Mein Kampf*—a ruthless war against European Jewry. Now came *Anschluss*. That's what the Germans called it. What did it mean? With the annexation of Austria, almost six million Jewish people were doomed in places where they were not wanted, for whom the world had become divided into countries where they could not live and countries that they could not enter. A favorite sport in Vienna was local residents looking on and cheering as prominent Jewish women were forced to scrub sidewalks on their knees in their lingerie. Their property and homes were confiscated, and those who couldn't leave were isolated and rounded up for slave labor and sent to a concentration camp called Mauthausen, in a small village in upper Austria. This was the end of illusion. The Germans were looking to expand their systematic march through Europe.

In the score of Kurt Weill's play *Mahagonny*, about a fictitious city that goes up in flames, actors carried signs stating, "Let's destroy the other fellow." They sang a song about not needing a typhoon or hurricane because "whatever damage they can do, we can do ourselves." With Stormtroopers already marching outside the theater, the final refrain must have been chilling: "There was a day and it's all gone by." The opera had its premiere in Leipzig in March 1930 and played in Berlin in December of the following year until it was banned by the Nazis in 1933.

How did the day go by? When did Hitler's drama begin? How did one man, one nation, one spirit draft the script for a war to end all wars? The historical origins of Nazi propaganda and Adolf Hitler's meteoric rise to power can be traced back to his *Mein Kampf*, where he devoted two chapters to analyzing the importance of propaganda and its practice. Hitler wrote about the aims of a propagandist in indoctrinating a population and the importance of ensuring the continued propagation of the message: "The first duty of the propagandist is to win over people who can subsequently be taken into the organization. And the first duty of the organization is to select and train men who will be capable of carrying on the propaganda." The organization's second duty "is to disrupt the existing order of things and thus make room for the penetration of the new teaching which it represents, while the duty of the organizer must be to fight for the purpose of securing power, so that the doctrine may finally triumph."

• • •

Adolf Hitler himself appeared in this latest production: the making of a dictator.

The footlights began illuminating the stage on a day in January 1923, when the Nazi Party started to recruit thousands of new members, many of whom were victims of inflation. Economic upheaval generally breeds political upheaval; Germany in the 1920s was no exception to this rule.

The Bavarian state government defied the Weimar Republic after Kaiser Wilhelm II abdicated, accusing it of being too far to the left. An army corporal who had served Germany in World War I declared at a public rally on October 30, 1923, that he was prepared to march on Berlin to rid the government of the communists and the Jews. A week later, he held a rally at a Munich beer hall. He stood on a table and, from his revolver, fired a shot into the air and proclaimed a revolution, leading two thousand armed "Brownshirts" into the streets in an attempt to take over the Bavarian government. The police resisted the putsch after more than a dozen were killed in the fighting. Adolf Hitler was arrested for high treason, received a five-year sentence, and was imprisoned at Landsberg Fortress.

During the trial, he took advantage of the occasion to transform the proceedings into a propaganda triumph. Acting as his own lawyer, he put on a dazzling display of oratory, taking full blame for the uprising. His courtroom behavior made a deep impression on many Germans who began to regard him as a force to be reckoned with.

Hitler served only nine months of his sentence at Landsberg am Lech. Within its walls, he lectured his fellow prisoners and walked in the garden of what was more a country home than a prison. With almost psychic intervention, in his quietest moments he was convinced that he could change Germany. Often, packages would arrive with the German black bread he loved so much, as well as sausages from a shop in nearby Munich that he had frequently visited because it offered the best-tasting bratwurst in the world. Loyal to its customer, the shop sent him a regular supply.

Hitler was convinced it was German black bread that sustained him and Richard Wagner's music that gave him inspiration; sweets were the icing on the cake. He loved plum pie and strudel made with Bavarian apples, which in the notably relaxed restrictions of the prison he was able to enjoy fully. He shared these delights over conversations with Rudolf Hess who, after hearing Hitler speak in 1920, was instantaneously and forever devoted to him. They had something in common, believing in astrology, and the stars must have been aligned to bond their friendship. After commanding the small SA battalion during the Beer Hall Putsch, Hess also served seven and a half months in Landsberg.

In these reasonably comfortable surroundings, acting as Hitler's private secretary and understudy, the receptive Hess transcribed and edited Hitler's book *Mein Kampf.* Eventually, Hess became, after Hitler and Göring, the third-most powerful man in Germany.

The first volume of *Mein Kampf* became the political script of the Nazi movement. It was dictated to Rudolf Hess, who, with his aristocratic underpinnings and education, afforded Hitler an opportunity to create his blueprint. Hitler told the story of his life, his philosophy, and detailed the proposal of the program he had resolved to achieve for Germany, a blueprint intended to restore the nation's honor after the Germans had been disgraced by the Treaty of Versailles, whose hard terms demanded reparations, a dismantled military, and the annexing of German territories.

He never failed to express his views regarding propaganda as if it were part of his genetic code. "Propaganda should not be addressed to the individual but always to the masses," he wrote. "For propaganda is no more an affair of science than an advertising poster is art. Propaganda should be directed to the emotions rather than the intellect, and must be popular and simple enough for it to impress itself on the average mind."

After his release from Landsberg, Hitler reconstructed his movement. Assisted by two cast members, met at party meetings, Dr. Joseph Goebbels, his propaganda wizard, and Captain Hermann Göring, a World War I flying ace, he went about the critical business of winning mass support.

At a national Nazi Party conference held in February 1926, Hitler and his comrades in Bavaria outmaneuvered northern party members led by Gregor Strasser, stripping the former leader of any influence in the growing Nazi movement. With rare political acumen, Hitler used his oratorical skill to attract both left and right. His propaganda appealed to the lower classes hit by the economic depression. At the same time, his insistence on attaining power by legal means gave him prestige with the military, the nationalists, and the conservatives.

This combination of insight into mass psychology and the willingness to work with the conservative right was a powerful factor in elevating Hitler to supreme political power. He gradually recovered the ground he had lost since the abortive Beer Hall Putsch. By 1930, he was the undisputed head of the Nazi movement. Money began to flow into the party's coffers from rich Rhineland industrialists who saw in Hitler their best safeguard against the unions and communism, which did not serve their aims, restricting profits and production. At the same time, Hitler drew increasingly solid support from Germany's polished society, as well as from discontented workers, to both of whom he promised security and relief, through revolution, from despoliation by Jewish financiers.

Germany was not alone, and international companies outside the perimeters of German Nationalism had much to gain, adding to their own corporate coffers. This participation helped Hitler gain both financial support and political power for the German people, as they had been in a depression.

A productive number of American road companies that earned hefty profits in Germany and industrialist Henry Ford made annual birthday gifts of 50,000 Deutschmarks to Adolf Hitler. With Hitler in power in the 1930s, the Ford production, known as Ford-Werke A.G., had no limits in Germany. On Ford's seventy-fifth birthday, in 1938, he received a Nazi medal, the Grand Cross of the German Eagle, designed for "distinguished foreigners." Henry Ford never returned the medal, and Secretary of the Interior Harold Ickes publicly denounced its acceptance.

Many American companies were complicit in Germany's rise to power, serving their own financial interests, as the Reich benefited from the influx of capital. General Motors owned Adams Opel. Wilhelm

Keppler, one of Hitler's top economic advisers, had deep ties in the Kodak Company. When Nazism was on the rise in the 1930s, Keppler advised Kodak to fire its Jewish workers. Chase Bank was also a prominent player. They froze European Jewish customers' accounts and cooperated by providing banking services to Germany.

Standard Oil set up an alliance with I.G. Farben, a division of the Bayer Company, to produce artificial rubber and gasoline from coal for the Nazis. William Randolph Hearst worked with the Nazi Party to help promote a positive image of the new Germany through the American media. In 1934, he traveled to Germany, where he was received by Hitler as a guest and friend.

• • •

Hitler's recurring theme in his script was that the Jews were involved with communists in a joint conspiracy to take over the world. He claimed that 75 percent of all communists were Jews, and argued that the combination of Jews and Marxists had already been successful in Russia and now threatened the rest of Europe. He also asserted that the Communist Revolution was an act of revenge that attempted to disguise the inferiority of the Jews. In one performance on July 27, he spoke to sixty thousand devotees in Brandenburg, to nearly as many in Potsdam, and that evening to one hundred and twenty thousand massed in the giant Deutsches Stadion in Berlin, while outside an additional one hundred thousand heard his voice over loudspeakers.

"We are on the threshold of history and a new Germany!"

# CHAPTER 1

# Introducing the Führer, Joseph Goebbels, and Heinrich Himmler

———— ∞∞∞ ————

Hitler, in his role as an actor, not only performed, but also personified an exorcism of a shameful past. He sought audience empathy and response, playing "Deutschland, Deutschland über alles" in specially constructed stadiums and halls, theaters, and open-air amphitheaters all over Germany. The stirring German national anthem, composed by Joseph Hayden, with lyrics by August von Fallersleben, contributed to the pageantry.

Within a theatrical framework that focused on his own destiny, Hitler was a proficient organizer and was brilliant in his application of impression management. He created a character that went well beyond the publication of *Mein Kampf*, and, in so doing, he assumed the role of director, casting himself as führer. Everything, from his personally designed uniform through an affected walk, usually with his hands folded behind his back, to well-staged photo opportunities with children documenting a kind and compassionate leader, and the outstretched arm giving a salute from his open-air Mercedes, became part of his persona.

Directing his struggle, he showed remarkable shrewdness in keying his message to the distress, the fears, and the hopes of other Germans. It was Hitler's skill as an orator that helped him first to become recognized within the party and then to become its most influential member. Indeed, his oratorical skills enabled him to make his mark quickly, as within only a few months he became a featured speaker of the infant National Socialist German Workers Party. One reason why his speeches were so effective at drawing crowds was that he spent a great amount of time before a mirror, perfecting his image and his movements while being photographed by the Nazi Party's official photographer, Heinrich Hoffman, and his assistant, Leni Riefenstahl, who was to become the legendary director of *Triumph of the Will.*

Hitler took his craft seriously. He knew that to hold an audience he must be persuasive, using techniques long perfected by classical actors. Drawing upon emotions and memory, appearing offstage as he did on, Hitler took as his inspiration Constantin Stanislavski, a Russian actor and theater director who styled the Stanislavski method that inspired numerous acting teachers in Europe. He treated theater-making as a serious endeavor requiring dedication and discipline. Collaborating with actors and with the great playwright Anton Chekhov, he perfected performance at the Moscow Art Theater, which supposed that the life of a character should be an unbroken line of events and emotions creating a convincing role: "The artist of the stage must be the master of his own inspiration, and must know how to call it forth at the hour announced on the posters of the theater. This is the chief secret of our art."

"I will become the greatest leader in Germany history," said Hitler. He willed it. He imagined it. He created it. He staged it. He rehearsed, as any actor would, each expression, each action, each movement carrying an effect to charm and to disarm. He would have no match, honing his performance for hours, turning, pausing, dancing through each expression, finding his own voice until he became master of his own style, ready to perform stunning oratory for a receptive audience. It would not happen by chance, but by will, by the mastery of circumstance and conditions.

His dress was carefully crafted: a brown shirt, a red and black swastika on its arm, not to be too elaborate, but instead unpretentious, appealing to the common *volk*. The swastika had a long, not ignoble history in Europe, reaching back to antiquity, and the Sanskrit symbol, with its meaning "it is good," was adopted as an emblem of the Nazi Party of Germany, an emblem of the Aryan race.

His appearance was immaculate, his gestures and salutes impressive, his walk confident. He always ensured that lighting was effective and every sound system perfect.

A setting was masterfully, meticulously created to project his message, a message carefully built in terms of tone and effectiveness, beginning with a soft overture and building in loud, pounding intensity. A hundred searchlights around a staging area, with elevated platforms, created what famed correspondent William Shirer characterized as a "cathedral of light."

His presentation finished as any great symphony would, climaxing in a flourish, reaching peak orchestral performance as you would find in a great musical composition. With this painstaking preparation, he would be ready to convince and inspire children, generals, and all who sat before him in this "cathedral of light." Germany was waiting, and onstage he would live in the hearts and minds of all Germans—he would never be outperformed by anyone.

Addressing enormous crowds, he was charismatic, and with diplomats, in one-on-one meetings, he engaged them with "the deepest and clearest blue eyes they had ever seen." Strange, almost mystical, he could enchant. It was a certain unexplainable attraction that actors carry both on stage and screen, an aura, a connection, a certain charisma.

He believed, as Goebbels did: *make the lie big*. He did this by building upon exaggerated economic conditions, Jewish inferiority, Nordic superiority; an over-scored legacy for a new Germany. Make it simple, keep saying it, and eventually "they" will believe it. Having rehearsed his style in Munich's beer halls, Hitler now modulated the tone and timbre of his voice to suit the acoustics of each occasion and place, timing his entrances until a kind of electric expectancy suffused his audience.

As a graphic artist in his early years, Hitler surely visualized the character he intended to portray in the unfolding drama: a Teutonic knight who had been sent to rescue his people. In outdoor theaters called *Thingplätze*, often constructed on sacred ground, an actor playing Hitler would descend as a deus ex machina, a device in Greek drama that allowed an actor to be lowered to the stage from the heavens or appear from the wings as a god. He speculated as to how future generations would portray his crucial role in the coming thousand-year Reich.

Hitler's dramaturge, Joseph Goebbels, edited the führer's script and co-directed the production. Goebbels was called the greatest press agent the twentieth century had yet seen; years before, anticipating his role in the Nazi play, he gave the führer a passage that he had written in his diary: "My department will be something immense, something the world has never seen before, a Ministry of Public Upbringing and Education in all fields of radio, film, news and photo services, art, culture, and propaganda."

The appointed minister assured Hitler that, under his direction, the ministry would create a comprehensive staged reality, and all Germans would regard it as the only real world.

Goebbels wanted his ministry to have complete and unified control over propaganda and related activities within the Reich. A wave of the hand from Hitler was at once an assurance and a dismissal. Hitler excluded particular propaganda functions from Goebbels's control. The revitalized Wehrmacht would supervise information given to the troops through a separate Propaganda Branch and security police; Hitler appointed Heinrich Himmler to lead the ruthlessly violent Gestapo.

With another player taking to the stage in a supporting role, Himmler became one of the most powerful men in Nazi Germany and as Reichsführer-SS, a special rank and title, he oversaw all police and security forces. Initially, Himmler was involved in the Beer Hall Putsch—the unsuccessful attempt by Hitler and the National Socialist Party to seize power in Munich. This event would set Himmler on a life of politics. In the intervening years until he came to power, Himmler searched for a worldview, came to abandon his Catholicism and focused instead on the occult and on anti-Semitism. Known for his organizational skills, he was the overseer of the concentration camps, the extermination camps, and the killing squads of the Einsatzgruppen. Himmler coordinated the killing of millions of Jews, three to four million Poles, communists, and other groups whom the Nazis deemed unworthy to live or were simply "in the way."

So Himmler took the part of *Reichsführer* of the Schutzstaffel (the famed black-uniformed SS Guards whose primary function was initially to protect the führer but who soon evolved into a terror organization), and inspector of the notorious Geheime Staatspolizei, the Gestapo, the State Secret Police. His primary function in Naziland was never to be seen onstage but, rather, to be felt offstage. The discontented merchant, the dissident party member, the persecuted Jew, the defiant churchman, and the too-independent army officer all with good reason dreaded his heavy hand and often landed in one of Herr Himmler's concentration camps.

Under Himmler, Germany soon became the most policed country in the world. He purged, sacked, centralized, and reorganized the regular German police. The working SS troops were not only entrusted with keeping German order, but also with producing a great race of supermen. SS marriages were arranged and the bride's physical qualifications and racial background were thoroughly investigated. SS colonies for young married couples were made attractive breeding grounds. Himmler made his police force not only a service but also an essential part of the drama, adding the elements to a script that create suspense and conflict.

With Himmler joining the cast, Goebbels labeled events and people with a distinctive new vocabulary that reflected both the policies and the rhetorical emphases of the new regime.

There was, for instance, the *Volksgerichtshof* ("People's Court"), a tribunal which condemned people accused of crimes against the state; verdicts were sometimes directed by Hitler.

The *Volkshalle* ("People's Hall") was a proposed gigantic domed building to be constructed in Berlin as the world capital of Germania, part of Adolf Hitler's vision for the future after the planned victory. It was designed by Albert Speer, the favored architect of the Third Reich.

*Volkswagen*, inspired by Joseph Ganz, a Jewish engineer, was the "people's car." The beetle-like automobile caught Hitler's attention in prewar Germany, and it is one of the most durable and popular legacies of the Nazi era.

The *Abwehr* was a German military intelligence organization and an espionage group within the defense ministry that gathered domestic and foreign information, most of it in the form of human intelligence.

*Aktion 1005* was the secret Nazi operation for concealing evidence about mass-killings.

Goebbels manufactured counter-conspiracies against anyone who might conspire against the nation, and the newly conscripted traitors were handed over to his co-director, Himmler. Chief among these were Jews, who were largely blamed for the country's perceived moral and financial decline. During a secret meeting with top SS officials, Himmler referred explicitly to the *Ausrottung,* the "extermination" of the Jewish people: "I also want to refer here very frankly to a very difficult matter. We can now very openly talk about this among ourselves, and yet we will never discuss this publicly. . . . I am now referring to the evacuation of the Jews, to the extermination of the Jewish People. . . . Because we know how difficult it would be for us if we still had Jews as secret saboteurs, agitators and rabble-rousers in every city, what with the bombings, with the burden and with the hardships of the war."

• • •

News policy was considered a weapon of war. Hitler insisted that one mistake of World War I was that newspapers under the control of Jewish capitalists misinformed the world (in fact Jewish editors had reported the news objectively and accurately). He would not take any such chance this time. Now news would cut a swathe for the Third Reich in a second and extended engagement, and propaganda became an engine of national expansion. Propaganda "is not a pejorative term for the German people. Indeed it inspires and electrifies them," Hitler wrote. Of course, some might dislike the term. "If need be, I will call propaganda by something

other than its name; I'll call it *Menschenführung,* the guidance of men."
Thinking the Nazi revolution could be accomplished in different ways,
Goebbels, too, reasoned he would transform the nation by a mental
revolution and win over the opposition instead of killing them.

But when necessary, Hitler certainly resorted to violent means—
supplemented by a proper narrative—to deal with possible threats, both
external and internal. One particular danger was ambitious party members like Ernst Röhm, an army officer from Bavaria who had been help-
ful to Hitler. He played the antagonist in Hitler's play, until Röhm's
brown-shirted Sturmabteilung outlived their usefulness. In any drama,
surprise, suspense, and conflict drive plot. A drama called "The Night of
the Long Knives" was no exception.

Röhm became a threat to Hitler's leadership, undermining him
offstage.

Hitler had already begun preparing for the conflict. In January
1934 he ordered the secret police to gather incriminating evidence
against Röhm and planned to reduce the SA by two thirds, leaving
them with only a few minor military functions. Röhm responded with
further complaints about Hitler and began expanding the armed elements of the SA. To many it appeared as though the SA was planning
a rebellion.

Although determined to curb its power, Hitler put off doing away
with his longtime comrade until the very end. His confidant and general, Hermann Göring, whom Hitler designated commander of the
Luftwaffe, used Röhm's published anti-Hitler rhetoric to support a claim
that the SA was plotting to overthrow the führer. By late June, this story
had been officially recognized and Himmler was giving protective orders
to the SS. With scant evidence, Himmler and his colleagues actually
convinced Hitler to think the plot was real.

Meanwhile, Röhm and several of his companions went away on holiday to a resort in Bad Wiessee, a beautiful spa on one of the loveliest
lakes in Germany. On June 28, Hitler phoned Röhm and asked him to
gather all the SA leaders at Bad Wiessee on June 30 for a conference.
Röhm agreed, apparently suspecting nothing.

That day and night, June 30, marked "the Night of the Long Knives" when the entire leadership of the SA was purged, along with any other political adversaries of the Nazis. At dawn that morning, Hitler flew to Munich, and then drove to Bad Wiessee, where he personally arrested Röhm and the other SA leaders. All were imprisoned at Stadelheim Prison in Munich. Hitler was uneasy authorizing Röhm's execution and gave him an opportunity to commit suicide. SS-Hauptsturmführer Michael Lippert, who laid a pistol on the table, told Röhm he had ten minutes to use it and left. Röhm refused. When Lippert and Obergruppenführer Theodor Eicke returned, he stood in the middle of the cell with his shirt open, theatrically baring his chest as they shot him. Röhm was buried in the Westfriedhof in Munich.

An article from *The History Place* provides a more detailed account about the drama that took place: "Saturday morning about 10 a.m. a phone call was placed from Hitler in Munich to Göring in Berlin with the prearranged code word 'Kolibri' (hummingbird) that unleashed a wave of murderous violence in Berlin and over 20 other cities. SS execution squads along with Göring's private police force roared through the streets hunting down SA leaders and anyone on the prepared list of political enemies (known as the Reich List of Unwanted Persons)."

That evening, Hitler flew back to Berlin and immediately immersed himself in the drama: "On his way to the fleet of cars, which stood several hundred yards away, Hitler stopped to converse with Göring and Himmler. Apparently he could not wait a few minutes until he reached the Chancellery. . . . From one of his pockets Himmler took out a long, tattered list. Hitler read it through, while Göring and Himmler whispered incessantly into his ear. We could see Hitler's finger moving slowly down the sheet of paper. Now and then it paused for a moment at one of the names. At such times the two conspirators whispered even more excitedly. Suddenly Hitler tossed his head. There was so much violent emotion, so much anger in the gesture, that everybody noticed it." It was not only the general masses who were the audience for the performances.

The purge of the SA was officially declared legal the next day with a one-paragraph decree, the Law Regarding Measures of State

Self-Defense. In an attempt to erase Röhm from German history, all known copies of the 1933 propaganda film *Der Sieg des Glaubens* [Victory of Faith], in which Röhm appeared, were ordered to be destroyed.

After this necessary diversion and preview of coming attractions, Hitler got down to redrafting the play at hand. There was more to do after the distraction of purging a renegade movement. He was confronted with a bigger revolution, a larger stage. Germany would not feel compelled to rationally justify the advantages and disadvantages of National Socialism in the coming war. Its people would be emotionally overwhelmed by the spectacles and extravaganzas—created with close attention to theater—and newsreels, without interference from the press. The people would become overwhelmed by oratory. A crucial part of this process would involve casting the Jews as villains in the unfolding performances according to a propaganda plan.

On January 30, 1939, speaking at the Reichstag about the future of Europe and the fate of European Jewry, Hitler took his cues from Himmler's script that had been discussed earlier and privately among a select group of officers and now became public policy. Ranting for two hours, Hitler performed a familiar tirade and gave a menacing forecast for the Final Solution.

The führer did not detail what he had in mind then, but while full-scale Jewish resettlement was at one time the objective, gradually total annihilation became the Reich's policy. Hitler gave his generals broad authorization to carry out his wishes.

• • •

When Nazi Germany annexed parts of Czechoslovakia, Prime Minister Chamberlain proclaimed that his government would resist further aggression; unfortunately, the vow came too late. Trying to flee the expanding Nazi web, Jews found increasing obstacles and restrictions in their way. The world press did not give much support. Leaders followed policy from World War I when the British government, under a League of Nations mandate, issued a White Paper, restricting Jewish immigration to Palestine.

Stepping on stage with perfect timing to add conflict to the drama, was Reinhard Heydrich, a high-ranking German Nazi official and one of the main architects of the Final Solution. In January 1942, he issued an invitation to German government lawyers, generals, and officials for a special weekend gathering at Grossen Wannsee 56/58, a comfortable, now infamous lakeside villa not far from Berlin. Fifteen men, many with doctorates from German universities, came to Wannsee to launch *Aktion Reinhard*, the implementation of "a final settlement" of the Jewish problem in places called Bełżec, Treblinka, Auschwitz. These were to become the killing fields of the Holocaust.

From Munich beer halls to wide-open stadiums, the message was simple and compelling: revenge. Hitler's aggressive drive burned in the hearts of his fellow veterans: revenge against the victorious Allies of World War I; revenge against the unacceptable Treaty of Versailles peace plan that impoverished all Germans; revenge against the Bolsheviks whose leveling plans for the entire earth were contrary to *Mein Kampf*; and, especially, revenge against the Jews.

Jews, he said, were found within the highest circles in England and France, were prominent within the Soviet Union, and dominated many fields within Germany itself—medicine, science, finance, and the arts—and as such, they had polluted German culture and purity, along with Jewish bankers whose "self-serving greed" had destroyed Germany's economy. He manufactured a compelling, convincing theme for his audience.

Of course, Jewish scientists, bankers, musicians, from Einstein to Mendelsohn, had contributed to Germany's rich heritage, and Heydrich had no foundation for his hateful commentary. The big lie was at the heart of the play with an ultimate consequence that the country's cultural life was diminished, even destroyed.

The Nazis' scenario, incorporating image management, could now facilitate aggression by specifying the targets. The Jews became the perfect character villains in Hitler's theater. They were different, they were separate, they were the enemy. Forced to carry identification cards with a prominent *J* on them, the Jewish population would be barred from civil service. Boycotts of Jewish stores were organized with the SA blockading Jewish-owned outlets and pummeling any who dared to cross their picket lines. Then an incident, the assassination of a German diplomat by a Jewish refugee from the Reich, would unleash wholesale destruction of Jewish commercial establishments. What could be more essential to stagecraft than dramatic violence, with a cast of angry mobs, with torchlight parades, with the shattering of glass?

The goal of performance, as Bertolt Brecht had written with bitter irony, was to "destroy the other fellow."

The pace of the drama accelerated and was given dramatic expression in this staged event: *Kristallnacht*, known in English as the "Night of the Broken Glass." The attack was intended to look like a series of spontaneous acts, but it was in fact all carefully orchestrated by the Nazi government. It was a massive nationwide pogrom in Germany and Austria on the night of November 9, 1938, and was directed at Jewish citizens throughout both countries. It was, for many, a hint of the Holocaust to come. The night damaged, and in many cases destroyed, over a thousand synagogues throughout Germany, many Jewish cemeteries, more than seven thousand Jewish shops, and twenty-nine department stores.

More than twenty thousand Jews were arrested and taken to concentration camps. A few were beaten to death while others were forced to watch. The number of Jewish Germans killed is uncertain, with estimates ranging from thirty-six to about two hundred over two days of rioting. The number killed is most often cited as ninety-one. The indiscriminate nature of the violence suggests some non-Jewish Germans were killed simply because someone thought they "looked Jewish."

From the elegant boulevard of Unter den Linden to broken cobblestone streets off the Kurfürstendamm, soon all German Jews were forced to wear a Star of David. Hitler believed that as each scene unfolded, Jews would be eliminated. German "racial purity" would highlight the Jews' congenital weakness and serve to prove the truth of his statements about their inferiority.

Once German armies swept eastward, labor resettlement camps would be set up and, to achieve this end, dramatic deceptions were staged. This in itself was connected to performance and an unfolding tragedy. The Jewish people were told they were being evacuated for their own good, and newsreels projected images of resettled Jews, with camp orchestras welcoming new arrivals. Instead, a labor force was created, and their stay in the camps would be terminal. When they arrived, the strong were chosen for slave labor and directed to the left, and all others to the right, to their doom.

A cast of hundreds of thousands of troops had been assembled to play in the theater of war. Hitler's script was ready for an out-of-town tryout. True to his dramatic orientation, he staged the reoccupation by the German army of the demilitarized Rhineland, a border area along France, and a peace condition inscribed in the Versailles Treaty. When the Wehrmacht marched into the Rhineland, German commanders were under orders to retreat should they encounter armed opposition. There was none. The out of town tryout was successful. While Hitler polished the production, inside Germany, life and theater merged, and the first act of World War II opened quietly without opposition. There were no reviews except a few favorable notices inside the nation.

CHAPTER 2

# The Road to the Third Reich

———— ∞∞∞ ————

The National Socialist Party continued to take measures that may have seemed unusual for an obscure faction on the fringe of German politics. On August 14, 1927, Alfred Rosenberg, the self-proclaimed philosopher of Nazi ideology, had joined the supporting cast and temporarily took over a director's chair. He needed to revise and restage a portion of the script, specifically *Kunstpolitik*; that is, cultural policy decrying the influence of "foreign" art, especially foreign theater, on German culture. He pointed to Piscator and Brecht as examples of the political left's contamination of German theater.

Rosenberg had been one of the most influential Nazi intellectuals, holding a number of important German state and Nazi Party posts and establishing the Institute for Research into the Jewish Question, designed to provide legitimacy for the regime's anti-Semitic policies by proving the existence of a "Jewish conspiracy" on the basis of books and archival materials confiscated from Jewish organizations at home and abroad. As a result, there was organized looting of Jewish libraries, art collections, and other such assets, and by the end of the war, the Reich had shipped an astonishing amount of looted artwork and artefacts from German-controlled Europe back to Germany. Stealing was introduced into stagecraft.

Once Hitler became chancellor, Rosenberg's activities were centralized through the formation of a *Reichskulturkammer* (The Reich's
Chamber of Culture), and Propaganda Minister Joseph Goebbels structured the Chamber of Culture as he had done in the Propaganda
Ministry, with separate departments for press, radio, film, and literature.
Goebbels directed German theater toward a "people's choric theater"
recalling the pageantry of Germany's Teutonic past dating back to the
twelfth century.

Objects and symbols reconnecting the country with its supposed
Aryan roots influenced the once-defeated Germans. By reminding them
of their proud past, Hitler promised them an invincible future. Spangles,
daggers, and medals, each bearing a swastika or an eagle, were devised by
a professional stage-set designer, as were uniforms worn by proud
German soldiers, who became a crucial part of Hitler's enormous supporting cast.

The führer supervised every detail of all items and insignia worn by
the military. The swastika of National Socialism with its red background
became a symbol of the nation's blood. The white circle highlighting the
swastika gave an impression of inexorable movement and power, of the
Reich rolling across the globe with mighty, irresistible force.

To add to the drama on Germany's home front, a repertory company
formed, applying tried and tested models from national history.
Goebbels's staff distilled mythological acts of Teutonic heroism into an
interpretation of medieval drama, with the same nationalism, backed by
the music of Richard Wagner and infused with the will to power inspired
by the poet and philosopher Friedrich Nietzsche.

Nazi theater with its concentration on dazzling and overwhelming
spectacle essentially reestablished an open-air theater tradition from the
Middle Ages. The drama combined myth and legendary deeds comple-
menting Nazi ideology, exploring the Nietzschean struggle between noble
and ignoble races and the supposition that the Nordic master race was
superior to "lesser" races, something Hitler had tackled in his writings.

A central feature of Nazi theater was the chorus, a device that allowed
the producers to enlarge the stage. The role of the chorus now included

watching the action onstage, becoming a "bridge through which audience members could transport themselves as part of the chorus."

With amphitheaters under construction, Goebbels's board commissioned appropriate plays. One writer was Kurt Heynicke, whose *Der Weg ins Reich* [The Road to the Third Reich] premiered in Munich on the summer solstice of 1935. The plot of *Der Weg ins Reich* is easily summarized: a Teutonic knight, a hero, returns to the Fatherland after a prolonged war abroad. The emphasis of the production was elsewhere. Audiences were greeted with a calculated piece of propagandistic spectacle before the opening act of Heynicke's play. Flaming torches, blood flags, and richly braided uniforms provided an introduction on the Platz, a public square near the Brandenburg Gate.

In the evening the familiar circle of searchlights shot upward into the sky, beaming out from the large open-air theater; they were visible many miles away. Before the performance began came the sound of a hundred drums; first a roll of small snare drums, then the heartbeat resonance of bass drums introduced a deeper and richer tempo until the cadence overwhelmed the senses, slowly at first, then a pause, then starting all over again in an unrelenting beat. When Germans, from nearby as well as from far-flung cities and villages, approached the open-air theater, the drums became louder still. There were long avenues of emblematic red and white banners with vast platoons of German soldiers standing to attention.

There was a call to arms, a call to the stages, a call to an event. An orchestra played, joined by a chorus of three hundred performers divided equally on each side of a main staging area. One group sang and the other responded, almost like a Mass, a holy celebration, profound and melodic, an overture to the evening, conveying Germany's heroic glory. Audiences of fifty thousand Germans sat quietly, obediently, their eyes glassy, their minds hypnotized as each note struck a chord in their Teutonic souls. In the final scene that deus ex machina, a godlike figure representing Hitler, was lowered into view, and the play was suddenly resolved. The audience burst into uproarious applause.

The orchestra, film, lights, sets, chorus, and actors all contributed to the performance, building to a climax, bringing thousands to their feet singing, "Deutschland, Deutschland über alles." Tears fell from each spectator. After a thunderous ovation, the drums began again, in a much softer tempo, and the führer's votaries brought the evening to a close. The spectators themselves had become components of a play representing Adolf Hitler, in scenes that were part medieval allegory and part biography.

Significantly, as this onstage triumph unfolded, a contingent of Hitler Youth placed among the audience within the amphitheater joined the chorus of warriors and women onstage, chanting, "Rise up, you German nation!" as party members distributed throughout the audience leaped to their feet. The curious mixture of Hitler's experience as a World War I veteran and medieval allegory formed the basis for many plays performed by the "people's choric theater" in the 1930s; more than half of them centered on the theme of the hero and his return to a homeland destroyed from within.

Heartened by initial success, Goebbels announced a huge building program that saw the completion of no fewer than sixty amphitheaters in Germany by 1938, each having a seating capacity of between ten thousand and fifty thousand. Some open-air theaters had survived World War I and were refurbished to meet Nazi staging requirements while others were built from scratch. Nazi theater became a powerful propaganda device enshrining German mythology.

Researching undocumented lore from the pre-Christian era, the Cultural Chamber unearthed the term *Thing*. A *Thing*, or *Ding* as it was formerly written, was a Teutonic assembly area reputedly used as a tribunal and chosen because it was located on the site of some great battle or feat of heroism.

Robert R. Taylor in *The Word in Stone: The Role of Architecture in National Socialist Ideology* and Orin Knapp in *Symbolic Leaders* have written about the "sacred" outdoor amphitheaters constructed in Germany to promote the German message, and were characterized by Fritz Gerlich, editor of the *Munich Post*, as Churches for National Socialism. The productions were extravagant and appealed to German audiences eager to celebrate a glorious cultural past and national heritage.

To encourage dramatic expansion, Goebbels planned four hundred *Thingplätze* that would serve as "cultic centers of National Socialism." He dispatched archaeologists throughout the German countryside searching for relics that indicated the location of hallowed ground.

One of the first *Thingplätze* was constructed at Verden an der Aller, where archaeologists allegedly discovered bones belonging to some 4,500 Saxons slaughtered by Charlemagne. These locations evoked visions of past German glory in the minds of playgoers, but their use was part of a broader and more insidious aim. Harkening back to a pre-Christian era of "pure" Aryan culture, the *Thingplätze* served as Nazi tabernacles, which would gradually replace Christian churches in German cultural life and thereby pave the way for Hitler as the cultic Messiah of the *people*.

Drawing upon tradition, the "Passion Play" festival of Oberammergau, a source of anti-Judaism and theological Christianity, was produced. (Oberammergau Passion Plays were first performed in 1634 as the result of a vow made by the inhabitants of the village that if God spared them from the effects of the bubonic plague then sweeping the region, they would perform a passion play in homage.) Casts from acting companies all over the Fatherland were auditioned. Hitler Youth doubled as ushers and chorus members, creating a "flesh and blood" bond between the audience and the performance on stage.

Curiously, when the first of these works was produced in 1933, neither the Protestant nor the Catholic clergy protested at this secularized revision of Christian doctrine.

From the very start, Goebbels and other members of the Culture Chamber sought to break down the illusory fourth wall separating audience from performance. Their decision to build only outdoor theaters and to situate them near sacred grounds was obviously inspired by the desire to blur the line between theater and reality. Party member Hans Brandenburg suggested that *Thingplätze* design include "a bordering stage thrusting outward into the auditorium as a tie between the stage and the audience, a playing area for the chorus."

There were revolving stages, whereby portions of the stage were divided into moving runners, in which colorful scenery passed; a cyclorama from behind projected black-and-white film. Each of these details was intended to amplify the impact of the ideological message and the "sacred spot" was reserved for the performer representing Hitler as the Veteran Warrior.

The *Thingplätze,* covered only by a ceiling of stars, were where German passions were aroused and where the people merged into a single, obedient, proud mass.

But *Thingplätze* were not immune from journalistic criticism. Fritz Gerlich, the editor from the *Munich Post,* noting how the productions elevated propaganda to a level that he had never seen before, reported on them, and paid the ultimate price for his honesty.

Seeing events before they happened, growing up in Munich, he studied history, and earned his doctorate. With poor eyesight, he depended on steel-rimmed glasses, a characteristic that came to identify him. A staunch patriot of Germany in the aftermath of its defeat in World War I, he offered unwavering support throughout Hitler's rise to power. When the Nazi agenda expanded into radical racial laws, Gerlich would have no part of it. Hitler had promised to peacefully restore and rebuild Germany, with rights for all its citizens. In time Hitler betrayed and blatantly lied to his former supporter.

Coupling his radical views with anti-Semitic policies—seizing property, internment camps, and violating the rights of Germans without trial— Hitler's actions were patently illegal. The *Post* was warned, but still the paper reported on political murders, on Hitler's willful falsifications of history, and on the propaganda stunt of using the newly constructed *Thingplätze* to promote Nazism. Gerlich wanted his fellow Germans to understand that Hitler's way—freedom of the press suspended, free assembly forbidden, civil rights violated, and any protest a crime punishable by death—was not the German way. Gerlich fought until Stormtroopers burst into his newspaper office, beat him senseless, and dragged him off to a concentration camp. A few days later, his wife received a message and a package. The Nazis had killed the journalist who had seen through them all. Inside the package were no words, just his blood-spattered, steel-rimmed spectacles.

# CHAPTER 3

# From Choric Theater to Party Rally

————∞∞∞————

Many of the dramatic themes and staging techniques developed by Goebbels and the Propaganda Ministry staff were replicated in an explicitly political setting. Nazi Party rallies were held in Nuremberg each year from 1933 onward, around the time of the autumnal equinox. In turn, the party rallies included innovations incorporated into the productions staged at the *Thingplätze* as art blended into political drama.

Hitler, as the leading dramatist of the Nazi show, endorsed and approved Goebbels's amphitheater projects, but ideological drama in and of itself would not be enough to convey the impression the führer wished to make upon the audience. Dramatized ideology would be required, and to that end the party rally was central. The rally grounds, like the *Thingplätze,* would become sanctified turf and a stage calculated to absorb participants' identities into one *volk.*

Toward this crucial goal, the same process of stage expansion was employed, with the entire Zeppelin Field in Nuremberg and its immediate environment becoming a part of the performance within a framework displaying party flags and emblems. The stadium was bigger than twelve football fields and provided space for more than four hundred thousand people. Here mass parades of the German Labor Service, the Wehrmacht, and of the "political leaders" (office bearers of the NSDAP) were staged before the führer. The "Cathedral of Light" provided spectacular effects, when over one hundred and fifty particularly powerful floodlights beamed toward the sky.

"I'm beginning to comprehend some of the reasons for Hitler's astounding success," wrote journalist William Shirer from Berlin in September 1934. "He is restoring pageantry and color and mysticism to the hard life caused by the economic depression." Hitler, empowered to lead the nation, had made a fine art of staging enormous spectacles that inspired a new Germany. In this mystical city of Nuremberg, hundreds of thousands of Germans cheered to the strains of martial music from brass bands. Battalions of Stormtroopers, fitted with field packs, goose-stepped in a display of precision marching; the bands led a regiment of Brownshirts into the city; and, saluting stiffly from his open Mercedes touring car, Hitler reviewed column after column of parading soldiers.

Inside the stadium of drums and light, linking arms across an immense athletic field, thousands of members of the League of German Girls danced in a celebration of "faith and beauty," a performance that required long and meticulous preparation. Young men demonstrated their strength and skill in a precision drill with heavy poles. Mock tank battles followed, thrilling the spectators. Albert Speer had designed a perfect setting with two adjoining grandstands, one a quarter of a mile long.

The first dimension of the Nuremberg Rally "frame" was its sheer size. Hitler emphasized the need for monumental architecture to reflect the "heroic scale of life" in the Third Reich. Author Thornton Sinclair witnessed the event and reported on the extraordinary scale of the 1937 Nuremberg rally:

The buildings and grounds of the Party rally reflected its grandiose character. What has already been done on them is impressive, but what has been planned is truly staggering.

The fields, the Luitpold Arena and the Zeppelin Field, were equipped with extensive stone stands and striking decorations. A vast area had been set aside for the army demonstrations, but these plans were now dwarfed by those projected for the congress building, the main hall of which will seat sixty thousand people. The German Stadium, which would accommodate four hundred fifty thousand spectators, was the latest undertaking to be announced.

Interviewed about the magnitude of the Nuremberg design, Hitler disingenuously asserted, "I do this to restore in each individual German his self-respect." Actually, the intent was exactly the opposite; monumentality was designed to awe the individual and to encourage mass-thinking.

Posing as a Nazi sympathizer, British journalist and author James Mayo wrote in a summary snapshot:

> The meeting was held at night, and to symbolize the greatness of the Third Reich, searchlights were aimed vertically, forming seemingly endless light walls. The mass of people attending the meeting were uniformly dressed and arranged in regimented rank and file.
>
> With appropriate music and the added oratorical capabilities of Adolf Hitler, a mystical sense to the greatness of the Third Reich was created in the minds of the participants. Germany's greatness was not only symbolized through Hitler, but also through the presence of the stage set. The stage became more than a stage; it became a realized heaven on earth, a political Garden of Eden.

Mayo reported about the customary distant drums rolling to a heart-pounding beat, with tall troops carrying torches and mystical banners through the wide lanes separating thousands of the faithful, loyal to the Nazi cause. In terms of dramaturgical perspective, while conventional theater allows for separation in performance, the Nazis intentionally blurred the line. The swastika, the Reich's eagle, and blood flags emblazoned the stage and were symbolically placed around and within the audience, breaking conventional performance walls.

While the pageantry of the *Thingplätze* productions were more fluid, involving and blending audience and performance on specially constructed stages, on fields of honor, a military parade became a hallmark of the Third Reich in a more controlled and disciplined way. They were exquisitely produced events, conveying a message of power, but in a different setting.

With its role in the Germanic myth, with its relationship to the Holy Roman Empire and its position in the physical center of Germany, Nuremberg was chosen by the Nazi Party as the perfect site for the extraordinary Nazi Congress rallies.

The rallies extensively used marching columns dressed in standardized military and paramilitary costumes. On each day of the weeklong booking, a different part of the Nazi movement was staged. Performances were set aside for the Brownshirts, the Hitler Youth, the SS and SA, National Socialist Motor Corps, the National Socialist Flyers, and the Nazi Labor Troops.

• • •

At an early hour, 110,000 men had filled the field except for a vacant stone center walk eighteen meters wide, running 240 meters from the speaker's tribune to the memorial to the valiant soldiers who fought in wars, on the opposite side of the field. The structure, built by Albert Speer, could seat five hundred dignitaries. Thousands of flags ran like red ribbons through the ranks. After the führer arrived, the leaders of the different organizations reported to him. The standard-bearers marched forward out of the ranks, then around the side of the arena to the rear, to flank the memorial, their ranks reaching to the corners of the field.

On "Labor Day," members of the German Labor Front, having marched past the führer, stood some 45,000-strong, reciting and occasionally singing in unison: "We are the troops of peace."

Hitler's entrance into the stadium was itself a masterpiece of timing and stagecraft. Long after the expectant audience had assembled, blasts of trumpets heralded the arrival of the führer who, with his retinue, made a triumphal entry, marching down the long center aisle to the stage to the strains of martial music, and shouts and cries of "Heil!" After the führer reached the stage, the blood flag was borne in, followed at a distance by banners decorated with eagles.

Guarded by three SS men wearing the medal of their exclusive order, evidencing their long membership and special service to the party, the blood flag was carried to a position in the middle aisle, between those sitting on the stage directly behind the speaker's platform, where it was held throughout the proceedings by its guardians standing to attention.

The führer's appearance was invariably synchronized with the symbolic climax of the blood flag's elevation, creating yet another bond between the Reich's leader and the mystical image that he had chosen for his movement. Sometimes Hitler delayed his entrance until the assembled crowd were starting to show visible signs of restlessness.

Once on the platform, the führer went through a short mime routine. His hand on his belt buckle, he assumed the speaker's podium and froze in a heroic posture. In this statuelike immobility, the führer listened to a Nazi dignitary and his welcoming words, displaying no overt emotion. With crowd expectancy at its peak, a carefully timed sequence was set in motion involving multiple cues that closely coordinated Hitler's movements to staging effects. Hitler stirred and suddenly shot out his chin; simultaneously, 150 antiaircraft searchlights thrust columns of light skyward. The entire field was enveloped in a bath of intense light as the beams diffused against the nocturnal cloud cover and a quarter of a million voices shouted, "Sieg Heil!"

In his speeches, Hitler pounded home his theme of an Aryan race destined to achieve its manifest historical destiny through the establishment of a leader state set against Bolshevism and Zionism. These were the themes of *Mein Kampf,* and they were central to the führer's oratorical pyrotechnics at the Nuremberg Rallies.

While the proceedings within the stadium occupied most of the world press's attention, another dimension to the Nazi Party rallies at Nuremberg tended to escape notice. Throughout the week, festivities, lectures, demonstrations, exhibitions, and amusements were scheduled on the rally grounds. Rosenberg, or even Hitler himself, would discuss the rudiments of Nazi *Kultur* theory, the relationship between art and government.

Demonstrations by a variety of Nazi organizations from the SS to the Hitler Youth delighted audiences with examples of precision marching, mock combat, and choral singing. The entertainment included sports, dancing, shooting, bowling, band music, beer tents, and elaborate firework displays. In addition, exhibitions set up on the field fulfilled explicitly propagandistic functions, with a photo gallery exhibit depicting the horrors of communism in Russia under the banner of "World Enemy Number 1, World Bolshevism." These more casual events, far from detracting from the nightly extravaganzas, served as yet another bridge between the clearly staged reality inside the stadium and the everyday life of those in attendance.

# CHAPTER 4

# From Party Rally to German Cinema

———∞∞∞———

An elaborate system of propaganda, making use of the new technologies, high-speed film, long lenses, and lighter cameras, provided the tools for German cinema to emerge as an art form. Directors had the opportunity to shoot events with as many as ten cameras before editing the scenes together. Film became a favored instrument of propaganda. Hitler and Goebbels took a great interest in filmmaking, and the use of film for propaganda was meticulously planned by the National Socialist German Workers Party when it took control of German studios.

Hitler intended to project his stage image and his definition of Germany's situation to an audience beyond those who could travel to Nuremberg. Virtually all of the führer's addresses were broadcast over the radio and reported at length in the daily press. Sections of the rally were specifically staged and tailored for filming. Special towers were constructed for Germany's most infamous filmmaker, Leni Riefenstahl.

From the time the Nazis assumed power, they sought to exercise a monopoly on the flow of public information. By controlling the news media, limiting public assembly, and attracting other ideological institutions, the Nazis converted and sensitized much of the German public. The German press remained in private hands during the prewar period of the Third Reich, but it was nonetheless censored. Each day a press conference was held in Berlin and a document given to each newspaper's confidential envoy with detailed instructions about what stories should appear in the next day's edition and how they should be presented. The disclosure of their contents to unauthorized sources had consequences.

One reporter, from the Berliner *Börsen-Zeitung*, leaked instructions to members of the foreign press and was subsequently sentenced to life in prison. As for foreign newspapers, most were classified as *verboten*. They could not be sold at newspaper kiosks or legally distributed within the Reich even before World War II.

For the most part, those who disagreed with Hitler's policies stayed silent. *Be Proud and Silent* was a slogan encouraging people to accede to Nazi policies.

The Nazis had their own in-house crop of moviemakers. Hitler had seen Leni Riefenstahl's *The Blue Light* and found its dynamic treatment of mountaineering gymnastics entirely consistent with his vision of physical culture in Germany. He requested that Riefenstahl turn her cinematic vision to filming the 1934 Nuremberg Rally, and effectively gave *Triumph of the Will* unlimited financial backing.

The film was more than a faithful cinematic transcription of the party rally, for the medium afforded Riefenstahl the creative freedom to intercut in striking montages key Nazi symbols with images of the crowd and of Hitler. The film begins with rows of raised arms that converge toward Hitler's car while it slowly passes, then from an overhead camera angle, there's a bird's-eye view of thousands of tents housing Hitler Youth, the shot ending with an ornamental pattern composed of torch-lights searching through a huge cloth banner in the foreground.

Throughout the film, the swastika and the Reich's eagle are coupled within the frame alongside Hitler, with symbolic power. In league with this use of symbolism, Riefenstahl borrowed devices that had been developed in the people's choric theater. The nation was at work for the Fatherland; the incredible number of military formations massed on the parade grounds overwhelmed the senses.

In this stunning documentary, the Nazis conveyed their message, the film being made in concert with the event. Riefenstahl participated in planning the Nuremberg Rally to amplify its power in cinematic form. While it is difficult to square Riefenstahl's longstanding insistence that *Triumph of the Will* was mere documentary, the central point once again is how the Nazis intentionally blurred the line between art and life.

Far more than any other political movement in history, the Nazis maximized the power of the newsreel. One of the favorite concluding shots common to Nazi newsreels was that of uniformed platoons marching towards eternity, the columns heading off into a distant sky.

Pictorial content was closely controlled. *Baptism of Fire* and *Victory in the West*, for instance, documented the Nazi conquests of the Low Countries and France. German newsreel editors invariably interspersed images of beautiful natural settings among the action shots. Indeed, despite the fact that it was now an occupied city, Paris in *Victory in the West* was shown as tranquil, even bucolic, with images of birds and flowing rivers intercut with the smiling faces of German soldiers and French civilians, cunningly juxtaposed so that the invading army appears to be welcomed by the French.

Uniformity was key in portraying both the unified Germans and the unified enemies. When the Nazi Party came out with the anti-Semitic propaganda film that posed as a documentary, *The Eternal Jew,* they used Jewish symbols like the Star of David and fonts that resembled Hebrew to show Jews as a single, culturally distinct population separate from the Germans.

As the enemy was framed and defined, it became easier for the Nazis to rally the masses, who were also being framed and defined. Given the humiliation of the Treaty of Versailles and the tumultuous economic times, the Nazis used their propaganda machine to rally the "Aryan" German family in supporting the Nazi cause. In the end, the Nazis succeeded in propagating what is now known as in-group bias, the tendency for people to give preferential treatment to members of their own group. This, in combination with the anti-Jewish propaganda, succeeded in distancing the majority of the German population from anyone who was not seen as a pure Aryan.

Between the beginning of September 1939 and mid-November 1942, Goebbels's Propaganda Ministry had a wealth of material at hand to demonstrate that Hitler's script was being performed and that its climax, the defeat of the Allies, was a dramatic given. Morale among German forces and civilians was high. Victories bore out Hitler's text and, even if there were lapses, they could be hidden and the Nazis could rely upon Germany to cast the players in their appointed roles. In town squares throughout the enlarged Reich, huge maps were displayed so that citizens could follow the progress of the Panzer units rolling across Western Europe and, after June 1941, into the USSR.

Graphic evidence of an inexorable Axis march was filmed by daredevil cameramen sending back newsreel footage, and after careful editing, shown to German audiences flocking to Nazi-controlled movie houses. While Goebbels governed his own speaker's bureau, sending delegates schooled in performance throughout the Reich to mobilize public support for their country's war cause, it was the cinema that carried the home front message.

Goebbels became increasingly attached to his self-appointed function as Nazi Germany's principal film producer. His focus had always been on cinema, but now the introduction of radio as a propaganda vehicle was too effective to overlook. Allied propaganda coming into German-occupied territory, both white and black, constituted a problem. If radio receiving sets were allowed to remain in private hands, a portion of the Allied propaganda message was bound to undercut the Nazi script, but if they were confiscated, the Nazis would be deprived of this means of getting their own message out, and effectively put into play.

No such conflict was involved in the use of film. Goebbels was especially attached to the motion picture; three evenings a week he previewed a feature film and newsreel not only to seek relaxation and the company of film people, but also to offer what he considered to be expert criticism.

Film dominated over radio. Goebbels's belief in the supreme importance of newsreels inspired him to provide his newsreel company with expanded headquarters after one of the heaviest air raids Berlin experienced toward the end of 1943. He assumed near-absolute control over what went into German documentaries, quasi-documentaries, and official historical films.

From files in the United States Holocaust Museum comes a report confirming that newsreels were indeed central to German Propaganda Minister Goebbels's efforts to form and manipulate public opinion. To exercise greater control over newsreel content as the war progressed, the Nazi regime consolidated the country's various competing newsreel companies into one, the *Deutsche Wochenschau* (German Weekly Perspective). Goebbels actively helped create each newsreel installment, even editing or revising scripts. Twelve to eighteen hours of film footage shot by professional photographers and delivered to Berlin each week by courier were edited down to 20 to 40 minutes.

Distribution of newsreels was greatly expanded as the number of copies of each episode increased from four hundred to two thousand, and dozens of foreign language versions (including Swedish and Hungarian) were produced. Mobile cinema trucks brought the newsreels to rural areas of Germany.

There were accompanying films about the Nazi conquests. *Bomber Squadron Lutzow*, for instance, was about centers of inhuman treatment at the hands of a Polish overlord, culminating in the rescue of a column of German POWs by the heroic Luftwaffe, which machine-guns and dive-bombs Polish guards while leaving their captives miraculously unscathed. German forces, under the führer's personal direction, wreaked havoc on Polish oppressors before a single drop of German blood was shed.

Propaganda framed the script to win over the majority of the German public; even those who had not supported Adolf Hitler in his design carried the Nazis' radical program, which required the acquiescence, support, or participation of broad sectors of the population. Combined with the use of terror to intimidate those who did not comply, Goebbels sought to manipulate and deceive the German population and the outside world. From shocking content about the rape of Aryan women, to the pollution of the German character brought about by the Jews, to appealing messages of a super race, at each step of the way, propagandists advanced the concepts of national unity and a utopian future that resonated with millions of Germans. Simultaneously, they waged campaigns that facilitated any theme that excluded the Nazi vision of the "National Community."

Goebbels's interest in film went beyond its content. Although *Gone with the Wind* seemed to contain an implicit antiwar message and may have served the isolationist cause in America, Goebbels was incandescent with envy at each screening. He was determined to produce an historical epic of equal sweep, directing his studio to make *Uncle Kruger.*

Emil Jannings, one of a handful of first-rank German actors who remained in the homeland during the war, produced and starred in this historical drama about South African Boer statesman Paul Kruger and his battle against British imperialism—Goebbels could never quite put aside the ideological push. When the film garnered the foreign film prize at the 1941 Venice Film Festival, the propaganda minister's envy of *Gone with the Wind* was temporarily assuaged. *Uncle Kruger* might not have reached the artistic heights of its American model, but Gestapo agents assigned to monitor audience reaction to it at home and abroad reported that the anti-British mood had been significantly increased and consolidated. Regardless of artistic merit, *Uncle Kruger* was clearly a success in Germany.

Eventually, when the Nazi drive toward Moscow faltered and the people of Leningrad did not succumb to the invaders, Goebbels needed a means of squaring the role of Hitler as the infallible Messiah with the setbacks occurring under his nominal control. He once again turned to film as his medium. *The Great King*, released in March 1942, provided a frame for the redevelopment of the führer's character.

Based upon the near-legendary eighteenth-century Prussian King Frederick the Great, not only was *The Great King* able to advance, albeit by analogy, Hitler as a military genius, but it also dramatized scenes of Frederick berating his defeatist general staff and included an explanation of recent events in the field. One could accordingly conclude that the failure of the Blitz to crush the Russians was not Hitler's fault but, rather, that of the generals who had departed from the füh-rer's outline.

Hitler was not only personified as a common man who broke bread with his troops but as a Messiah as German Romanticism took on a Byronic tinge. German audiences, at least, liked it, and *The Great King* was a sterling instance of Nazi integration propaganda.

Joseph Goebbels also carefully implemented Hitler's vision. Following Hitler's *Mein Kampf,* he advocated the use of propaganda to spread the ideals of National Socialism—racism, anti-Semitism, and anti-Bolshevism. Germans were reminded of the struggle against foreign enemies and Jewish subversion. During periods preceding legislation or executive measures against Jews, propaganda campaigns created an atmosphere tolerant of violence against Jews and establishing the Nuremberg Race Laws, prior to the barrage of anti-Semitic economic legislation following *Kristallnacht.*

Propaganda also encouraged passivity and acceptance of the impending measures against Jews, with the manufactured appearance that the Nazi government was stepping in and "restoring order."

Films played an important role in disseminating racial anti-Semi-tism, the superiority of German military power, and the intrinsic evil of the enemies as defined by Nazi ideology. Nazi films portrayed Jews as "subhuman" creatures infiltrating Aryan society. For example, the afore-mentioned film *The Eternal Jew* (1940), directed by Fritz Hippler, por-trayed Jews as wandering cultural parasites, consumed by sex and money.

The Nazi regime used propaganda effectively to mobilize the German population to support its wars of conquest until the very end of the regime. It also served to secure the acquiescence of millions to racially targeted persecution and mass murder.

Excelling at organizing masses on the screen as well as on the street, the Nazis' filmmakers devised a characteristic sequence in which the image of the crowd figured centrally. This trope, found time and again, starts with an establishing shot of a crowd photographed with a tele-scopic lens. It then moves to extreme close-ups of individuals observing the crowds, normally the faces of women and children rather than men.

In the last stage, the camera returns to the crowd, implying that the individuals appearing before have now joined its ranks and have voluntarily traded their individual existence for membership of the masses. There is, as one might anticipate, an exception to this editing guideline. Hitler alone appears as an individual and never loses his individuality in a sea of waving arms and bobbing heads.

With a carefully designed strategy to promote the will of the nation, the German script was complete. With the invasion of Poland in August, the war moved into actual performance, and Hitler's extensive impression management, reinforced by staged popular rallies and the careful use of film, had a powerful effect on the German military and civilian populations. For Germany, there was no turning back. German politics and propaganda were projected onto an international screen. The drama of the Third Reich would be played out and the conflict developed on the world stage.

• • •

Films were a useful tool, but in this powerful, indeed overwhelming drama, Adolf Hitler exhibited the timing and sleight of hand of a skilled magician. The speed, precision, and orderliness with which he moved should have no longer surprised the world, but he outperformed even himself. His culminating campaign in Czechoslovakia lasted exactly three days.

Edvard Beneš, the president of Czechoslovakia, was forced to resign, and on October 5 he left for England after a trip to Berlin. Emil Hácha was sworn in as the new president. The men of Prague were voicing their anger and humiliation.

On the evening of March 14, Hitler invited the newly appointed President Hácha, who had been a respected jurist and judge, to the Reich Chancellery, the office of the chancellor of Germany, in Berlin.

Hitler sent a message to the president: "You have two options, my friend and President, for the safety of your country. One is to cooperate with Germany, in which case the entry of German troops will come peacefully. Two, if you should choose not to cooperate, resistance will be broken by force of arms."

By four o'clock, Hácha collapsed with a mild heart attack and was treated by Hitler's physician; then he effectively signed over Czechoslovakia to Germany, believing that collaboration was the only way he could help his people and nation.

When, in September, Britain met with French and Italian leaders to resolve the political status of Sudetenland Germans, no Czech leaders were allowed to participate. England had a treaty obligation to support Czechoslovakia in the event of an attack. After meeting with Hitler, Chamberlain returned with a paper proclaiming that he had brought peace with honor.

The Czechoslovak state president issued a statement that trustfully laid the fate of the Czech people and country into the hands of the führer of the German Reich.

The army's march on Prague began. "Attention! Attention!" blared Czech radios every five minutes all day. "German army infantry and aircraft are beginning the occupation of the republic. The slightest resistance will be met with utter brutality. All commands have to obey the order."

Meanwhile, Nazi troops seized the remainder of Czechoslovakia. In Prague, Germans began arrogant demonstrations. Stormtroopers posted themselves outside German schools. Squads of German students in jackboots and armbands jostled their way through the bewildered crowds shouting, "Heil Hitler! Sieg Heil!" Repeatedly warned that resistance would be futile and fatal, crowds greeted the first armored cars in Prague's streets in mute despair. Later in the day they grew defiant. Groups sang the Czech anthem and wept openly. Some shouted "Pfui!" ("Go back home!"). But the only physical resistance Herr Hitler's tanks met was a volley of snowballs.

For Prague's Jewish district there was terror. By the week's end the number of documented suicides had risen to one hundred. The soldiers, acting under incredibly detailed orders worked out weeks in advance, closed all banks, took over hotels, invaded barracks to disarm one of the best-equipped armies in Europe, and began to arrest political prisoners from a list of over two thousand.

Adolf Hitler, having snatched a few minutes' sleep on a train from Berlin to the border, had then driven in swirling snow and over icy roads through Sudeten villages and Czech towns to Prague.

Aware that the last German Emperor, Kaiser Wilhelm II, had lost the First World War, the monarchy was tainted with the loss. Hitler had come to power with a constitution giving authority to sweep away the old order and had no desire to return to any form of monarchy. If Hitler had declared himself Emperor, it would have diminished his image, and while he avoided that political assumption, he used stagecraft to establish an image of victory. But in Prague he had an emperor's entry exactly eight hours after the arrival of his vanguard, exactly twenty-five hours after having summoned Dr. Hácha to Berlin, exactly one year and a day to the hour after his triumphal entry into Vienna. At dusk his car climbed the hill to ancient Hradčany Castle. Slowly he ascended its stairs to his suite. Adolf Hitler's personal gold-bordered swastika was unfurled overhead. He stepped up to a window and looked down on the twinkling lights of the city. Then he announced the previously-devised organization of Bohemia and Moravia as a protectorate. Thus, aside from the mopping-up operations, the campaign was completed. When he arrived back in Berlin, Stormtrooper units and loudspeakers sang out all day a song with the refrain:

"Today we own Germany. . . . Tomorrow the world."

# CHAPTER 5

# Theater of the Absurd

—◆◆◆◆◆◆—

In time, Hitler was concerned as to how the world might perceive Germany's treatment of Europe's culturally accomplished Jewish population. To counteract any bad publicity, he devised a ruse to distract any negative perception.

He looked for another solution, a place for respected authors, musicians, composers, actors, Jewish officers, and Jewish World War I veterans who had distinguished themselves.

As Nazism and newly enforced racial laws spread across Europe, the Reich found a small town in Czechoslovakia that would suddenly become an outpost for learning and culture. The attractive former military fortress built by the Habsburgs was an area nine blocks long and five wide. Past the gates, faded yellow buildings with red tiled roofs housed officer quarters. Each group had a park, a quadrangle and green lawns, and in the center, a large square for parades. From a bird's-eye view, the camp looked like an eight-pointed star.

In return for the requisition of homes, and the order for financial account holdings to be placed under German care and supervision until the end of the war, Hitler offered accommodations, a spa just outside of Prague, to both German and European Jewry. They turned over their bank accounts, homes, and art collections for "safekeeping" until hostilities ceased and they could return home. Here a family could enjoy the finest music, attend lectures, and receive fairly good medical care. To the unsuspecting, living side by side with many of Europe's more distinguished composers and conductors, statesmen and soldiers, scientists and scholars, along with numerous celebrities from stage, screen, concert halls, and other walks of life, seemed an attractive package.

The prominent personages shared one common characteristic: all were Jews escaping the Nazi menace. Because of their stature and connections within their respective countries, they could not be marked for execution, at least not right away. Their total disappearance might occasion disturbing inquiries abroad as well as within the Reich itself. Instead, they would be given an entire city in which they would be safe. The city was Theresienstadt, and the Nazis described it as Hitler's gift to the Jews.

In this way, Theresienstadt, a drama unto itself, became a showplace; a unique, self-governing concentration camp designed to cover up the Jewish extermination program. Its inmates were not only allowed to receive packages from friends and relatives, but also from Jewish relief agencies operating in neutral countries.

Within the world's press, there came reports of brutal war crimes committed in German concentration camps and intolerable conditions that violated the Geneva Convention. News of gas chambers began to spread. Britain and America appealed to the neutral Swedish government to intervene and the Red Cross in Switzerland to inspect. To every official diplomatic channel, Joseph Goebbels, German minister of propaganda, denied reports of extermination as outrageous rumor.

A letter given to the International Red Cross concerning Theresienstadt, also known as Terezín, the community that had been widely reported to be a model concentration camp, brought humanitarian concern. It was written by Baroness Bleichroeder, granddaughter of Bismarck's most noted financier, and received by Peter de Pilar, undersecretary of the International Red Cross Headquarters in Geneva. She reported intolerable overcrowding and appalling lack of medical attention and food rationing. Her husband, General Bleichroeder, a decorated German veteran in World War I, had been transported to a work camp in the east, her family of five lived in one small room, and her daughter suffered a long illness after repeated appeals for medical attention were ignored.

The family had turned over their considerable fortune to the Germans for safekeeping, in return for a place to live in dignity for the war's duration, a place widely promoted by the Nazis. De Pilar, a friend of Baron Bleichroeder's before the war, funded charitable foundations, including the Red Cross. That organization's charter monitors countries needing emergency assistance in war and peacetime. Copies of the letter were sent to the leaders of the World Jewish Congress and to the Czech government-in-exile in Britain. Outraged, de Pilar issued a statement from Geneva: "If this is accurate, it cannot stand."

To quash rumors about the killing centers, the Nazis permitted a visit to Theresienstadt by representatives of the International Red Cross. Hitler could not allow such reports staining the honor of German virtue, so he put into play an elaborate scheme that would be unmatched in illusion and deception.

"What you will see here is a normal provincial village," the commandant said to the visiting representatives. The delegation was made up of: Franz Hvass, of the Danish Foreign Office Political Section; Dr. Eigil Juel Henningsen, a director from the Department of Health; Maurice Rossel, director general of the International Red Cross; his deputy and others. The visitors, eighteen in all, set out to see Terezín for themselves. A fleet of Mercedes drove them along a predetermined route. The cars stopped by the park and at the shopping street, and then the inspection party continued on foot. They visited the bank; Terezín now had its own banknotes with a picture of Moses engraved upon the currency.

It was a clear day, perfect for sightseeing. The landscape was interrupted only by signs reading "To the School," "To the Café," "To the Theater," "To the Baths." The newly constructed bandstand had a uniformed brass ensemble playing marching songs, with just enough of a tempo for anyone to step in time to their tunes. The conductor bowed. Leading the inspection, Rossel remarked to the delegation, "The camp band. They play well, don't you think?"

Women in clean coveralls with rakes over their shoulders, looking as if they had stepped out of a poster, marched past on cue. On a farm that had been cultivated just outside the village, the workers had been ordered to arrange a "market" of lettuce, tomatoes, and cucumbers to ripen. "We grow most of our own vegetables here," they said. To produce enough for the village population would have taken miles of cultivated fields, but still it appeared reasonable enough.

The smell of freshly baked bread invited the delegation to meet a line of cheery bakers in white hats and gloves, dispensing slices of pumpernickel loaves fresh out of the oven.

Hvass and Juel Henningsen checked their fellow Danish residents and dropped in to see their refurbished quarters, bringing greetings from King Christian and the bishop of Copenhagen, and spent enough time to observe their well-being so they could report back to church and state.

The group walked past chess players studiously plotting their next moves. On a converted park square, spectators joined soccer fans and cheered as a goal was scored.

Hearing the voices rehearsing Verdi's *Requiem*, for which the world-famous Raphael Schächter had recruited soloists and a fifty-member choir, they listened to the last refrain, a rising crescendo of *Libera Me*, which was beautifully performed.

The delegation went to remodeled living quarters and the newly supplied pharmacy.

"I imagine it's a sacrifice for the German army to give up necessities," said Rossel, the head of the delegation. Distributing medicine to civilians was *verboten* by the German high command.

Terezín was a play, a stage-managed deception, and Rossel had come to observe, but he was selective, seeing things as he wished. Even during the tour, when a passerby pressed a folded piece of paper into the hand of one of the delegates—"Was Sie sehen hier ist nicht wahr. Bitte helfen sie uns." ("What you see here is not true. Please help us.")—it was ignored.

What was meant to restore a measure of decency to Hitler's promise and reputation was no more than an elaborate hoax. Theresienstadt was a transition camp whose residents were systematically transported to Auschwitz. The Nazis launched a *stadtverschönerung*, a stunning Hollywood production, but a moral failure by any standard. The camp had been beautified, gardens planted, houses painted, sidewalks washed, buildings refreshed, barracks remodeled, a village green seeded with new turf, postal services improved, a bakery installed, concerts played, a beautiful children's opera, *Brundibár*, composed by Hans Krása, was performed in a grand hall, art and fashionable items displayed in store windows. It was a Potemkin village, much like the fake settlements that were specially constructed at the direction of Russian minister Grigory Potemkin to deceive Empress Catherine II during her visit to Crimea in 1787. Potemkin, who led the Crimean military campaign, built villages of hollow facades, false fronts along the desolate banks of the Dnieper River to impress the monarch and her court, demonstrating his conquests, securing his position, and winning admiration from the empress.

In Geneva, Rossel, head of the International Red Cross, issued his fifteen-page report. He told his staff and advisers, "Living conditions are a little crowded, but the food is terrific, and I should comment I saw some of the most attractive ladies in Europe, wearing silk stockings, hats and scarves, carrying handbags." He concluded, with misguided assurance, "After our inspection and tour of Theresienstadt, we report an extraordinarily high standard of care, outstanding medical facilities attended by European doctors in residence, and that the number of Jews sent to labor camps is exaggerated."

Rossel and his delegation did not know that the men playing chess so studiously in the park had never played chess in their lives. They did not know that the patients in the hospital under clean white sheets had arrived just a few weeks before. They didn't know that the pharmacy rarely if ever dispensed medicine. They did not know that the school marked "Closed for Summer Vacation" had never been a real school. They did not know that the dolls the little girls were joyfully playing with had been given to them just hours before, or that the banquet they so enjoyed was organized for their benefit only. And they certainly did not know that sentries had preceded their every step, giving signals so that the young women with rakes over their shoulders would be marching past the visitors, or the soccer goal and cheering spectators were laid on for them, or that the finale of the Verdi *Requiem* would be sung on cue as they arrived.

Director Maurice Rossel was the most misinformed or the most nearsighted man in Europe.

After the inspection, the entire chorus who had sung Verdi's moving *Requiem* were transported to Auschwitz. In time, all but three of the children who performed in the cast of *Brundibár* were sent east on trains.

In hundreds of other camps "transport" became the dreaded synonym for death. Many asked in a questioning indictment, "Why weren't the railroads serving the extermination camps bombed as so many leaders requested?"

World War II had many stages and sets. Terezín was certainly a stunning example of performance in action.

• • •

Away in the peaceful Bavarian Alps underscored by Wagnerian music, was another theater of diplomatic drama with performances by a select group of actors. Adolf Hitler's Berghof at Berchtesgaden was a setting in a mountain hideaway fifteen miles from Salzburg, six hundred miles from Danzig, 1,300 miles from Moscow, and three thousand feet above sea level. Facing the cloud-capped mountains, the brown and white Berghof itself, with its huge echoing rooms, bedrooms for forty guests, guards' turrets, machine gun nests, seemed as unreal as the home of the troll kings. At this ethereal haunt there arrived German Foreign Minister Joachim von Ribbentrop, sundry legal experts, advisers, and retainers.

The chalet, high in the Bavarian Alps, was designed by Hitler himself. On the second floor, leading off from a pine-paneled living room, there was a terrace with large red umbrellas. Inside, past a telephone switchboard, a study, and in the center of the room, a globe. Beyond it, a floor-to-ceiling window with views that reached as far as the eye could see. Wearing lederhosen and embroidered braces, often with his mistress Eva Braun at his side. After a pause, the führer treated his lunch guests to the prologue to a drama that would include slanderous words timed to the second, a bombardment of rumor, blankets of lies, provocations exploding like mines before advancing troops, flank attacks of economic reprisals, and promises and threats launched simultaneously. His road company arrived in Poland.

Germany's journalistic big guns poured an unceasing barrage on that country. Führer Hitler said that part of Poland should be returned to the Reich and if the Poles cooperated there would be no need for an act of war. Leaving this riddle for the world to ponder, he then vanished into the mountains again like a figure from Wagnerian mythology.

The proud old Hanseatic city of Danzig worked and played so normally that uninformed visitors could scarcely have guessed what international storms were gathering about it. Thousands relaxed on the gloriously white sands or swam in the cool waters of Danzig Bay. The Nazi-operated radio station invited listeners to "come and see Danzig and spend your summer holidays here."

Filtering into the Free City were German "tourists," all of them men aged between twenty-five and forty. The Poles estimated that seven thousand of them arrived in one week. They were housed in barracks and were soon observed installing machine guns and building fortifications on the Bischofsberg, the hill to the city's southwest. The seizure of Danzig by Germany would mean no more than another of Hitler's conquests, another large Baltic seaport, and 407,000 more Germans added to the Reich. To Poland, the loss of Danzig would probably eventually mean the loss of the Polish Corridor if not absolute political domination by Germany.

The city, which had once been a part of Poland but later became the capital of West Prussia, was declared a Free City under League of Nations protection at the end of World War I. As such, it provided Poland with a guaranteed outlet to the sea. The city's population remained largely German.

At the end of August 1939, for the seven most momentous days of Europe's modern history, Adolf Hitler did not leave his Chancellery. Alone in spirit, he slept little, ate little, spoke little. He rose promptly at seven o'clock each morning, put on his brown uniform, breakfasted on fruit, zwieback, and a glass of milk. Throughout the day he conferred endlessly, stopping for twenty-minute meals of vegetables, bread and butter and his special 1 percent beer. For half an hour in the morning, and again in the afternoon, he strolled through the Chancellery gardens.

Until deep into the night he talked with the closest of his confidants, leaving them for bed at four or five in the morning. Whenever a decision was needed, he went off to brood alone. His nerves grew taut. By the last Wednesday in August, when he gave Sir Nevile Henderson his demands for a Polish settlement, none was offered, and Hitler would not have patience mistaken for weakness. He waited no longer. He sat alone in his study, a portrait of Bismarck looking down at him from the opposite wall. The night wore on; milk wagons began to rattle through the streets. He called for Göring and Hess and issued his directive, then instructed Himmler to produce an opening scene.

It was a curious request to make of the German army, and Chief of Staff Franz Halder noted the fact in his diary. Heinrich Himmler, head of the SS, the party's own armed force, wanted a supply of Polish military uniforms. Puzzling or not, Himmler's appeal was honored by the army with its usual efficiency: the uniforms were swiftly procured and delivered.

Probably neither Halder nor any other Wehrmacht officer was aware of the reason for the clothing at the time, but before long they understood it all too well. Sometime during the last two weeks of August, thirty-four inmates were taken from a concentration camp in eastern Germany and installed in a nearby schoolhouse. On the last day of the month, all but one of the prisoners were ordered to dress themselves in the Polish uniforms, then they were injected with a fatal poison, taken to a small forest near the German-Polish border, and shot. Their bodies were arranged as though they were Polish soldiers who had died while advancing into Germany.

Later that day, the thirty-fourth inmate was hustled off to the nearby town of Gleiwitz. Wearing Polish civilian clothes, he and other similarly disguised SS security men commandeered the local radio station and broadcast an inflammatory statement announcing Poland was attacking Germany and urging all Poles to join the colors. A simulated scuffle with station personnel then ensued before an open microphone, leaving the inmate who had impersonated the firebrand "Polish" broadcaster lying dead from gunshot wounds on the studio floor.

On September 1, at 10:00 a.m., Hitler stood before the Reichstag and cited the charade at Gleiwitz as an instance of Polish aggression on German soil. By then the first phase of his meticulously planned military campaign against the Poles had already been launched by sea, land, and air, and every sign indicated a quick German victory. World War II had begun.

• • •

Adolf Hitler picked up a pen. At 5:11 in the morning of September 1, Germany was at war. Later that morning, worn and harried, he stood before the Reichstag. No one in Germany, not even the kaiser, had ever spoken as Hitler spoke that day. It was the speech of a man persecuted beyond endurance, a man driven by some mystical inner necessity, a man who was alone with his fate.

"My love of peace and my endless patience should not be mistaken for weakness. I am now determined to talk the same language to Poland that Poland has been talking to us." All of his psychic forces drove Adolf Hitler into war, though it was an exhausting undertaking: "All my life I have wanted to be a great painter in oils. I am tired of politics, and as soon as I have carried out my program for Germany I shall take up my painting." Somehow, a failed artist forgot, just for a moment, his self-imposed destiny. Could he have known he was playing the role of one of the most ruthless dictators of all time? Was he overpowered by the beauty of the Alps, the freshness of the air, the companion of a woman who was devoted to him? Perhaps he remembered for an instant where he had come from? At that moment, that brief interlude from reality, he expressed, "I feel that I have it in my soul to become one of the great artists of the age and that future historians will remember me, not for what I have done for Germany, but for my art."

# Entr'acte

———∞∞∞———

I n his sixth year as the dictator of Germany, Adolf Hitler scripted the *Lebensraum* that he had promised the Germans. After annexing Austria, he signed the Munich Pact with Britain and France on September 9, 1938, which awarded Germany the Sudetenland area of Czechoslovakia. The pact guaranteed new boundaries for the rest of Czechoslovakia. By March 1939, Hitler had violated the pact and seized the rest of the country in a swift, bloodless takeover. After protecting himself against Russian interference by signing a nonaggression pact with Stalin, Hitler sent his troops marching into Poland—and the drama called World War II began in 1939, a history book year.

That September, Europe was plunged into a war that would last six years, embroil most of the world, and cause the deaths of more than fifty million people. There were other major, and occasionally violent, international occurrences as well: the end of Spain's Civil War, Russia's bloody invasion of Finland and bloodless conquest of the Baltic states, Italy's seizure of Albania. The outbreak of war overshadowed most other events, but life went on—the United States had World's Fairs in New York and San Francisco; heavyweight-boxing champ Joe Louis beat challenger Tony Galento; Major Bowes was presiding over radio's *Original Amateur Hour*; the king and queen of England came to visit and have tea with President and Mrs. Franklin D. Roosevelt.

In August 1939, after Hitler had signed the nonaggression pact with Stalin that divided Eastern Europe into zones of influence and left Germany free to take over the rest of Europe without Russian interference, Hitler's propaganda machine was in high gear, and on the home front Hitler's march of tyranny throughout Europe was hard for Americans to imagine, much less prevent.

Franklin Delano Roosevelt's New Deal measures had made him highly unpopular with many of the nation's businessmen and had aroused opposition even in the Democrat-controlled Congress. But in the fall of 1940, Roosevelt had defeated the Republican presidential candidate, Wendell Willkie, by an overwhelming margin. With this new mandate he began to lead the United States away from its traditional isolationism and to align the nation more and more with Great Britain and later Russia in the war against Germany. America's involvement would take time. Franklin Roosevelt began collaboration on a script with Winston Churchill. But Britain was already at war.

Britain experienced the real threat of invasion. Local Defence Volunteers (later known as the Home Guard) were formed to support the regular army in the event of attack. They also undertook security patrols of installations, were on the alert for downed enemy aircraft, helped rescue services, and supported antiaircraft batteries. Air Raid Precaution (ARP) units were established prior to 1939. ARP patrols located bomb "incidents" and coordinated responses from fire and rescue services. Policemen, Auxiliary Fire Service (AFS), Heavy Rescue, and stretcher teams were often required to recover the dead and wounded from buildings damaged by air raids. Women served in a range of civil defense roles: as ARP wardens, in the Police Force, as ambulance drivers, and AFS telephone operators. Additionally, the Women's Voluntary Service (WVS) assisted in evacuation schemes.

In Europe it was total war. In the United States it was shock: the grim event had finally arrived. Roosevelt, who had the benefit of a forewarning from the US diplomatic corps, returned to Washington three days before the Nazi thrust and thus had an opportunity before other men to consider with the cold light of reason an even more momentous event: a change in the visible shape of things to come. The first and the most controversial possibility was that the United States might, within a few months if not a few weeks, have to decide whether or not it would go to war in still another theater. If German victory began to look probable, it was possible that Japan would move to seize the Dutch East Indies. If Germany moved to destroy the British Empire, Japan would seize British Malaya.

Those far-off lands meant little to the United States, except that from these outposts came the major portion of the rubber and tin on which the country depended. There was no other present source from which the United States could get an adequate supply of these necessities. However the US decision went, it would be serious, and may well be made on short notice. Wrote Walter Lippmann, a gifted American writer, reporter, and political commentator, "If the offensive which Hitler has now launched in Poland succeeds, we shall know no peace in our lifetime. Our duty is to begin acting at once on the basic assumption that the Allies may lose the war this summer, and that before the snow flies again we may stand alone and isolated, the last great democracy on earth."

On New Year's Day 1940, though Germany had clamped an iron fist around Central Europe and Japan was raping China, most Americans were peaceably preoccupied with their own homegrown affairs. They had been lining up at movie theaters since 1939 to see the film version of *Gone with the Wind*, Margaret Mitchell's romantic novel of the Old South. They were betting on whether a nimble, bantamweight Tennessee eleven would trounce the brawny 220-pounders of Southern California in the Rose Bowl. They were feeding nickels into roadhouse jukeboxes to hear Wee Bonnie Baker warble, "Oh, Johnny! Oh!" And they were looking ahead to the nation's quadrennial circus, the presidential conventions, where the biggest question would be whether "That Man in the White House," never a stickler for tradition, would shatter yet another precedent and run for a third term, a question on which the subject himself kept smilingly silent. To many Americans, there seemed little else to worry about. True, some big trouble had been brewing overseas.

But US citizens assured themselves that they were "two broad oceans" away from foreigners' ancient quarrels. The Japanese would never dare to invade America. China was what Japan wanted, and China was on the other side of the globe. Besides, the European war now appeared to be at a standstill. Four months had passed since the Nazi dictator Adolf Hitler had sent his panzers into Poland.

Since the quick destruction of Poland in September 1939, so little had happened that Idaho Senator William E. Borah, a devout isolationist ever since World War I, dubbed this one the "phony war." While the war stood still, American sentiment remained where it had been in the 1930s, when the US government had pledged itself, by a series of neutrality acts, to remain aloof from European entanglements. A poll conducted by Elmo Roper in December 1939 showed that 67.4 percent of the American people were opposed to taking sides.

Yet in the United States, as far back as 1937, the Young Communist League was formed, and no one worked harder at being American than the American communists. Cast as sympathizers, they created organizations made up of plain ordinary people, who wanted to cooperate with other patriots.

The sudden transformation began not in America, but in Moscow, where the Russians shelved their traditional anti-capitalist dogma, and convinced freedom-loving nations around the world to form an alliance to protect the Red motherland.

The new line of thinking was called the Popular Front, and in the United States the *Daily Worker*, a communist paper, was inaugurated to support Russia, attracting Americans with WASP names and a *Mayflower* lineage, and extending its reach, citing equality and the plight of the "American Negro" in black churches. At its peak, the Front had more than seven million members, representing thousands of affiliated organizations, acquiring a measure of respectability. Communism took precedence over Nazism.

Hollywood was where the party thrived, plush Beverly Hills neighborhoods buzzing with zealous activism for a variety of causes. Members of Hollywood's Anti-Nazi League and the Screen Writers Guild, and assorted writers and stars in their ambit, threw open their hearts, their homes, their swimming pools, so that the Hollywood branch of the Front with its seductive tang of celebrity became hard to resist. Where else could so many liberals rub bosoms and shoulders with such stellar characters as Myrna Loy, Joan Crawford, Edward G. Robinson, James Cagney, and Melvyn Douglas? The film community relished the sensation of being involved with history in the making, and gave generously of their time and money. It was a heady mix while it lasted, but on August 23, 1939, in another spectacular turn of events, Russia signed with Germany the Nazi-Soviet pact and Stalin toasted Hitler's health: "I know how much the German nation owes to the führer."

With those shocking words, the ideological ground beneath the Popular Front gave way. Within months, the American Communist Party had lost most of its members, and many thousands of other Americans who had been pursuing "the good cause" under a Red banner awoke to the realization that they had been duped.

Then the landscape changed in 1940 as Russia and Germany were on the move, taking one country after another: Finland invaded by Stalin's Russia; Norway, Denmark, Belgium, Luxembourg, the Netherlands, and France by Hitler's Germany. In June, under the pall of smoke that turned light clothes gray and made eyes smart, European life went on. The omnibuses and tubes in Paris continued to run, though less frequently, the radio stations broadcast only martial music interspersed with news bulletins and communiqués, and people journeyed out to the suburbs to see the damage caused by Nazi bombers. The cafés and the Bank of France remained open, and people stood in queues at local banks to withdraw their savings. Two American films ran on the Champs-Elysées theaters: *Going Places* and *You Can't Take It with You.*

Germans, who had been nourished on a staple diet of promises and threats, took a moment to relax. Adolf Hitler rescinded his ban on dancing and decreed that his countrymen could dance on Wednesdays and Saturdays between 7:00 p.m. and curfew. He also granted them permission to tune into Nazi-occupied Norway, Belgium, the Netherlands, and

France, but still forbade them under the threat of death to listen to Radio Denmark, which broadcast anti-German sentiment.

Hours after the invasion, the German minister in Oslo demanded Norway's surrender. The Norwegian government refused, and the Germans responded with a parachute invasion and the establishment of a puppet regime. Norwegian forces refused to accept German rule and continued to fight alongside British troops. But an accelerating German offensive in France led Britain to transfer thousands of soldiers from Norway to France, resulting ultimately in a German victory.

On the fall of France, Hitler dictated that the French capitulation take place in a forest north of Paris, the same spot where twenty-two years earlier the Germans had signed the armistice ending World War I. Hitler intended to disgrace the French and avenge the German defeat. To further deepen the humiliation, he ordered that the signing ceremony take place in the same railroad car that had hosted the earlier surrender. The armistice was signed on June 22. Under its terms, two thirds of France was to be occupied by the Germans. The French army was to be disbanded. In addition, France must bear the cost of the German invasion.

On a sunlit and still day, many a traveler had driven through the green aisles of the forest of Compiègne to see the wagon restaurant where the armistice of the First World War was signed. Compiègne is a very formal forest; unlike the deep woods of Germany, always a little wild and mysterious, the old trees of Compiègne stand in straight, neat rows. Planted long ago, they are a witness to a history of German order.

Hitler could not resist this theatrical curtain for the second act of the Promethean drama he had set in motion. He could not resist appearing in person to hear the terms of capitulation of France to the delegates on the spot where the Germans had made their surrender under the WWI German Armistice.

William Shirer, a radio reporter for CBS News, stood in the clearing in the forest of Compiègne next to the railroad car where the ceremony took place, broadcasting quietly the following commentary in hushed tones: "The time is now three eighteen p.m. Hitler's personal flag is run up on a small standard in the center of the opening. Also in the center is a great granite block which stands some three feet above the ground. Hitler, followed by the others, walks slowly over to it, steps up, and reads the inscription engraved for all time in great high letters on that block which he had composed: HERE ON THE ELEVENTH OF NOVEMBER 1918 SUC-CUMBED THE CRIMINAL PRIDE OF THE GERMAN EMPIRE . . . VANQUISHED BY THE FREE PEOPLES WHICH IT TRIED TO ENSLAVE. Hitler reads it aloud, and Göring reads it. They all read it, standing there in the June sun and the silence."

Hitler paid careful attention to the emotions he performed: "He glances slowly around the clearing, and now, as his eyes meet ours, you grasp the depth of his hatred. But there is triumph there too—revengeful, triumphant hate. Suddenly, as though his face were not giving quite complete expression to his feelings, he throws his whole body into harmony with his mood. He swiftly snaps his hands on his hips, arches his shoulders, plants his feet wide apart. It is a magnificent gesture of defiance, of burning contempt for this place now and all that it has stood for in the twenty-two years since it witnessed the humbling of the German Empire."

Hitler was increasingly aware of his place in history; even before the heady victory over France and the Lowlands, he had begun to talk as if his mission was no longer to smash Versailles and extend German power, but to correct in one lifetime the mistakes of the past. The staid, level beauty of the countryside was where Hitler's dominance over France must have been as incredible to him as to the rest of the world. He had gone a long way since his first territorial conquest. Now France was a defense against England.

How did Hitler achieve such remarkable success? Was there some black magic, some secret weapon or infallible prescription that enabled this World War I corporal to win Napoleonic triumphs? Perhaps he was not constricted by any moral standard? He simply knew what he wanted and got it.

For seven years Hitler had mobilized all the moral, military, and economic resources of Germany for "the sole purpose of waging war with all means."

In his own mind, the Nazi chancellor was unmistakably a man of destiny. At Compiègne, he delivered terms to the French from the same chair occupied by Marshal Foch years earlier. When he entered Paris, in a light brown duster over his uniform, he did an uncustomary jig on a terraced landscape reaching toward the Eiffel Tower.

The former corporal, the struggling artist, the despised dictator, the former state prisoner, the man who had bluffed most of Europe, had realized a grand ambition.

• • •

After the continent fell to the Nazis, Hitler turned his full attention to afternoon tea, to a battered Britain—only twenty miles distant from occupied France, without allies, and with an army much reduced and almost completely without arms after the debacle at Dunkirk.

In Britain, Winston Churchill came to power, and with eloquent speeches and a trickle of help from the United States—some aircraft along with fifty superannuated destroyers—he steeled his country for the long battle to come.

Churchill responded to Hitler's aggression: "If we are now called upon to endure what they have suffered, we shall emulate their courage, and if final victory rewards our toils we shall share the gains, aye, freedom, that shall be restored to all. . . . Upon it depends our own British life, and the long continuity of our institutions and our Empire. The whole fury and might of the enemy must very soon be turned on us. Hitler knows that he will have to break us in this island or lose the war."

In Churchill's compelling style, he continued, urging his countrymen, as he had done before with concern.

"If we can stand up to him, all Europe may be free and the life of the world may move forward into broad, sunlit uplands; but if we fail, the whole world, including the United States, including all that we have known and cared for, will sink into the abyss of a new Dark Age. . . . Let us therefore brace ourselves to do our duties, and so bear ourselves that, if the British empire and its commonwealth last for a thousand years, men will still say, 'This was their finest hour.'"

• • •

In the United States, President Roosevelt did indeed use the war as an argument for running for an unprecedented third term, and in the November election he defeated an unconventional and energetic Republican candidate, Wendell Willkie. The front lines were far away on a distant horizon, and at home, a seven-year-old horse named Seabiscuit became racing's biggest all-time moneymaker; Wagnerian soprano Helen Traubel made her debut at the Met; and Ernest Hemingway published his new novel, *For Whom the Bell Tolls.*

But in time, the United States would go to war, when the democracies were faced with a defeat as serious as the fall of France or the possible loss of the entire Far East. For Franklin Roosevelt and Winston Churchill to meet in Washington face-to-face at this juncture was an elementary step in the co-authorship of a script for the playing fields. Never before had a wartime prime minister of Great Britain visited the United States. Cloaked in secrecy, Churchill dropped out of the sky with breathtaking suddenness. The day after his arrival, Winston Churchill sat beside Franklin Roosevelt behind the broad desk of the Oval Office, waiting with the poker-faced calm of a veteran political speaker while two hundred–odd US and foreign newsmen gathered for a press conference unique in White House history. Those who crowded up front saw a pudgy man with cheeks like apple dumplings, blue eyes beneath restless crooked eyebrows, the merest foam-flecking of sandy gray hair on his bald pink pate, a long black cigar clenched at a belligerent angle above his bulldog jaw. From the sleeves of his blue sack coat extended long cuffs, half hiding the small hands folded placidly across his middle.

Franklin Roosevelt, less jaunty than usual, his style a little cramped by appearing as one of a duet, introduced his guest. There were shouts from the rear from newsmen who couldn't see. Churchill stood up, grinned, climbed on his chair, waved his hand. The applause and cheers rattled the windows. It was Churchill onstage, at his best.

On Christmas Eve, Winston Churchill stood bareheaded while Franklin Roosevelt, on the south portico of the White House, went through the annual ceremony of turning on the outdoor Christmas tree's lights. Then Churchill joined the president in broadcasting Christmas greetings to the nation. Said the prime minister: "I spend this anniversary and festival far from my country, far from my family, yet I cannot truthfully say that I feel far from home. . . . In God's mercy, a Happy Christmas to you all." His warm expression was a bond, a seal of friendship, a foundation of a partnership in the production that would effect the European Theater of War.

The real Churchill eloquence came later, at a joint session of Congress. Congressmen who had gone home for the Christmas holiday scurried back to Washington for the historic occasion. There were tears in Churchill's eyes at the ovation that greeted him, from isolationist and interventionist alike. He shoved his thick, horn-rimmed glasses over his nose, blinked, balanced himself like an old sailor. Then he let go—the growling, galling scorn for his enemies, the passages of noble purple for his friends: "I avow my hope and faith, sure and inviolate, that in the days to come the British and American peoples will, for their own safety and for the good of all, walk together in majesty, in justice, and in peace." When Churchill had finished, white-haired Chaplain Barney Phillips leaned over and whispered: "Mr. Prime Minister, you are the most perfect master of the English language in all the world."

• • •

While the Soviet Union was not a major player in political theater on the world stage, understanding the role it played suggests a broader perspective surrounding the country's historical background.

In Moscow, standing as a testament to the greatest revolutionary in Russian society is an impressive building on Moscow's Red Square. It is the tomb of Vladimir Lenin, the architect of the Soviet state, the man who led the Bolshevik Revolution expanding upon the concepts of Karl Marx, the man who effectively created a communist worldview. Following his Marxist perspective, humanity would become a vast, interconnected, classless, and collectivist society, a "society of abundance," with every citizen bearing their own individual need.

Before the war, the ideology of the Soviet Union had been based on the doctrines of Karl Marx and Vladimir Lenin, to promote reform. In a whirl of propaganda and spin, Lenin's fiftieth birthday had been marked by widespread celebrations across Russia with the publication of poems and biographies dedicated to him. Twenty volumes of Lenin's *Collected Works* were published. Shortly after, when he was in failing health, H. G. Wells and Bertrand Russell came to honor him at the Gorki palace, his exquisite home.

Despite his illness, Lenin still wished to be active in political developments, dictating *Lenin's Testament*, in which he discussed the personal qualities of his former comrades, favoring Leon Trotsky, the founding leader of the Red Army, and being particularly critical of Joseph Stalin, who despite his lack of confidence, would become the dictator of Russia, urging that he be removed from the position of General Secretary of the Communist Party: "Stalin is too crude, and this defect is . . . unacceptable in the position of General Secretary. I therefore propose to comrades that they should devise a means of removing him from this job and should appoint to this job someone else who is distinguished from comrade Stalin in all other respects only by the single superior aspect that he should be more tolerant, more polite and more attentive towards comrades."

It was not to be. Stalin defeated his archrival Trotsky, who fled, exiling himself to Mexico, and had already begun enhancing his power by appointing his supporters to prominent positions, taking responsibility for the Politburo, and by consolidating territories within Russia, changing the name of the newly proposed state to the Union of Soviet Socialist Republics.

While Lenin had been a keen supporter of world revolution, believing that the concept of national borders was an outdated one, Stalin sought to increase his own power, focusing on Russian nationalism, through cunning use of spin and subterfuge. He had always contended that with the struggle to build a socialist society, the necessary class struggle would intensify as enemies grew more desperate, and all opposition leaders were described as traitors and agents of foreign, imperialist powers.

His Five Year Plan further intensified this struggle, adding to the Great Terror. Those who spoke against the state and any who profited from public property were characterized as "enemies of the people" and rounded up for the gulags (labor camps).

Instilling hope, faith, and certainty, bringing solidarity among the population, the Soviet Union did its best to try to create a new society in which the people of Russia would unite as one, a society carefully depicted in posters and newsreels to inspire and enthuse the Russian people. One word was more effective than any other, and that word was *tovarish* ("comrade"). All the peoples of Russia were united so as to constitute a single great family.

But who was this man Stalin, wreaking havoc through terror supported by political propaganda within his nation and at the same time reaching across borders so that western nations were taking notice?

In 1878, on the year's shortest day, in Gori, near Tiflis, he was born to a poor hardworking Georgian cobbler named Vissarion Dzhugashvili. The boy's humble mother christened him Joseph. The family name would not stick very long, for in time, in revolution, and by clever political manipulation, he acquired the pseudonym of Stalin, "Man of Steel." Throughout his life, Stalin would leave an imprint on the world.

In 1940, *Pravda* declared: "Metal workers of Detroit, shipyard workers in Sydney, women textile workers of Shanghai, sailors at Marseille, Egyptian fellahin, Indian peasants, all speak of Stalin with love. He is the hope of the future of workers of the world." He advanced the communist cause, in his own country and abroad, winning support and courting controversy.

To further his aims, he maintained an iron grip on the production and dissemination of information. Propaganda and censorship were advanced through speeches, radio, and film to every segment of the population in schools, universities, and labor. A central censorship body called Glavlit, the General Directorate for the Protection of State Secrets in the Press, was established to prevent publication of information that could compromise state secrets in books, newspapers, and other printed matter, as well as in radio and media.

Not only did Glavlit monitor all printed materials, at home and abroad, but it also ensured that ideological spin was applied to every published item. Departing from the "party line" was punished by imprisonment or through courses of punitive psychiatric treatment. Journalist and playwright Isaac Babel once said to a trusted friend, "Today a man only talks freely to his wife—at night, with the blankets pulled over his head."

From the beginning, Russian politicians felt that the most effective way to indoctrinate people's minds was to begin with children through education. Communist youth organizations were launched in order to create a new man, a new way of thinking, a collective way of life. Just as with the Hitler Youth in Germany, so it was with the Soviet Pioneers—the underlying idea was to create a new generation to serve the nation, to "rescue children from the harmful influence of the family," to "nationalize them."

To build a utopia of equality and justice, Stalin, the godlike founder of the Soviet state, preserved the class struggle at the heart of Marxism, and he never failed in that mission. Radio was put to good use, with receivers in communal locations, where the populace gathered to hear news. Posters were widely distributed depicting the Red Army's triumphs. Films were heavily propagandistic. When war broke out, there were film dramas, like *Girl No. 217*, which told the story of a Russian girl enslaved by the inhumanity of a German family. Propaganda films were projected from specially equipped trains that rode the rails of Russia, stopping at remote villages and towns across the union.

Literature, visual art, and the performing arts drew on heroic realism, filled with images of health and happiness; paintings teemed with busy industrial and agricultural scenes, and sculptures depicted devoted workers, sentries, and schoolchildren all happily toeing the party line.

The essential instrument of news was *Pravda*, the official national newspaper of political discussion that scrupulously controlled news content.

Revolutionary theater was used to inspire support for the regime and hatred of its enemies, particularly agitprop theater, "noted for its cardboard characters of perfect virtue and complete evil." Many Soviet works depicted the development of a "positive hero" and promoted the hard discipline appropriate for the "socialist way of life."

The notion of an enemy, both internal and external, was a pervasive feature of communist propaganda.

# ACT II

# Curtain Going Up: The Lion Roars

———∞———

*Transitioning swiftly from Germany's ever-growing appetite for world conquest, the still-unsuspecting Great Britain sees the British Prime Minister Neville Chamberlain stepping sheepishly off the stage to make way for the dramatic genius of a new prime minister, Winston Churchill, who is charged with the daunting task of redrafting the German script, a script that now threatens his homeland. He is challenged to draw into the conflict isolationist, stubbornly neutral America, and take advantage of new technology, particularly radio, to develop the propaganda and espionage techniques that have obsessed him for a lifetime, including the newly framed "black propaganda."*

*Black propaganda is a means by which information and material that purports to be from a source on one side of a conflict is actually from the opposing side and used to vilify, embarrass, or misrepresent the enemy. White propaganda is not as deceptive, but an honest way to enthuse the nation with patriotic programs, good news, inspiring films, and stirring oratory. The "white" approach was long held by the British Broadcasting Corporation as a moral and ethical way to fight the war. The BBC did not subscribe to black.*

*Realizing the desperate need to awaken his countrymen to the threat posed by their neighbor as Poland falls, Churchill speedily mobilizes state programs to oppose Germany. Noting that the English are traditionally averse to the message of propaganda, Churchill encourages the involvement of mass media in satirizing and demonizing Hitler. The BBC's popular program* It's That Man Again *stars the brilliant Tommy Handley. The beloved Vera Lynn and Gracie Fields sing hits of the Blitz, and distinguished actor Noël Coward writes and appears in films. The country is galvanized by this combined patriotic message. The English lion soon awakens, and the bombing of Britain brings the drama into the citizens' living rooms, creating for the first time a sense of national unity.*

*Germany realizes the threat of this unified United Kingdom and seeks to present a counter-message in the most alarming of ways: one "William Joyce," the English caricature and radio star created by the Germans, is born on the airways (and quickly counter-named "Lord Haw-Haw" by the suspicious Brits). Painting the war effort as one that is financed on the backs of the working stiffs even as the upper crust retreats to their country mansions, Lord Haw-Haw mocks the notion of "One England." A despised English traitor, Joyce chillingly advances propagandist wartime information.*

*England in turn counters with propaganda of its own with the fictional star "Gustav Eins," an over-the-top German personality who takes to the airways. Purportedly broadcasting from a van inside Berlin, he spreads rumors of the essentially anti-populist nature of the Reich to resisting German patriots. Other, still more effective "German" stations are launched in the wake of Gustav Eins and spread a propagandist message that gains credibility among its large target audience of Germans—civilian and military—by disseminating news reports that the listeners were otherwise deprived of. Additionally, black propaganda is utilized at its most effective via special Fraktur Gothic type, coined by the Reich, and used in ersatz ration books and on fraudulent leaflets, denouncing top leaders of the movement.*

*Churchill, having successfully rallied his compatriots, smartly realizes that to ensure a successful production to this worldwide drama, a major new player needs to be engaged, and soon. He sets his sights on America and upon Franklin Delano Roosevelt, comfortably hosting his "fireside chats."*

• • •

London had not yet taken news from the continent seriously, and was dancing in the heady, sparkling bubbles of the decade. Theaters thrived in the Strand, charity balls at the Savoy were in full swing, the economy was encouraging, and on warm afternoons, sunbathers with their pale blue and white striped folding chairs were out in the parks in full force. Life in Britain looked almost like a travelogue.

England had her own reminders of a triumphant past. The empire that had made London the capital of the world had been won in many a battle, and a grateful nation honored her heroes with adulation. None received more glory than Nelson and Wellington, the great admiral and the great general, who, at the beginning of the nineteenth century, defeated France at sea and on land, assuring Britain's status as master of the globe for the next hundred years. Their victories were still recorded in bronze and stone in Trafalgar Square and at Hyde Park Corner—a park not unlike Tiergarten in Berlin—where Britain's *Winged Victory* celebrated Wellington's Waterloo triumph, and in front, a memorial honored World War I artillerymen. Nearby, across another park, the Palace of Westminster housed two grand seats of government, the House of Commons and the House of Lords. Nor had Londoners ever stormed the Bastille, or taken the roof off a conclave of cardinals to force them to elect a pope in Rome. For decades leading into decades, England had expanded democracy and staged noble civilization, with calm and optimistic ingenuity. It seemed to be inherent in the British script.

English conversation was about fog and not war. And to combat the weather was Anthony Eden's famed black homburg and Prime Minister Neville Chamberlain's furled black umbrella. An admirer once sought out the establishment from whom Mr. Chamberlain bought it. With characteristic British clarity, the salesman described it: "It's what one might call a Rolls-Royce of an umbrella, natty but quiet, solid but a light dasher. The sort of umbrella which becomes part of a man, if I may say so." Mr. Chamberlain came to regard his gamp as a necessary part of his journeys abroad, and before pursuing "appeasement" on one such mission, he told friends the story of an old lady with an umbrella, who, pursued by a lion, suddenly turned, unfurled her weapon, and scared the beast away. Concluded Mr. Chamberlain: "I am taking my umbrella to Munich." Mr. Chamberlain had a chance to unfurl his umbrella but once during a thunderstorm, which passersby said had been ordered by God to show that the rolled umbrella really did open.

At home, Britain was almost calm, methodical, at times whimsical. Hospitals ringed the city, and well-staffed first-aid stations were dotted throughout the metropolis. Evacuation plans were published for all non-essential workers, for mothers and children, senior citizens, invalids. Beauty parlors were crammed with women seeking one last hairdo. The late August moon rode alone over a darkened sky. Parliament sat. The government asked for war powers—powers for the government to confiscate property, order arrests, search premises, control railways, conduct secret trials. Debate began. At 5:30 p.m., Prime Minister Chamberlain, his older voice steady, started his speech. If war came in spite of Britain's efforts for peace—"God knows I have tried my best"—Britain would fight.

What would motivate the British show? It was optimism, steadfastness, and balance. When the soldiers went off to the Great War, they had left singing, "Keep the Home Fires Burning." They came back singing an ironical song that went, "It wasn't the Yanks who won the war, it was my son Billy." But that balance would change. Despite warning voices and the dreadful impact of Hitler's blitzkrieg tactics against Poland, England was slow to appreciate its own peril. Then, in the early summer of 1940, came the fall of France and a miracle that there were any survivors at all at Dunkirk.

On a Sunday morning the day dawned bright and clear over the British Isles, the early autumn sun shining down from sparkling blue skies. It was, however, to be quite unlike any other Sunday.

In the space of a few sunny weeks, the play became obvious. Although the clouds of war had been steadily gathering around the nation, as the situation became more desperate, politicians and military men began to say, "Winston is the only one who can get us out of this mess." When he became prime minister on May 10, 1940, Churchill, at his most eloquent, took to the stage declaring that he had nothing to offer but blood, toil, tears, and sweat. Great Britain listened.

As London's church bells ceased ringing, radio listeners all over the United Kingdom heard the prime minister say: "I am speaking to you from the cabinet room at No. 10 Downing Street." His voice was slow and steady. "This country is at war with Germany." The PM was eloquent only when he ended: "Now may God bless you all. . . . For it is evil things we shall be fighting against—brute force, bad faith, injustice, oppression, and persecution. And against them I am certain that right will prevail." Then the prime minister hurried to the House to make a five-minute speech: "It is a sad day for all of us, but for none is it sadder than for me. Everything I had worked for, hoped for, and believed in during my public life has cracked into ruins. There is only one thing left for me, and that is to devote what strength and powers I have to forwarding victory of the cause for which we have to sacrifice ourselves. I trust I may live to see Hitlerism destroyed, and a restored and liberated Europe re-established." The House rose and cheered.

Then the king spoke: "In this grave hour, perhaps the most fateful in our history, I send to every household of my peoples, both at home and overseas, this message, spoken with the same depths of feeling for each one of you as if I were able to cross your threshold and speak to you myself. . . . We are at war."

CHAPTER 6

# The Home Front: To the Airwaves

The Germans were not alone in their focus on the media as the most important means of shaping perceptions of the war. From 1939 on, prime ministers Chamberlain and Churchill filled the BBC's airways with their familiar voices, providing the popularly accepted counter-script of the war's actors and events to the empire and the world beyond.

In September 1939, families huddled around radios, eager to hear news of the German invasion of Poland. From their receiving sets they were alerted to Prime Minister Neville Chamberlain's words. In carefully measured tones, Chamberlain told his listeners that Great Britain was determined to honor its bilateral defense treaty with Warsaw and that his nation was now engaged in war against Hitler's regime, fighting what he referred to as "evil things."

Chamberlain's voice betrayed a note of personal anguish. Barely a year before, he had returned from Munich bearing a document inscribed with the signatures of the führer, Mussolini, Clemenceau, and himself, in which Hitler's *Anschluss*, Germany's annexation of Austria, had been approved in exchange for an Axis warranty of peace. The value of this guarantee had already been diminished by the invasion of Czechoslovakia on the pretext that atrocities had been committed against citizens of German ethnic background living there. Clearly the piece of paper that

Chamberlain waved from the tarmac on that windy day upon his return from Munich in 1938 was entirely worthless. In a speech announcing Britain's entry into World War II, Chamberlain had named the headliner who would replace him in the director's chair and author of the British wartime counter-script.

During the next nine months, Britain and its continental allies were engaged in a "phony war" as Hitler delayed his assault on Western Europe. Known as the *sitzkrieg* in European circles, this quiet period ended in the spring of 1940, when German panzer units rolled through the Benelux countries, portions of Scandinavia, and France. From the beginning, the British attempted to protect their country and its comparatively small armed forces from air attacks by Göring's Luftwaffe, but in April, the bombing of British airfields was intense.

The war became real following the German invasion of Poland, and the British Expeditionary Force (BEF) was sent to the Franco-Belgian border. By May 1940, when the German attack continued, it consisted of ten infantry divisions in three corps, a tank brigade, and an RAF detachment of about five hundred aircraft. Although constituting only a tenth of the defending Allied force, it sustained heavy losses during the German advance and most of the remainder (roughly 330,000 men) were evacuated from Dunkirk in June, leaving much of their equipment behind. However, the 51st (Highland) Infantry Division was left behind at Saint-Valéry-en-Caux, as the Germans did not trap it at the time; it surrendered along with elements of the French 10th Army later in June. The short-lived second Expeditionary Force commanded by General Alan Brooke was evacuated from Western France. Only a brave rescue mission could ferry troops back to Britain, saving British land forces from annihilation.

After the abrupt surrender of Belgian King Leopold, some 600,000 survivors of the northern Allied armies were locked in a triangular trap along the North Sea. The result was a scene of carnage and valor more concentrated in space and time than anything modern history had ever seen: men by the hundreds of thousands in a desperate bid to live. It could be guessed that no fewer than 500,000 men were killed, wounded, or captured in seven days on a patch of earth about the size of an average US county (970 square miles). At least a thousand airplanes were shot down. Every town and hamlet was shattered by explosives or leveled by fire. Virtually every acre was stained with blood and strewn with corpses. But it was an orderly withdrawal with wounded men first; a courageous and masterful rearguard action conducted in full cooperation with the French. When the Belgian surrender fatally exposed the British left flank, German tanks, infantry, and artillery crunched ever closer, climbing over heaps of their own dead, toward the port of Dunkirk, a man-made harbor cut into a sandy tidal plain.

Just before getting there, the retreating Allies opened canal flood-gates to the east and west. But German aircraft continued their assault with bombs and machine-gun slugs in devastating sheets. French and British warships lay offshore, protecting themselves and covering the land troops' retreat with a flowing dome of projectiles from their heavy guns. Ashore, they sent seamen, marines, and engineers to construct gun emplacements for the soldiers to fall back on. The battle was appalling. Inside the blazing line of warships lay transports of every description; from big merchantmen and passenger steamers to channel ferries, private yachts, fishing smacks, tug-drawn coal barges. Embarkation had to be carried out at low tide by shallow-draft ships, whaling boats, dories, and rafts, surrounded by wreckage bobbing in the surf. A calm sea and bright sunshine made the rescue ships perfect bomb targets for two days and dozens of them were smashed, burned, sunk. Britain admitted a loss of thirty warships. Then a blessed fog rolled in for forty-eight hours, saving countless lives. When the soldiers reached the sea they hid—one of them said later—"like rabbits among the dunes." They were in smoke-grimed rags, many shoeless, others empty-handed in their underclothes after swimming canals. One squad of men carried a machine gun snatched from a crashed German plane with which they kept on shooting at new attackers; they got two. The walking wounded joined the rest in staggering into the oil-scummed waves, floundering about to reach the rescue craft amid spuming bomb-geysers. The crossing to Dover, Ramsgate, and

Sheerness was a vast, stupefying nightmare with German motorboats racing alongside them, firing torpedoes. Each successive boatload that came in safely seemed so precious and triumphant that out of the jaws of death British morale suddenly soared.

To celebrate his victory, Führer Hitler ordered flags flown throughout Germany for eight days, bells rung for three. And German officers called the stench of death on the beaches "the perfume of battle."

Since the outbreak of war, Winston Churchill had been serving as the First Lord of the Admiralty, but now a chorus of hopeful whispers arose simultaneously in British households hoping for a leader to carry them on. As the Luftwaffe waged unprecedented war against Britain, it became evident that Chamberlain was not up to the job and in May 1940, Churchill was elected prime minister. Three days later, he appeared before the House of Commons and, in response to questions regarding British war aims, said: "You ask, 'What is our aim?' I can answer in one word: Victory! Victory at all costs, victory in spite of all terror, victory, however hard and long the road may be." Later, he would insist that "every trace of Hitler's footsteps, every stain of his infected and corroding fingers will be sponged and purged and, if need be, blasted from the surface of the earth."

The drama unfolded. If Chamberlain led his country against "evil things," Churchill personified the Nazi evil in a single human form: Adolf Hitler. Compared to his nemesis, however, Churchill placed far less reliance upon propaganda, saying before his elevation to prime minister, "If words could kill, we would be dead already." Still, with his oratorical brilliance and distinctive stage presence, Churchill became a master of impression management. When he spoke or wrote, it was always an event. Churchill mobilized the English language and sent it into battle to steady his fellow countrymen and hearten those Europeans for whom the curtain on the stages of tyranny had fallen. The theater dark, the lighting effects of the theater were dim until the British lion roared, and now the British had a wartime leader for whom dramaturgical techniques came easily, a man who could oversee his country's revision of the Nazi script, and an actor capable of holding his own against

Hitler's compelling histrionics. Churchill was a playwright, a performer, an orator, fully able to write a script to be reckoned with. The curtain was rising on the battlefields of Europe.

In a fighting speech to Parliament, the eloquent prime minister admitted British losses of "over 30,000" men killed, wounded, and missing, nearly a thousand guns "and all our transport and all the armored vehicles that were with the army." But he said that the Royal Navy, "using nearly 1,000 ships of all kinds, carried over 335,000 men, French and British, out of the jaws of death." He concluded:

> We shall not flag nor fail. We shall go on to the end. We shall fight in France and on the seas and oceans; we shall fight with growing confidence and growing strength in the air. We shall defend our island whatever the cost may be; we shall fight on the beaches, we shall fight on the landing grounds, we shall in the fields and in the streets, we shall fight in the hills. We shall never surrender. And even if, which I do not for a moment believe, this island or a large part of it were subjugated and starving, then our Empire beyond the seas, armed and guarded by the British Fleet, would carry on the struggle until, in God's good time, the New World, with all its power and might, steps forth to the rescue and liberation of the Old.

Having forestalled the destruction of the BEF in hope that a lopsided peace agreement could be reached with the English, Hitler altered the German military script. A handful of British bombers had completed a woefully ineffective run on Berlin and, while this attack's military significance was negligible, having British planes enter German airspace did not play well. Hitler instructed Göring to re-target his Luftwaffe raids from the Royal Air Force military installations to British population centers, zoning in on London to destroy the people's will to fight. Neither the observation balloons that hung in the sky like huge silver necklaces nor land-based antiaircraft defenses could hope to stem the tide of the Luftwaffe attacks. Yet the führer was adamant: he felt a "blitz" on London should be initiated in order to convey the German war message directly to the British populace. On September 7, 1940, the methodical and relentless bombardment of London began, and any talk of a "phony" war ended.

The first air-raid warning wailed over the British capital. Some eight million unhurried Londoners tramped down the steps of their air-raid shelters, among them George VI and his Queen Elizabeth. The queen had gone down into the Buckingham Palace dugout wearing a morning gown of her favorite soft blue. Twelve days later, by the king's command, she assumed the title of Commandant-in-Chief of the Women's Royal Naval Service, Women's Auxiliary Air Force, and the Women's Auxiliary Territorial Service. A large part of her new life would be devoted to leading Britain's women-at-war, and the uniforms of these organizations were added to her wardrobe, the first warlike garments to be worn by the future Queen Elizabeth.

On the whole, it was Britain's fifteen million women who persevered. Hardest hit were typists, stenographers, and clerks, sacked when firms folded or reduced their staff as they deserted the big towns and hundreds of shops dropped shop girls as retail trade slumped badly. Even ladies of the evening had unemployment problems due to the nightly blackouts. With good will, mothers sent their children to live with strange families in the countryside.

When the alarm came, no one in London took it particularly seriously; just another nuisance raid, most people thought. A few firebombs began falling, people drove to watch them for a lark, then the flares began to float down, long graceful chain flares, star flares, and flaming onions. From all directions the planes began to dive-bomb, lower than usual, and then the citizenry suddenly realized: it was an ominous visit in return for a big fire-raid the R.A.F. had bestowed on Berlin the week before. Wherever they were—on roofs dousing incendiaries, in basements trying to forget—Londoners could hear the terrible falling bombs, like ripping muslin at a distance; and then the thuds. Some tried to read; most turned their radios off, because it was intolerable only to half-hear the bomb each thought had his or her initials on it.

During the bombing the orchestra at London's Café de Paris gaily played "Oh, Johnny, Oh, Johnny, How You Can Love!" At the tables, handsome flying Johnnies, naval Jacks in full dress, guardsmen, and plain civilians sat making conversational love. Sirens had sounded, but to those in the cabaret, leave time seemed too dear to squander underground. Then the hit came. What had been a nightclub became a nightmare—heaps of wreckage crushing the piles of dead and maimed, a shambles of silver slippers, broken magnums, torn sheet music, dented saxophones. But some of the carefree survived. They dragged themselves out, went with their bruises and grime to a West End hotel. They washed up. They went to the hotel ballroom and ordered food and drinks. Again, they asked the bandleader for a number they never forgot: "Oh, Johnny, Oh, Johnny, How You Can Love!"

The raid continued for eight hours, until 4:50 a.m. Everyone hurried to bed for a few hours of bottomless sleep before getting up to work. London was defiantly hopeful the next morning; women had on their cockiest spring hats, the men their brightest ties. Amid the shoveling of shattered glass was the sound of phonographs.

London was bombed, first by airplanes, then flying bombs and rockets. Thirty thousand people died in such attacks, fifty thousand were injured, and acres of the great city were devastated. Night after night, Londoners slept in air-raid shelters, and when the bombing began, no one knew what the outcome would be. After the roar and whistle of the bombs, the fires, the immense flames, Londoners emerged from their shelters, picked their way over the debris, and quietly went about their business. Those living on the outskirts, commuters all, who could see the sky red with destruction, got up as usual, kissed their wives, and caught the usual train. Often when they arrived at their shops, there was just a vacant hole in the ground, and they waited patiently, until someone told them what to do, where to go. Winston Churchill, with all his gifts of eloquence and oratory, never found the words to describe this astonishing calm. But the citizens around him could: "London can take it."

At first blush it might appear that little propaganda was needed to mobilize Britain's support for the war. This was not entirely accurate.

Even as German bombers streamed over the British countryside, Parliament was in a state of confusion about a response to the German attack on Poland. With a goodly portion of London already destroyed by the Luftwaffe, a motion was introduced into the House of Commons calling for the conclusion of a "soft peace" with the Axis powers. Granted, the British were at war, and Churchill's resolve would not be changed, but the question of whether all the populace could be enlisted to achieve the prime minister's goal of total victory remained problematic long after the struggle had commenced. Göring's attack on the Royal Air Force diminished Britain's ability to defend itself, and the Nazis were gathering their forces to launch "Operation Sea Lion," a landing of German troops on English soil.

• • •

A few weeks later, destiny was cruel to 1,450 Canadian and US travelers who sought to get home from thunderous Europe. In the 13,581-tonne SS *Athenia* of the Donaldson Atlantic Line they embarked at Glasgow, Belfast, and Liverpool for Montreal. At 8:59 p.m. on a Sunday, about two hundred miles west of the Hebrides, a mortal explosion suddenly rocked and ripped the *Athenia*'s hull, killing more than a hundred passengers and crew, and sinking her fast. One of the first ships to rescue survivors was the *Southern Cross*, the private yacht of Swedish tycoon Axel Wenner-Gren. The Norwegian freighter *Knute Nelson* picked up many more. British war boats raced toward where the *Athenia* was left to sink. World headlines screamed the news.

The House of Commons listened as the First Lord of the Admiralty announced: "The *Athenia* was torpedoed without the slightest warning. She was not armed." Berlin officials suggested the *Athenia* might have run into a British mine. To this the British Admiralty retorted there were no British mines off the west coast of Ireland. Berlin replied: "It is likely that a British submarine fired the torpedo as a propaganda measure to influence United States neutrality." Churchill was furious.

John Kennedy, twenty-one, son of Ambassador Joe Kennedy, was dispatched by his father from London to Glasgow to help interview survivors of the sunken SS *Athenia*. Franklin Roosevelt had just announced his decision not to furnish US naval convoys to returning refugees and John Kennedy was taken aback. Fresh in their memories were scenes when the torpedo struck: oil spurting into the air from exploded tanks; the bodies of firemen hurtling through a hatch; seasick, half-naked passengers rushing for the decks; and later, when the lifeboats were launched, passengers and crew picking their way over bodies toward the rails. They had been ten or twelve hours in the boats. They had waited anxiously for rescue. And, when rescue was at hand, they had seen one boat swamped and most of its occupants drowned before help could reach them, another one smashed to kindling by the propeller of a rescue ship. And so they were in no mood to take "No" from Mr. Kennedy. A college girl gave young Harvard man Kennedy the ultimatum: "We definitely refuse to go without a convoy!" Back to London went John Kennedy to tell his father.

Serious action needed to be considered, and back on Britain's seafront, the nation, profiting by past experience, took measures developed in World War I, introducing a convoy system for merchant shipping to assist the Merchant Navy in its duty of ensuring the overseas traffic of the British Commonwealth and its allies. As First Lord of the Admiralty, Churchill established control lanes. Merchant ships whose last port of call was British had to have a special war clearance. Ships bound toward European ports or en route to Northern Scotland would call in at Kirkwall on the Orkney Islands, just off the coast of Great Britain. Ships bound for the Strait of Gibraltar would call in at Gibraltar. The Royal Navy became fully mobilized.

• • •

Winston Churchill declared, "The Royal Navy is hunting the U-boats night and day and we fervently hope that by the end of October we shall have three times as many hunting craft at work as we had at the beginning of the war." Editor-in-chief of the Nazi broadcasting services, Hans Fritzsche, frothed at the mouth for thirteen minutes over the air, replying to Mr. Churchill's claim of a scoreless week for the U-boats. His critics in Germany reinforced their disdain for the prime minister, in language not befitting the English character.

"So that is what that dirty gangster thinks! Who does that filthy liar think he is fooling?" he reported. "So Mr. Churchill, that bloated swine, spouts through his dirty teeth that in the last week no English ship has been sunk by German submarines?"

• • •

Paradoxically, one thing England had in its favor on the home front was that the Second World War, unlike the First, was a "total" war. In contrast to the previous conflict, with its stationary slaughter of soldiers in the trenches while civilian populations were safely beyond the range of enemy fire, World War II was a war of movement and of peril for civilians and military personnel alike. During the five-and-a-half-year war in Europe, many Brits had to leave their homes that were either bombed or in danger and in the pathway of destruction. There were sixty million address changes in England and Wales, and during the period between September 1940 and September 1941, more British civilians than soldiers were killed.

The government initiated a "casting" call to all British civilians to assume a role and do their bit for the cause. It was a summons that few could refuse. Total war meant that the government would assume tasks normally left in private hands. Food supplies were severely rationed, homes had to be found for civilians bombed from their dwellings, and confiscatory taxes had to be coordinated to effectively siphon private incomes into the British war effort. Confronted with the vast uncertainties attending total war, the British public did what was necessary to effect the final outcome as scripted by their leader. Churchill captured the spirit of the "common man" essential during the Blitz in the pages of his multi-volume *The Second World War,* recalling that it was important to remember that the men and women at home were just as brave and steadfast as those fighting on the front lines:

> This was a time when all Britain worked and strove to the utmost limit and was united as never before. Men and women toiled at the lathes and machines in the factories till they fell exhausted on the floor and had to be dragged away and ordered home, while their places were occupied by newcomers ahead of time. The one desire of all the males and many women was to have a weapon. . . . Nothing moves an Englishman so much as the threat of invasion, the reality unknown for a thousand years. Vast numbers of people were resolved to conquer or die.

In London, one would be hard-pressed to find an individual over eight and younger than eighty not actively engaged in the fight against Hitler. Some Britons thought that the greatest battle of World War II would still be fought on English soil. If so, one of the many ways that Hitler could be defeated would be to heighten the drama, to create new and ever-growing productions and enlist as members of the cast the British People's Army, with makeshift weapons, in much the same way that von Seeckt's troops had honed their field skills in Germany. However, the Home Guard were never called upon to resist a German advance.

• • •

Thomas Wintringham was a British soldier and military historian, journalist and poet. After the outbreak of war, in 1940, and Dunkirk, he began to write in support of the Local Defence Volunteers, who would soon become the Home Guard. Strongly committed to protecting the home front, he opened a private training school, set on a former country estate in Osterley Park, near London. In a sense, he became a director leading a complementary battle, writing in *The New Ways of War*, "The only way to beat the Blitz is for four million civilians to teach themselves how to fight democratically, efficiently, and free of the myths of military convention. Britain must fight now not to the last Frenchman, not to the last British soldier, but to the last courageous Briton." To his Home Guard School flocked a growing army of Minute Men, traveling salesmen, shop clerks, and coal miners, with just two days of instruction.

After that, they went home and rehearsed on their front lawn or a neighbor's meadow. Tom Wintringham's methods were anything but orthodox. Drill, he considered as vestigial as the human appendix: it taught men how to stand up, walk stiffly, and be shot. At school, he and his recruited colleagues offered his "volunteers" a regimen for how to keep themselves fit by swimming, dodging from bush to bush, playing soccer, and American football. He taught the Minute Men how to take cover, how to throw grenades from a lying-down position, how to dig themselves in while on their bellies, how to face down when planes were overhead. He showed how a brave man could stop tanks with homemade grenades or crowbars or lengths of rail to spike the bogie wheels. He showed how to render service station gasoline pumps useless to German mechanized forces by setting fire to the gas, or putting sugar or linseed oil in it. He made diagrams of deep trenches in which men were quite safe from ground strafing by airplanes. He demonstrated how to hold up motorcycle forces by rigging up boards full of nails and strewing glass. Above all, Tom Wintringham explained, "Commands are not enough. You do not make a People's War by ordering people to do things. It is done by playing with convincing strength." But the companies never had a chance to fully perform on stage.

Before Hitler revised his war script, abandoning "Operation Sea Lion" and turning his sights eastward to Russia, the Home Guard stood at the ready to protect their homeland. They made up more than a million local volunteers who were ineligible for military service or too young, too old to join the services, and earned the nickname "Dad's Army." Their role was as a cast making up a secondary defense force, in case of a German land invasion. They fought fires and directed British antiaircraft fire toward the silhouettes of German planes in the skies above London and the countryside. Women volunteered for munitions production work and were drafted into uniform, the first instance in which British females were subject to conscription. Schoolchildren took part; women ran eyewitness dispatches back and forth from key countryside sightings to war rooms at Whitehall.

Acting as sentries during the day and night and as observers for military intelligence, they checked that people were carrying their identity cards. Local Home Guard units would know who lived locally and any strangers to an area would be subject to a check, especially as there was a genuine fear of fifth columnists. The Home Guard was also responsible for taking down road signs and any local clues that might help the enemy should they invade.

The *Home Guard Handbook* published in 1940 stated that the main duties of the Home Guard were:

Guarding important points.
Observation and reporting—prompt and precise.
Immediate attack against small, lightly armed parties of the
    enemy.
The defense of roads, villages, factories, and vital points in towns
    to block enemy movement.

Every member of the Home Guard was expected to know:

The whole of the ground in his own district.
The personnel of his own detachment.
The headquarters of his detachment and where he is to report for
    duty in the event of an alarm.
How to dispatch reports concerning enemy landings or
    approaches, what the reports should contain, and to whom
    they should be sent.

The Guard did valuable work. A special unit, the Auxiliary Unit, was created to fight behind enemy lines should an invasion occur. They would have lived and fought out of secret bases in the countryside. Their job would have been to sabotage anything that might have been of use to the Nazi invaders. Their knowledge of the local terrain would have been an invaluable asset in any fight against the Nazis.

In Churchill's own words, "The force is of the highest value and importance. A country where every street and every village bristles with resolute armed men is a country against which the tactics that destroyed the Dutch will not succeed, a country so defended is not liable to be overthrown."

His calls for unity were reinforced by the context in which his people found themselves. The populace was united and girded for war against a sharply etched adversary.

To add a lighter note, as the girding was taking place, the changing shapes of many leading ladies were not pretty, but young British women had to face it. In their years of dedicated work in war factories and the services they had become bigger in the wrong places: hands, feet, and hips. The average girl of twenty-five wore gloves and shoes at least one size larger than previously. Around the hips she was a thirty-eight, two inches broader than her older sister had been six years earlier. Costume designers rallied to fight the battle of the bulge, with greatly exaggerated squaring of shoulders, nipped-in waists, flaring skirts.

• • •

As British ladies adjusted to wartime fashion, the home front waited in readiness.

A date was set by Adolf Hitler for the completion of his conquest of Great Britain. An Overseas League tea party on August 15 for His Majesty's forces from overseas was little more than a fifteen-minute intermission. Adolf Hitler decided to attend. Huge German air assaults lasting from dawn to dusk began. Four or five hundred Nazi raiders came over Britain every day; no hour was without its dogfight. For two days German planes ranged widely over the British Isles on scattered raids in small formations. On the third day they staged another big show on Dover's balloon defenses. Supported in the air with steel cables strong enough to smash the wings of any plane striking them, they looked like a herd of docile elephants high in the sky. A squadron of fifty or sixty dive bombers circled at 30,000 feet, coming down singly in steep power dives out of the sun's eye to take pot-shots at the elephants with 37-mm cannon. Antiaircraft fire got the raiders' range and drove them off. British fighters ambushed the Stukas on their way home, when their ammunition was spent.

The war over Britain, and the battle in the skies, were not without delay and complication. Heavy mists often hung over northwest Europe and so did heavy suspense. The most terrific military force in the world, the German army, had been idle for months, and on Christmas Eve its commander, Field Marshal Walther von Brauchitsch, visited camps on the Channel coast. Near the long-range guns which sporadically hurled shells into England, he told his men, "The Channel will protect England only so long as it suits us." The British army and Royal Air Force took no chances. And just after Christmas Day, Germany's "invasion ports" were thunderously plastered with bombs night after night, from Norway to lower France. While the Nazis' other plans matured, the Luftwaffe returned to its central task with a freshly furious fire raid on London. Hundreds of huge blazes severely taxed the courage of London's thousands of firemen and volunteers. The Guildhall and other ancient monuments went down in avalanches and up in flames. It was the most dangerous conflagration in modern history—and London's water pressure was low.

But it was not only cities like London the Luftwaffe bombed. On bright moonlit nights, enough German planes were feinting at London to keep the night-flying defenders there preoccupied. Meantime, wave after wave of heavy-laden bombers passed around the city and headed northwest to Coventry. All night the drama played until they had dropped tons of high-explosive incendiaries on the old city where Lady Godiva had once, according to legend, ridden naked.

There was scene after scene of destruction. Coventry, a city of 200,000 on the southern edge of the Midlands, became one solid, seething mass of fire. Not just the factories on the outskirts, but the entire heart of the city, square miles of workmen's homes in long neat rows;

block upon block of shops and banks and pubs and offices; lovely old St. Michael's cathedral, all fell under the most concentrated rain of destruction yet loosened from the skies by mankind.

There were players under this marquee who dared resist the German bombers. Londoners sometimes saw an appealing leading man striding through the restaurants and bars with an air of careless majesty. There, the onlooker instantly felt that this was somebody. He was somebody: Brendan "Paddy" Finucane, Irish leader of Australia's famous No. 452 Fighter Squadron. To twenty-one-year-old Squadron Leader Finucane's credit were twenty-five German planes shot down, scores of fighter-bomber attacks on Nazi shipping in the Channel and on Nazi targets in occupied France. In compiling this record, Paddy had had a lot of luck. His plane had been badly shot-up only once. He limped for a while, but not from enemy bullets: he had fallen off a wall in Croydon, while celebrating an RAF victory. Then Squadron Leader Finucane's luck turned. Two Focke-Wulfs attacked him and Pilot Officer Richard Lewis while they were harrying a Nazi steamer. One of the Focke-Wulfs riddled Finucane's plane and wounded him in the leg and thigh. By radio he ordered Lewis to run for home. Lewis disobeyed. He hovered behind Finucane's tail, fought off repeated Focke-Wulf attacks while they both scurried back to their home aerodrome. Squadron Leader Finucane taxied his fighter up to the line and then collapsed at the controls.

His leg wounds mended, he returned to action, downed two more Nazis, raising his score to twenty-seven in his personal Battle of Britain.

He died after his heroic performance, becoming another member of a cast that never had a chance to take a final bow. Paddy Finucane was just another player who stood out from an enormous cast, who indeed played a small but heroic role in his nation's narrative. There were hundreds of men and women like him who played their roles selflessly, sometimes unnoticed. His was just one story that contributed to the nation's will, to stand steady, to stay the course.

All through a winter of dirty flying weather—too dirty for big-scale raiding—British airpower had been bristling, waiting. Now the open season was on. One night a force of more than a hundred British heavy bombers bore down on Cologne (chemicals, munitions, transportation). The raiders saw scores of fierce fires knitting a red blanket for the city. Equally devastating attacks were made on Essen, home of the vast Krupp works, and the vital port of Kiel. With fighter protection, RAF day raiders hammered factories, ports, and rail yards in northern France, as well as Nazi aerodromes in France, Holland, and Belgium.

In direct contrast to the underlying spirit of unity that animated England's wartime efforts, sustaining public support was made difficult by the traditional British aversion to spin. The British people's distaste for government involvement would ultimately work in Britain's favor by enabling other contributors instead of current government officials to fashion it. In the war's first stage, war news was delegated largely to the media, although with strings attached: editors were free to print what they wished for domestic consumption. However, should they publish any information that could help the enemy, they risked serious sanctions. Defense Regulations—D-Notices, as they were called—gave the editors guidance on what could officially be released. In addition, various branches of the British armed forces exercised censorship over information coming from the front. The bulk of these efforts were given over to recruits who monitored any information that might help the enemy.

Early in the Blitz, British analysts prepared a comparative assessment of the Nazi propaganda drive that had contributed to the fall of France and Britain's own propaganda potential. They concluded that British propaganda had to counter this formidable onslaught. Most worrisome of all, given the centrality of radio as Britain's news medium, was the fact that the German army now possessed far more radio transmitters as a consequence of its military conquests, which meant that the Allied efforts were likely not to be as effective for some time. Even if a cohesive British "counter-message" could be composed, its voice would be far softer and more circumscribed in range. Germany also had the capacity to reduce the volume and territorial scope of British propaganda by jamming.

While not all British households had a radio receiver, some 8.5 million radio sets were licensed to private citizens. The British Broadcasting

Corporation (BBC) reorganized, and launched the BBC Home Service and a Forces Programme intended for men and women in the armed services.

The BBC's services on behalf of the Allied cause were deemed to be of crucial importance. Nonetheless, news concentrated on the impact that the war had on the nation, rather than the BBC's influence on the war. During the war itself, the position of the BBC in the official British organizational chart's "Home Front" branch was barely visible. Fewer than ten references to the BBC can be located in all six volumes of Winston Churchill's *The Second World War*, and, despite their near-legendary eloquence, Churchill was silent in this history about his own wartime broadcasts.

While the BBC's loyalty or willingness to support the national cause with white propaganda was not in question, its conditioned reserve and tradition of understatement seemed impotent when compared to Goebbels's no-holds-barred approach to information management, and Churchill had a plan for disseminating news theatrically to his advantage.

Almost immediately after war was declared, and according to the *London Chronicle* and the *Sunday Referee*, he chastised the BBC for its halfhearted efforts. At a time when daily air raids had prompted the closure of Britain's theaters, movie houses, and concert halls, and the British people by most accounts were "thirsting for the superb in music and drama, and the rib-tickling from their favorite entertainers, the BBC programming was considerably bland." The *Times* reported that BBC officials were only intent upon news and producing white and mild features, like *The Spirit of Poland*, *The English Pageant*, *The Home Front*, and *The Shadow of the Swastika*, programs that would differentiate the British from their adversaries and unite Britons in the war effort.

One vital ingredient was missing from its home-directed broadcasting recipe at the war's onset—war-related entertainment.

Realizing it was essential to fuel the home front support, and responding to the criticism leveled by the print media, the BBC produced a wider range of wartime programs. Comedy shows became especially popular, with the *Garrison Theater, Hi Gang!* and *Much-Binding-in-the-Marsh,* a comedy originally based at an RAF station, lifting British spirits and helping listeners cope with wartime conditions. Towering above them all was a BBC radio comic strip entitled *It's That Man Again* and known to its ever-expanding audience simply as *ITMA,* the title referring to a contemporary phrase concerning the ever more frequent news stories about Hitler in the lead-up to the Second World War. It was later described as "probably the finest morale raiser of the war."

Its star, Tommy Handley, a beloved British comedian, became Britain's "Minister of Aggravation and Mysteries at the Office of Twerps." With no subject safe from its ripping barbs, *ITMA* featured a veritable rogues' gallery of British and German nincompoops, from the hare-brained charwoman Mrs. Mop to the besotted Colonel Chinstrap to Funf, a bungling German spy. At the height of its popularity, *ITMA* boasted in excess of sixteen million listeners, and gave a much-needed break from the grim business that comprised lives under the shadow of the Nazi boot.

Heartened by the results of its turn to popular entertainment, BBC personnel, without prompting from Whitehall, engaged popular entertainers like Tommy Handley, Vera Lynn, and Gracie Fields to record rousing popular songs. Vera Lynn's show *Sincerely Yours,* while dismissed by some MPs as "sentimental slush," earned her the appellation of the "Forces' Sweetheart." As for her songs, recorded as the *Hits of the Blitz,* many became standards—and while some have fallen by the historical wayside, each played a part in uniting Britain's public, and each song carried with it heart, wish, and memory, with such thematic lyrics as "I'll be seeing you," "When the lights go on again all over the world," and even lines about a nightingale that sang in the gardens of London's lovely Berkeley Square. The first songs released ten days after the war began were more patriotic: "We're Going to Hang Out the Washing on the Siegfried Line" and its immediate successor, "There'll Always Be an England." Other staples of the BBC's musical broadcasts were "Run,

Adolf, Run" and the Grace Fields seasonal piece, "I'm Sending a Letter to Santa Claus."

When Vera Lynn sang "I'll Be Seeing You," her audience hushed, remembering the times before the war:

> I'll be seeing you,
> In all the old familiar places,
> That my heart embraces
> All day through.

*The* song of the London Blitz was "A Nightingale Sang in Berkeley Square":

> The streets of town were paved with stars,
> It was such a romantic affair.
> And as we kissed and said goodnight,
> A nightingale sang in Berkeley Square.

Vera Lynn's songs offered not only memories, but also hope. Her signature song, "We'll Meet Again," promised:

> We'll meet again
> Don't know where
> Don't know when
> But I know we'll meet again
> Some sunny day.

The songs were aired and beloved on the home front and front lines, each of them in their own way somehow conveying to the listener a shared message, that essential, inalienable right to live freely and in peace.

The BBC was not alone in shifting toward more popular program content during the war's early stages. In 1939, the classical-oriented Council for the Encouragement of Music and the Arts (CEMA) was founded, chiefly to recruit artists effectively furloughed by the Blitz.

With virtuosos like Dame Myra Hess in its cast, the drama impacted British audiences. She was an English pianist, who had studied at the Royal Academy of Music, making her London debut in 1907. Her playing was acclaimed for both virtuosity and poetic sensitivity, and in 1939, doing her bit for the war effort, she organized a series of lunchtime concerts in the National Gallery. Under the extraordinary circumstances of wartime Britain, she became a musical heroine. Her leadership in bringing music to her countrymen from this iconic location was an act of considerable bravery. In defiance of German air raids, Hess, along with hundreds of other musicians, performed classical music concerts as bombs fell on the city. Ironically, the music most often featured at these concerts was that of German composers, which sent a strong message to the enemies of democracy, that Britain could admire the culture of the German people while abhorring the political realities of the Nazi Reich. In these remarkable times, Myra Hess became a symbol of British resolve to withstand the attacks, and she earned a special place in the hearts of the people and in the history of music.

CEMA took to Britain's highways and country lanes, with a gang of "music travelers" making their way across the UK on concert tours. Many performances were held during break times in Britain's armaments plants, and by 1943, CEMA artists were holding some 4,500 factory concerts a year.

In *The People's War*, one account from a CEMA member from the BBC Archives reported on his theatrical touring life in behalf of the forces:

> In 1941, at the age of seventeen, I was the stage manager of a second rate touring revue, "Bonjour Paris," and one of the acts was Ted Andrews, the Canadian Troubadour, with Barbara, the mother and stepfather of Julie Andrews.
>
> In May 1945 we were playing at the Wimbledon Theater and in Piccadilly Circus I saw the well-known musical actress Zoe Gail singing, "I'm Going to Get Lit Up When the Lights Go Up in London" written by her husband, the actor Hubert Gregg, and

there she was on the balcony of the Criterion Restaurant in a blazing spotlight, projected from the Palladium across the way.

It failed to mention that across the way from the Criterion, London was being relentlessly bombed.

Although CEMA was popular, theatrical producer and film magnate Basil Dean organized his own corps of music hall artists. Drawing upon his World War I experience entertaining Allied troops at the Crown's behest, he founded the Entertainments National Service Association (ENSA) to provide lighthearted comic relief from the drudgery of assembly lines. Dean also continued the tradition in which he was involved in two decades earlier by giving performances for British troops abroad, with shows in Dunkirk in 1939 and in Normandy in 1944, less than two months after the invasion. Artists staged shows for the "Tommies," illuminated by jeep headlights. Of the leading lights in the ENSA Company, none was more popular than Gracie Fields, one of Britain's greatest stars in both cinema and music halls.

Hers was a rags to riches story—in an era dominated by Mayfair accents, she was one of the few working-class women to keep her identity and translate it into worldwide success. Fields was universally loved and was in time awarded the title of Dame Commander of the British Empire. This honor was in no small part a result of her indefatigable wartime efforts. Even though at the outbreak of the war, she was recovering from a serious illness, she signed up with ENSA, and as a loved and revered trooper and morale-booster, traveled to France to entertain the troops in the midst of air raids, performing on the backs of open lorries and in war-torn areas. She was the first artist to play behind enemy lines in Berlin.

• • •

In many essential matters—arming its soldiers, arresting its dissidents, and invading other countries—the outbreak of the Second World War saw Nazi Germany with an insurmountable head start. Along with brainwashing its inhabitants, Joseph Goebbels and his well-financed Department of Film had been pumping out propaganda since the Reichstag burned down in 1933, preparing its citizens for genocide, global domination, and the general triumph of the will. Leni Riefenstahl was arguably the most talented woman ever to direct a documentary.

Britain's counter to Riefenstahl in artistic ability was Humphrey Jennings, poet of the 1930s documentary movement. His great trilogy of war films—*Listen to Britain, Fires Were Started, A Diary for Timothy*—were just as amazing as the propaganda films produced by the Ministry of Information.

Writing for the *Independent* in Great Britain, journalist Gerard Gilbert argued: "In the Second World War filmed propaganda came into its own, and the Government was determined to keep the country's 4,000 or so cinemas open. First World War propaganda was mainly waged by poster art—indeed, it was Hitler's belief that Great Britain's poster campaigns had helped win the war and that was one reason that spurred him on to create Germany's own formidable propaganda apparatus."

Not that the British were entirely slow off the mark in 1939. As soon as the Ministry of Information first officially manned its desks on Monday, September 4, it began planning scripts for stars. A newly restyled department called the Crown Film Unit looked to the country's most popular talent. The composer Benjamin Britten and poet W. H. Auden premiered one of the most enduring and first films, *Night Mail*, while elsewhere writer J. B. Priestley rallied the moviegoing public, reciting Churchill's "We Shall Fight on the Beaches" speech.

Many films aimed at British audiences weren't only shown in cinemas, but also in factories and social clubs. During the earliest phase of the war, the British government had ordered the closure of the country's movie theaters for fear of German air raids, but soon reversed this edict when the contribution of the movies to the home information campaign was seen to be indispensable. Prior to the showing of feature films, short reels were presented, pieces describing air-raid precautions, the need for increased national savings, energy conservation measures, and other tactical considerations. But what these shorts could not supply was propaganda that would prompt the British people to maintain their commitment to the defense of their homeland even as military casualties, civilian deaths, and wartime shortages mounted.

Despite the fact that film stock was rationed (nitrocellulose was needed for the manufacture of explosives), the film industry and its sister sectors throughout the British Empire produced documentaries and purely fictional films to convey the British war script to the public. One of the first of these to arrive at local movie houses was *The Lion Has Wings* in 1939, produced by Alexander Korda, a Hungarian-born film director and producer. He was a leading figure in the British film industry, the founder of London Films, and the owner of British Lion, a film distribution company. His semi-documentary work was dedicated to the RAF. Its aim was to underscore the capacity of the Royal Air Force to counter Göring's Luftwaffe. Another documentary-like film was *Fires Were Started*, chronicling the routine of a London fire station. These films joined such purely documentary pieces as *Target for Tonight,* taking the audience through the planning and implementation of an RAF bombing raid on occupied territory, and *Western Approaches*, which followed the journey of a convoy crossing the peril-fraught Atlantic to resupply Britain with food and weapons. Another key British propaganda film was *The Way Ahead*, directed by Carol Reed and starring David Niven, about a British platoon from call-up into combat. Unlike their darker, more strident German counterparts, these British propaganda films generally focused on the gentle and hopeful qualities of man.

Many British propaganda films were marked by a near-seamless blend of fictional narrative and documentary-style underpinnings. The model for such work was *In Which We Serve*, a film based on the exploits of Lord Mountbatten's destroyer, HMS *Torrin*, whose skipper was played by Noël Coward. With its story of quiet, understated courage and dogged determination, *In Which We Serve,* a story about a ship at sea, a family at home, and a classic example of wartime British cinema through patriotic imagery and national unity, set a standard of excellence that other British war films sought to emulate.

There were, to be sure, facets of the war at home that never reached the silver screen. Not shown, as one of King George VI's biographers later noted, were instances of cowardice and draft-dodging, of anti-Semitism, and, most particularly, of the looting that routinely occurred in the wake of Luftwaffe attacks. Nicholas Monsarrat, the English novelist and ambulance brigade member, described the aftermath of a bomb attack upon the London nightclub Café de Paris, on March 8, 1941:

> The first thing which the rescue squads and the firemen saw, as their torches poked through the gloom and the smoke and the bloody pit which had lately been the most chic cellar in London, was a frieze of other shadowy men, night-creatures who had scuttled within as soon as the echoes ceased, crouching over any dead or wounded woman, any *soignée* corpse they could find, and ripping off its necklace, or earrings, or brooch: rifling its handbag, scooping up its loose change.

Plainly, if the British integrationist message were to attain its maximum impact, then certain reports would have to be avoided. British news media, whether under D-Notice authority or not, successfully repressed unattractive issues on the home front, allowing the central war messages of unity and victory to be heard loud, clear, and without distraction.

# CHAPTER 7

# A Counter-Message Gets Through

———— ∽∞∽ ————

While the British media impressed on the public who the British themselves and who their "enemy" were, another voice rang through the diode crystals of household radios. The broadcast's origin was Hamburg, and its speaking voice was that of Lord Haw-Haw. After the first broadcasts, listeners wondered, *just who is he?*

They guessed that he might be Norman Baillie-Stewart, the famously treasonous British army officer. But soon, British officials identified him as William Joyce, an Irish-American, transplanted to England at an early age, and a brilliant student of languages at London University. He became propaganda director of Sir Oswald Mosley's Fascist Union and finally, in 1937, head of his own National Socialist League. He was described in the press as having a receding chin, a questing nose, thin yellow hair brushed back, a monocle, a vacant eye, and as regularly sporting a gardenia in his buttonhole. Joyce did not fit the comforting image of the cartoon villain. Thin-lipped and determined, he bore, as a souvenir of a Fascist brawl before the war, a scar gashed deeply from mouth to ear.

It was the *Daily Express* who tagged Joyce with the sobriquet Lord Haw-Haw, explaining, "He speaks English of the haw-haw, dammit-get-out-of-my-way variety."

Joyce continued to put forth his curious amalgam of peril, puns, and pap until his station was captured by Allied troops. Having signed off, drunk, before escaping to Northern Germany, he was captured by the British, tried for treason in London, and executed shortly thereafter.

The tone of the show was set with his opening line, "This is Jairmany calling," as Joyce distended his syllables for conscious comic effect. His show was chock-full of malapropisms and misfiring colloquialisms, filled with skits and chillingly accurate news of war damage in Britain. His aim, on the whole, was limited to undermining British integrationist propaganda and exploding the carefully wrought impression that Britons were united in their stand against the Nazis.

One recurrent skit pitted "Smith" against "Schmidt," the latter being a neutral "second banana," acting as a foil for Smith's barbs. Smith himself was a typical upper-class Englishman, hell-bent on winning the war and equally intent on not soiling his hands in the process. Smith did not reside in England, but awaited the war's outcome in a Swiss chalet. He returned to his native country twice in the course of Haw-Haw's tenure: once to keep evacuated London children from being quartered on his country estate, and once to invest in armament shares that paid dividends of 20 percent. Smith and Schmidt were periodically joined by other Haw-Haw characters: Sir Izzy Ungenheimer, a nouveau-riche Jewish noble who advised Smith on avoiding taxes; and Bumbleby Mannering, a sanctimonious clergyman maintaining an opulent lifestyle from munitions-industry profits.

Despite the amusement of the English public, Haw-Haw's mocking of a unified Britain was probably more effective than His Majesty's government cared to admit.

There was, however, a dramatic change in Haw-Haw's broadcasts from Hamburg after the German invasion of Norway. Haw-Haw became less amusing, pared down his upper-class- and government-baiting, and began to pound home a theme to British audiences far more ominous than the misadventures of Smith. The message was that the German war machine was unstoppable and that further resistance to Nazi domination of Europe was stupid. The British public were almost amused . . . and fascinated. Via these broadcasts, the Reich Ministry of Public Enlightenment and Propaganda attempted to discourage the British population within radio listening range, to suppress the effectiveness of the Allied war effort through propaganda, and to motivate the Allies to agree to peace terms leaving the Nazi regime intact and in power.

Among many techniques used, the Nazi broadcasts prominently reported on the shooting down of Allied aircraft and the sinking of Allied ships, presenting discouraging reports of high losses and casualties among Allied forces. Although the broadcasts were widely known to be Nazi propaganda, they frequently offered the only details available from behind enemy lines concerning the fate of friends and relatives who did not return from bombing raids over Germany. As a result, Allied troops and civilians frequently listened to Lord Haw-Haw's broadcasts despite the sometimes infuriating content, inaccuracies, and exaggerations, and consequently gave more attention to these broadcasts than to the official reports of British military casualties.

With Haw-Haw's popularity, the German Propaganda Ministry adapted some of his characteristic concepts for their new station. Propaganda intended to dispel the unity theme was handed over to the New British Broadcasting Station, which put forth similar stories of war exploitation by the rich. The New British Broadcasting Station subtly moved further into black propaganda with cleverly disseminated information. Little did the Germans know, however, that many radio scripters in Britain were already at work on a black production of their own and would soon become expert in this deceptive craft.

# CHAPTER 8

# The British Rewrite the German Script

—∝∝∝—

The Elizabethan playwrights used double plots to represent life's variety and complexity. Two stories were told concurrently; the lives of one group of characters affected the lives of the other.

So it would be with both white and black propaganda as major instruments in political warfare campaigns launched by the opposing sides in World War II. Unregistered on any government organization was a body called Electra House where hundreds of counterfeiters, forgers, and other technicians of black propaganda rehearsed their trade by producing fake documents and leaflets with the look and feel of authentic German originals. Just outside London, a British estate was home to brilliant agents who were matched in variety by the many carefully cultivated plants and flowers present in its gardens.

Hard at work at Electra House was Hugh Dalton, who had been educated at Eton and King's College, Cambridge. During World War I, he had served as a soldier on the French and Italian fronts.

Winston Churchill appointed him minister of economic warfare from 1940 and he established the Special Operations Executive. A skilled propagandist, he was determined to help liberate Europe's working classes from Nazi occupation. Dalton was convinced that a significant blow could be struck from inside the greater Reich. He told his staff that they must organize movements in every occupied territory comparable to the Sinn Fein movement in Ireland, to the Chinese guerrillas now operating against Japan, to the organizations that the Nazis themselves developed so remarkably in almost every country of the world. He told them that they must use many different methods, including industrial and military sabotage, labor agitation and strikes, continuous propaganda, terrorist acts against traitors and German leaders, boycotts, and riots.

This was delicious news for Sefton Delmer, a German-born reporter of the *Daily News*, loyal to King and Country. Sitting in his "local," he longed to be part of Churchill's newly formed Political Warfare Executive (PWE), a secret British body created to produce and disseminate both white and black propaganda, with the aim of damaging enemy morale and boosting the morale of the occupied countries. He came up with a scheme to produce programs in perfect German and broadcast them into Germany via powerful transmitters in the south of England. There were afternoon concerts, soap operas, and news. He imagined what mischief he could cause, much to the disapproval of the conservative BBC. The corporation was staid, grounded in ethics, and discouraged dirty tricks. But Electra subscribed to the notion that all's fair in love and war.

Ultimately, Dalton came to head PWE with a staff formed from Electra House and Special Operations 1. PWE was responsible for all forms of propaganda, black and white, targeted at the Axis powers or Axis-controlled lands. From SO 1, Dalton recruited students and experts steeped in German culture, and to oversee black propaganda aimed at the enemy, Dalton found his man, Sefton Delmer. In the crucial area of "black" radio broadcasts to German troops and civilians, Delmer personally ran the British show, with an uncanny ability to put himself in the shoes of his prospective listeners, to identify with the enemy's wants, needs, anxieties, and discontents. Like a skilled dramatist, Delmer understood the kind of presentations that were likely to have the maximum impact upon his audience. He relished every minute.

He had been born in Berlin, the son of an Australian father who taught English at Berlin University. His high school years were spent in Germany during World War I. In 1917, the family repatriated to England, where he took a degree at Oxford. Delmer returned to Berlin on assignment as a correspondent for the *Daily Express*. In his role as a journalist he met Ernst Röhm, head of the Nazi Stormtroopers, and, through Röhm the Nazi elite, including Hitler, Goebbels, Himmler, and Göring. In 1940, in the early days of the war, Delmer decided to move from reporting to taking an active role. Knowing the military wouldn't accept him, as he was grossly overweight, Delmer approached two friends in secret intelligence—Ian Fleming, of British Naval Intelligence and future author of James Bond, and Leonard Ingrams, a colorful financier, who had flown around Europe in his private plane prior to the war and had a plan to assassinate Himmler. Suspected, at first, of being a German agent, Delmer was in time cleared and joined the newly formed PWE at Woburn Abbey, another counter-intelligence center near London.

Electra House engaged in undercover activity. It was also known as Paris House, which was originally an exhibit at the Paris Exhibition of 1878. The Duchess of Bedford fell in love with the building and had it dismantled and transported to Woburn. During the war, the head of Electra House shuttled between there and his London headquarters in a Rolls-Royce. There was a rumor that a tunnel led from Paris House out into the surrounding countryside, supposedly an escape route for the king and queen in the event of invasion, as one of the staging posts on their evacuation route to the coast.

Helping Dalton penetrate the German mind and heart was an eminent Canadian psychologist, Dr. John T. MacCurdy, author of the seminal *Problems in Dynamic Psychology*. He was a tall, quiet, tweedy man sporting horn-rimmed glasses, who offered up innovative insights into and approaches to propaganda, and doubled as a lecturer in psychopathology at Cambridge University.

While much of the SO 1 and PWE radio work was black, it did not mean that the content of its transmissions was uniformly distorted. In fact, the bulk of the "German Service" broadcasts were straightforward news stories and bulletins. The dominant view held that people who were listening—through German jamming of the signal at the risk of their lives—did not want entertainment or speculation.

A main strategy was to provide accurate and interesting information rather than statements of policy, appeals, or discussions of the postwar world. Propaganda broadcasts toward the continent were based upon real news, diligently assembled from a variety of sources, notably the "Daily Digest" of German broadcasts supplied by the BBC's Monitoring Service. As more black stations came online, the search for news that would have the ring of authenticity, of being gathered within Germany or occupied territory, became even more intense. Presentation of straightforward news was a valuable technique leading to an audience that grew as the news broadcast in Germany lost credibility. At the same time, once a reputation for accurate reportage was secured in listeners' minds, then false tactical information could be integrated into the broadcasts and be received as perfectly credible in this context.

The aim, before and after D-Day, was to concentrate on the experience of the ordinary German soldier, his plight, the economic conditions in his country, and the mismanagement of the war by his leaders. The broadcasts focused on: disasters on the Eastern front; the growing weakness of German war production under the stress of bombing, blockades, and recruiting demands; the diminishing importance of the German air force as protector of their homeland; battlefield confusion; and the breakdown of authority. Nevertheless, the challenge of black propaganda was to drive wedges into those themes and ideas that Hitler and Goebbels were at such pains to impress upon the German mind. Rumor and suspicion were spread, tales of luxurious living by Nazi bosses reported, and an atmosphere of war-weariness and defeatism emphasized. Above all, the goal was simply to win, and black propaganda played a part in the great game of deception and confusion.

The two main forms of impression management were printed leaflets and radio transmissions. Electra House/PWE produced numerous leaflets that claimed to be of German origin, as well as what appeared to be an official publication of the German military. Among the individuals who proved invaluable to Dalton and Delmer was a specialist in typography named Ellic Howe. Howe was a student at Oxford who left without taking a degree to become a printer. During his travels abroad, he collected type fonts used by foreign printers across Europe. While visiting the Monotype Corporation at Horley in Surrey, he found a vast collection of type punches in their inventory, including many of the German Fraktur Gothic design, some used exclusively by the Reichsbank in Berlin. Combining his own talents with Monotype's holdings, he was able to produce phony government documents, planning memos, duplicate ration cards, and counterfeit currency. He also hit upon the idea of creating rubber stamps to support the authenticity of his bogus output.

Howe turned out to be a gifted manager. Through his prewar publishing contacts, he proceeded to make arrangements for the PWE with Fanfare Press in London, to do the forgers' printing; with Spicer's, Ltd., to supply the paper; and with Monotype Corporation, to provide typography and other materials. Before the end of the war, his unit had produced hundreds of forged German documents. He once remarked that he could supply "anything from a few forged letterheads to several million forged German ration cards."

Sefton Delmer recognized the potential value of Howe's machinations for sabotage, as psychological warfare, as an ancillary type of black propaganda to reinforce his propaganda radio transmissions. Except in special cases, leaflets were not dropped from aircraft but were disseminated behind enemy lines by agents belonging to SO 1 and other organizations. Pamphlets that were simply dropped were usually white propaganda that indicated their actual origins. They were usually truthful, dropped to manipulate troop morale, to highlight poor military positions, to encourage the reader to stay alive for their family's sake, to promote the reasonableness of an honorable surrender. One such leaflet read, "Die Festung Europa Hat Klein Dach" ("Fortress Europe Has No Roof"), documenting the increasing size of bombs dropped between 1940 and 1943.

Subtler, more covert methods were used to put these bogus black leaflets into circulation in target reader circles and German military units. They ranged from placing handsome reward notices and stickers on walls showing officers who had abused the war effort to ingeniously disguised booklets giving advice on ways of avoiding war work. There were also a number of forgeries of bank notes and direct mail ration cards, including postage stamps bearing Himmler's head instead of Hitler's, adding a dash of uniqueness to the German Postal Service—a combination of sabotage and propaganda. Flooding the German marketplace with bogus ration cards floated inside Germany caused a run on sparse but essential German goods. Officially stamped letters were dispatched with appropriate government seals and signatures:

Dear Fraulein,

To reward your loyalty, the Führer wishes to express his appreciation and award you additional ration cards for the duration of the cause. You will find them enclosed. Please accept the confidentiality of this arrangement.

Thousands of cards were gratefully received and redeemed, causing chaos in the rationed economy.

Wehrmacht generals had doubts about the leadership capacities of the Waffen-SS commanding officers as a result of the high casualty rate among troops and officers and the blunt manner of operations, and both were suspicious of each other regarding the use of operating funds. Ellic Howe participated in the entire gamut of black propaganda and sabotage operations. To help create mistrust between the Wehrmacht and the SS, he created a Bremen criminal police poster offering a ten thousand-mark reward for the arrest of a fictitious SS officer on charges of desertion and embezzlement of army funds. Many Germans responded to local officials claiming to know the officer's whereabouts and to collect their reward.

A twelve-page pamphlet entitled *Europa in Gefahr* ("Europe at Risk"), created by Howe, was credited to the fictitious Lieutenant

Colonel von Seckendorff. He penned a letter dated February 27, 1942, to the Nazi Party's representative in Shanghai, identified only as Party Comrade Puttfarken. The "publisher" of *Europa in Gefahr*, as revealed in a brief prefatory note, purported to be "a group of patriotic men who considered it their duty, in spite of the serious political situation, to bring this document, which came into their possession by chance, to the notice of the public." The inflammatory pamphlet was designed to divide Germans from their Japanese allies, describing in graphic detail "atrocities" committed by Japanese troops against both British and German citizens in the Far East. The author claimed knowledge of Japanese war aims calculated to disturb the pamphlet's readers: what the Japanese sought was a war among the white races of Europe that would weaken all parties and pave the way for Japanese domination of the entire globe.

In another Delmer-Howe production, an "SS brochure" purported to be of German origin detailed how women who volunteered for the Reich's social services were apt to wind up as factory workers who were exploited, not fully utilized for their talent or skill, worked without rest, and caused family hardship. Supposedly printed by concerned Wehrmacht personnel, the pamphlet's objective was twofold: to alienate women from war work lest they be pressed into hard labor, and to encourage a growing rift between the army and the SS. The pamphlet spoke of SS members as Bolshevists in Nazi garb who sought to collectivize labor and place German workers under centralized authority.

# CHAPTER 9

# Two British Radio Stations

———— ∞∞∞ ————

O f the various black propaganda activities scripted by Dalton and Howe for the Political Warfare Executive, radio was the centerpiece.

Early in 1941, as Delmer directed the newly created special section of the Political Warfare Executive, he started with a secretary and one assistant, but from these small beginnings developed one of the war's most curious and fascinating applications for impression management, one that helped influence the dramatic calculus of the war. His stations included such disparate personalities as a history don, an inspector of schools, a banker, a newspaper editor, and an assortment of German refugees launching broadcast propaganda that purported to come from a German station inside Germany. Again, much of what was broadcast was the truth, gleaned from the tapped conversations of German prisoners, so rich in information that sometimes it even deceived the American allies, always suggesting that it originated from patriotic Germans eager to expose German weaknesses and corruption, which were impeding the efforts of a noble führer.

"Accuracy first," Delmer told his writers. "We must never lie by accident. Or through slovenliness, only deliberately."

Dramatic and theatrical in every respect, Delmer and his team broadcast with practiced deception, and disseminated lies and disinformation through such new and effective techniques that they were able to take over the wavelength of German radio stations, thus diminishing their effect.

In time Delmer struck airwave gold. A premier British black radio station effectively aimed at German troops was Gustav Siegfried Eins. It was both the name of the station and that of its leading cast member. The station broadcast on military shortwave frequencies from May 1941 to November 1943 and was said to transmit from a mobile van inside Nazi-occupied territory. In actuality, programming was broadcast from a London suburb. Gustav Siegfried Eins was on the air for ten-minute sessions prerecorded each day and sent out twice over two different frequencies. In part owing to its racy character, GSE became one of the best-known British black propaganda stations. Gustav Siegfried Eins and "Der Chef" won a large audience in Germany, and theories were spread as to his identity and the location of his transmitter. Hitler's Foreign Office floated a notion that the Chief operated from a barge on the River Spree. Another was that he kept on the move through Hitler's Europe, dodging from hideout to hideout.

On June 8, 1941, after GSE had been broadcasting for a fortnight, Delmer summarized the subversive objectives of the station.

The primary aim of the GSE was to press German soldiers and citizens to intentionally deviate from Hitler's script. The broadcast did not give explicit sabotage instructions to its listeners, although it did give phony instructions to members of an imaginary organization. GSE did not attempt to alter the attitudes of its listeners but to create a situation in which some listeners felt compelled to act, and the character of its transmissions appealed to the lowest common denominator in the German psyche.

In Delmer's view, the attempt to convert the Germans to rebellion against Hitler by argument and appeal was a waste of breath and electronic power. The Germans, he was convinced, would begin to feel and react only when they realized that the war was lost and it was better to abandon Hitler than to fight on. To stimulate German thinking into action hostile to Hitler before this stage had been reached they would have to be tricked. Trickery and deception were beyond the parameters of the BBC. A new weapon of psychological warfare was needed for this purpose. Delmar issued a memorandum to his staff: "We must appeal to the will and self-interest inside every German in the name of his highest patriotic ideals, appealing to an inner core of insecurity, talk to him about his führer and his Fatherland, and in a way that is contrary to the efficient conduct of Hitler."

To add a special touch of irony, Delmer decided that the nameless leader should be introduced as "Der Chef," the same moniker that Hitler's entourage used to refer to their leader.

In his first broadcast, "Der Chef" began to announce very soberly his call sign and dictated some code signals.

Who, in fact, was Gustav Siegfried Eins? He was played by Peter Seckelman, and Delmer accomplished a casting coup in finding this journalist and writer. The announcer was played by Johannes Reinholz, a German prisoner of war who had a clipped baritone voice, and who hated the Nazis from his very soul. He was so bitter that he would have been unusable in most programs, but he fitted GSE to perfection. Further, his inexperience as a broadcaster was an advantage; nobody could expect smoothness or persuasiveness from him after listening for a few moments to his convincing hard breathing, rough intonation, and general bull-in-a-china-shop way of denouncing his despised opponents.

While various inducements were offered by the Allies to other German POWs to get them to work on black radio propaganda beamed to German-held areas, Reinholz essentially volunteered to be in the program because, in reality, he was a right-wing German who believed that Hitler's script was being perverted by his left-wing cronies.

"Here is Gustav Siegfried Eins . . . here is Gustav Siegfried Eins," Reinholz repeated monotonously for about forty-five seconds. There followed a number code, to add a note of authenticity, the Germans were always fond of number codes; Gustav Siegfried 18: "Willy meet Jochen Friday row five parquet stalls second performance Union Theater."

There were hundreds of Union Theater cinemas all over Germany and Delmer fondly imagined leather-coated Gestapo thugs attending every one of them on the lookout for Willy and Jochen. The Gestapo would be quick to fix the signal coming from Britain with their detection instruments, but they could not ignore the possibility that Willy and Jochen were British agents, and that the message to them was genuine.

Then at last, with code declaration completed, it was time for "Der Chef" to launch into his special address. He was answering queries, he announced, which had followed his last message. Of course, there had been no previous transmissions, and this only caused confusion and frustration for the German Security monitors, who would have assumed they'd missed this broadcast, creating muddled confusion.

"Der Chef" had been warned, and he wanted it to be understood that he had been warned, by a deputy führer, and had to lay low because of this witch hunt, and stay off the air for a few days as a consequence. But now the coast was clear and he could report clearly and accurately and respond to a few subtle questions, which suggested the flight of Rudolf Hess, a *deputy führer* who had flown to Scotland to negotiate a peace.

"First, let's get this straight," rasped "Der Chef," "this fellow is by no means the worst of the lot. He was a good comrade of ours in the days of the Free Corps. But like the rest if this clique of cranks, megalomaniacs, and parlor Bolsheviks who call themselves leaders, he simply had no courage in crises. As soon as he learns of the darker developments that lie ahead, what happens? He loses his head completely, packs himself a satchel of hormone pills and a white flag, and flies off to throw himself and us on the mercy of that flat-footed bastard of a drunken old Jew, Churchill. And he overlooks completely the fact that he is the bearer of the Reich's most precious secrets, all of which the obscene British will suck out of him as if he was a bottle of Berlin's favorite beer."

Dramatic pause.

"I must however deny one thing that some of the rumors in the führer's headquarters have suggested," "Der Chef" went on, namely that "the fellow flew to Britain under orders of the führer. I am convinced that this is quite out of the question. Our führer would never authorize a man with such an intimate knowledge of our operational plans to go into enemy country. And that is proved too, by their negligence in permitting this grave blow against the Fatherland to be struck, namely by the security snoops who, if they had been anywhere near as good as they say they are, would have stopped the poor idiot in time."

After a few more salacious details about the stupidity of the security system, "Der Chef" finished off his transmission with a dramatic: "That's all for now. I shall repeat this, all being well, every hour at seven minutes to the full hour. *Immer sieben Minuten vor voll.*"

Delmer particularly liked the denunciation of Churchill as a "flat-footed bastard of a drunken old Jew." With one phrase he had won credibility as a genuinely German station. No member of the German public, he was convinced, would ever suspect that a British propagandist could be capable of such outrageous language about their prime minister.

When Germany invaded Russia, it provided new material for "Der Chef." As an entirely plausible broadcaster, he ranted against the Russian Bolsheviks in Moscow, and the Party Bolsheviks at home. When things went wrong, he blamed all the mishaps on the generals. With each new carefully detailed story, he told of the scandalous private and party life of officials: "While our brave soldiers are freezing to death in Russia, because of the corruption of the contractors, who delayed getting the army's winter clothing ready in time because they are out for bigger profits, these same traitorous swine are having a wonderful time feathering their nests in soft job billets far from danger and privation." The party was to blame, the Wehrmacht were good men, as were the decent Germans, the true patriots.

"Der Chef" told how party officials used their inside knowledge to secure privileges and provisions for themselves, mentioning the names of the wives who had rushed to stores, also named, to acquire all the woolen goods and textiles: "these treacherous whores" of our trusted party. Sure enough, a few weeks later, a Kiel newspaper published an article on the run at department stores.

Often, too, newspaper articles provided inspiration for a Gustav Siegfried story. A featured article in one of Dr. Goebbels's periodicals praised blood transfusion units of the Nazi medical service and obligingly singled out for special mention, by name, meritorious doctors and nurses. It was fodder for "Der Chef" to cite criminal carelessness, fabricating the fact that the tainted blood had come from Polish and Russian donors, and not good clean Germans, polluting Aryan purity.

Creating some of the most convincing stories, "Der Chef" denounced the made-up and sybaritic life of the Parteikommune, Municipal Party, and their goings-on when he learned that Dino Alfieri, Mussolini's ambassador to Berlin, was shortly returning to Rome for consultation. In justification of the demand that Alfieri must be removed from diplomatic circles, "Der Chef" recounted how a German officer had come home unexpectedly, even giving his home address, on leave from the Eastern Front. In his Berlin flat, the officer discovered his wife in flagrante delicto with the ambassador. The officer drew his service revolver and would have shot the ambassador there and then "had the cringing coward of a Macaroni not gone down on his knees and pleaded 'diplomatic immunity.'" The account of July 3, 1941, crept into *Ciano's Diary*, the journal of Benito Mussolini's son-in-law. "Alfieri's star appears to be on the wane in Berlin." Il Duce laughed heartily when he heard of such diplomatic protocol. Some stories were characterizing the moral fiber of Germans and Italians as simply outrageous and salacious, which many German listeners found oddly attractive, and the scandals held their attention, adding to amusement and comic relief at Electra House.

Gustav Siegfried continued to build a substantial audience in Germany, and stories told by "Der Chef" were getting around. "Der Chef" continued to defy the Gestapo with sulfurous broadcasts until the end of 1943. Delmer decided to expand his operations and make better use of impression management. Eventually "Der Chef" had to die, and on air: he was "caught at last" with the sound of a tommy gun salvo and shouts of "Got you, you swine!"

A transmitting engineer knowing no German and unaware of the very final nature of the broadcast went through his routine and repeated the broadcast an hour later. "Der Chef" died twice.

On February 5, 1943, Sender Atlantik, Delmer's new station, was launched with a crew of hardworking perfectionists. It reached a broader audience with such news as that Nazi Party functionaries were exempt from front-line duties, quoting from a decree issued by Goebbels's propaganda ministry. The station encouraged listeners to engage in acts of defiance and disobedience, not by appeals, but by news items showing the duplicity of the German authorities. They never gave up trying to make their listeners worry about what was happening at home. And Delmer mixed things up a bit. For instance, a decree about divorce: Hitler had learned that it was a great scandal that women who had been unfaithful to their soldier husbands could be saved from the consequences of their adultery if the husband was killed. He issued an order that all divorces should be carried through to the end just as if the soldier was still alive. A soldier's faithless wife could bear her husband's name, inherit his worldly goods, and even collect his pension.

These initial efforts were addressed primarily to civilians living in Germany and Nazi-occupied territory. However, Sender Atlantik expanded into an "official" German armed forces entertainment station; its target audience becoming German U-boat crews operating in the Atlantic. Much of Sender Atlantik's output was simple news bulletins, but it established a theme that the infamous Gustav Siegfried Eins had developed. The station carefully avoided any direct criticism of Hitler himself, indeed even defending the führer against real and imagined domestic enemies.

A main focus was Heinrich Himmler, one of the most powerful men in Nazi Germany. As Reichsführer-SS, he controlled the SS and the Gestapo. Himmler had become the leading organizer of the Holocaust. As founder and officer-in-charge of the Nazi concentration camps and the Einsatzgruppen death squads, Himmler held final command responsibility for implementing the industrial-scale extermination of between six and twelve million people. Sender Atlantik implied that Himmler and the SS were busily undermining Hitler's script and composing their own scenario for the outcome of World War II in which Himmler would emerge as the "star" of a pan-European Reich structured along Bolshevist lines. In time, this puncturing of the Nazi unity theme by Allied black propaganda would widen the rifts within the highest levels of the Nazi Party.

Delmer's Soldatensender Calais (the Soldiers' Station) German Service, which was pitched to German soldiers on the western front from a bogus point "near Calais," was an offshoot of Sender Atlantik. But there was a major technical difference. Whereas other British-run black radio stations worked shortwave frequencies, Soldatensender Calais could be heard over standard medium-wave receivers. In May 1941, at the suggestion of Electra House and Special Operations 1 personnel, Winston Churchill authorized the purchase of an extremely powerful radio transmitter from the United States under the code name Aspidistra, borrowed from the popular song "The Biggest Aspidistra in the World."

Coming online in the fall of 1942, Aspidistra, in southeast England, was the medium through which Soldatensender Calais reached German troops stationed throughout Western Europe. Claiming to be an official armed-forces entertainment/news station, Soldatensender was also heard by civilians inside Germany who were starved of news as a consequence of the Nazi Propaganda Ministry's stringent censorship of disturbing reports from the front.

Soldatensender Calais, just as its predecessors had, pretended to be a station of the German military broadcasting network. The station was in operation from October 24, 1943, to April 30, 1945, broadcasting on the medium-wave band 833 kHz, with an associated shortwave station Kurzwellensender Atlantik. The station used a 600-kilowatt transmitter originally built for American broadcaster WLW, in Cincinnati. This transmitter had been unused at the factory after the Federal Communications Commission, FCC, imposed a 50-kW power limit, and so the Radio Corporation of America, RCA, was glad to sell it overseas. The transmitter was installed in a huge underground bunker, where it was briefly the world's largest medium-wave station, and perfect for a deceptive "black" operation.

The Soldiers' Station was in a sense the successor to Gustav Siegfried Eins, and was an inherently more plausible operation. An isolated group of German army men represented themselves as having established intelligence connections with the home front. While party scandal was broadcast, the chief basis for the high credibility of the Soldiers' Station was the accurate news that home conditions provided. Weeks before mail reached the front, soldiers learned from the Soldiers' Station just what streets had been bombed out in the towns from which they came, and the news was almost always correct, for it came from Allied air reconnaissance. The Soldiers' Station counseled sabotage, among other things, and even gave detailed instructions on how to make explosives and how to use incendiary packages dropped by Allied planes.

Operating from 6:00 p.m. local time to dawn, the station broadcast music and coverage of sports and other events of interest to a German serviceman during which the listener was receptive to propaganda items aimed at decreasing morale. One example was a warning that confidence men were swindling German soldiers being transferred from France to the Russian front. This approach could be compared to those used by Tokyo Rose and Axis Sally, without the heavy-handedness of the Axis programs. Both Rose and Sally were generic names given by Allied forces in the South Pacific to approximately a dozen English-speaking female broadcasters of Japanese propaganda. Their intention was to disrupt the morale of Allied forces listening to the broadcast near the Japanese mainland and, according to rumors circulating among GIs, Tokyo Rose routinely identified American units on air, sometimes even naming individual soldiers. Her purported predictions of impending attacks were, according to many, unnervingly accurate.

As part of its cover, Soldatensender Calais relayed speeches by Adolf Hitler and other Nazi officials. During the D-Day invasion of June 6, 1944, Soldatensender Calais broadcast information intended to convince German intelligence officers that the invasion area was wider than it actually was. After the Pas-de-Calais area was overrun, the station changed its call sign to Soldatensender West. Soldatensender's broadcast was repeated in print the next day in the PWE/OSS *Nachrichten für die Truppe*, an air-dropped newspaper for German troops.

As was the case with many Allied black stations, the general drift of Soldatensender transmissions over time was toward explicit tactical advantage. It boasted a large audience of uniformed and civilian listeners. Interrogations later held by intelligence units found that fully 50 percent of captured POWs said that they had heard the "German" station.

In the war's closing stages, the station broadcast deceptive reports of Allied troop movements, warning civilians of approaching enemy assaults, advising them to leave their homes, and thereby impeding the retreat of the Wehrmacht along clogged German roads. Some presume that German soldiers and civilians caught on to Soldatensender's game, yet even though many believed that these transmissions were scripts written by the enemy, listenership remained high and relatively stable. Soldatensender did furnish accurate news that was not available to its audience from Axis sources. Aspidistra's power produced a clear, constant signal while other stations were weak and vulnerable to jamming. The station closed on April 30, 1945, without any official announcement.

The British began writing an alternative script for World War II from the war's start, but this competitive scenario was intended solely for domestic audiences. At the same time, through the black propaganda activities of the Political Warfare Executive and its predecessors, the British sought to discredit the *Mein Kampf* script through a combination of embarrassing facts, innuendos, and falsehoods that undermined the definition of the situation that the Nazis were trying to impress upon German soldiers and civilians.

Ultimately, the British began to compose a fully-fledged alternative to Hitler's script, one that encompassed and spoke to a worldwide audience, but before they tackled this task, the British needed a collaborator, and that co-author was the United States.

# Act III

# Point/Counterpoint:
# Dramatic Conflict

———❦———

*The Third Act follows with Franklin Delano Roosevelt, and in 1939 he is faced with a populace who are opposed to taking a side in World War II. Even as he himself proclaims his disinclination to become involved in any "foreign wars," he studiously works behind the scenes with Churchill to influence public sentiment.*

*Roosevelt, aided by a platoon of poets and an alphabet of organizations, goes about the job of swaying a reluctant American audience.*

*Outmaneuvering the isolationists on the home front requires careful cultivation of Roosevelt's audience, and "The Good Ship Reuben James" gives a calculus to international events. This sinking, courtesy of a German U-boat, plays right into FDR's script.*

*Casting Hitler as a zealot hell-bent on world domination, reminding Americans subtly that the Atlantic Ocean is not as big as it seems, FDR quietly stokes American fears and suffuses his fellow citizens with sympathy for the British cause. Conveniently aiding him in this mission is the entertainment industry.*

*Orson Welles's famous prewar radio production of* War of the Worlds *becomes a realistic foundation for coming attractions. In the movie Mrs.*

Miniver, *a beautiful, dutiful English housewife valiantly struggles against the Blitz, protecting her hearth and children.* Sergeant York *stirs the patriotic American and helps the audience to understand the transition that they must make from a noninterventionist position to military engagement with an expansionist enemy.*

Soon after the attack on Pearl Harbor, stars from Hollywood and radio read the Bill of Rights in its entirety. We Hold These Truths *is wildly popular, drawing sixty million listeners and the government asks all four participating networks to spin off a thirteen-week series.* This Is War! *includes news from the front told by great voices from the entertainment industry, celebrating each branch of the armed services. As James Cagney's distinctive voice booms over the airwaves, "All over the world, the fight is freedom versus slavery."*

The message is recycled and reinvented for many political purposes and in America in 1941, it rings loud and clear. The third major player joins the drama: America is at war. Ed Murrow brings the reality of the front line, the experience of the Blitz into the homes of millions of Americans. On the home front, the Americans expand their role into "black propaganda" with a cowboy who rides in at the end of the act. His name is Wild Bill Donovan.

Nazi Stormtroopers singing to encourage a German boycott of the allegedly Jewish Woolworths Department store in 1933. *Courtesy Rare Historical Photo Collection.*

One of thousands of book burnings that took place in Germany beginning in 1933. *National Archives.*

Adolf Hitler strikes a pose for his personal photographer, Heinrich Hoffmann, whilst rehearsing and listening to his recorded speech. *Courtesy Rare Historical Photo Collection.*

SA troops parade past Hitler. Nuremberg, 1935. *National Archives.*

Nazi Rally in Nuremberg in 1937. The "cathedral of light" consisted of 130 antiaircraft searchlights aimed skyward to create a series of vertical bars surrounding the audience. It was designed by Hitler's architect, Albert Speer. *Courtesy Rare Historical Photo Collection.*

Germania, the proposed Third Reich World Capital designed by Albert Speer. *Courtesy Deutsches Historisches Museum.*

Ovation for Adolf Hitler in the Reichstag after his announcement of the *Anschluss*, March 1938. *Courtesy Rare Historical Photo Collection.*

Joseph Goebbels congratulating a young Hitler Youth on receiving the Iron Cross in 1945. *Courtesy Rare Historical Photo Collection.*

From young German students to Hitler's Youth, the image of strong and idealistic fighting power enhanced the German cause and message. *Courtesy Deutsches Historisches Museum.*

Standing up gloriously amid the flames, St. Paul's Cathedral after being bombed by the Luftwaffe. London, 1940. *National Archives.*

This photograph represented the spirit of Britain, embodied by a single milkman performing his duties among the rubble and destruction with selfless determination. 1940. *Courtesy Rare Historical Photo Collection.*

British motivational slogan and poster. The Brits were known to keep a stiff upper lip, meaning that they stood with pride to defend their homeland and carry on despite hardship. *Courtesy The Imperial War Museum.*

British women did their part, if not in active military service, then through their work in hospitals, war rooms, and factories producing aircraft, tanks, and weapons. *Courtesy The Imperial War Museum.*

Record album cover of Vera Lynn, the Sweetheart of the Forces. Lynn's songs were both inspirations and sentimental. *Courtesy Decca Records.*

RAF salute. *Courtesy The Imperial War Museum.*

An assembly line of students assigned to copy World War II propaganda posters. New York, 1942. *National Archives.*

*Harvesting a Bumper Crop.* Poster of film actress Rita Hayworth promoting scrap metal for the war effort. Many in the Hollywood community volunteered their services to enforce the war effort through activities like selling bonds and entertaining troops. 1942. *National Archives.*

American poster supporting the war effort. Famous artists were enlisted to create posters, and funding the war through contributions was considered a patriotic duty of every citizen. *Library of Congress.*

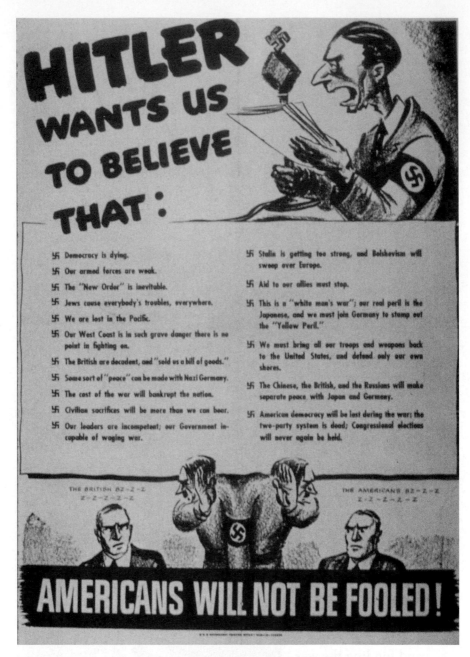

To counteract the German propaganda machine, posters were introduced to the American public to set the record straight and discredit false information distributed by radio and printed posters and pamphlets. *National Archives.*

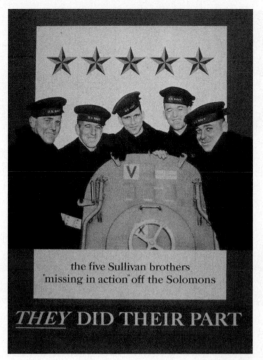

the five Sullivan brothers
"missing in action" off the Solomons

*THEY* DID THEIR PART

The five Sullivan brothers lost their lives serving together on the USS *Juneau*. A poster was created to represent the ultimate sacrifice for the sake of the nation. 1942. *National Archives.*

For your country's sake today—

For your own sake tomorrow

GO TO THE NEAREST RECRUITING STATION
OF THE ARMED SERVICE OF YOUR CHOICE

American propaganda poster encouraging women to fight and defend. *Courtesy Dover Poster Collection.*

*This Is the Army* by Irving Berlin, with an all-star soldier cast performing for the Army Relief Fund. *National Archives.*

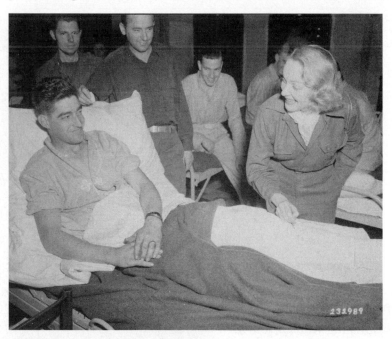

German-born American actress Marlene Dietrich visiting the troops to help morale. *Library of Congress.*

Roosevelt and Churchill, allied grand strategy meeting, 1943.
*National Archives.*

An American
photojournalist, Edward
Steichen, aboard an
aircraft carrier in World
War II. *National Archives*

НА ВСЯКОЕ НАПАДЕНИЕ И УДАР МЫ БУДЕМ
ОТВЕЧАТЬ ТРОЙНЫМИ УДАРАМИ ВСЕЙ МОЩИ
НАШЕЙ ДОБЛЕСТНОЙ КРАСНОЙ АРМИИ

Russian propaganda poster emphasizing the might of the Russian army.
*Courtesy Museum of the Great Patriotic War.*

ДОГОВОР ДРУЖБЫ

As the war changed, posters like these depicting the Soviet soldiers
fighting along with Great Britain and the United States raised morale.
*Courtesy Museum of the Great Patriotic War.*

## SUPREME HEADQUARTERS
## ALLIED EXPEDITIONARY FORCE

Soldiers, Sailors and Airmen of the Allied Expeditionary Force!

You are about to embark upon the Great Crusade, toward which we have striven these many months. The eyes of the world are upon you. The hopes and prayers of liberty-loving people everywhere march with you. In company with our brave Allies and brothers-in-arms on other Fronts, you will bring about the destruction of the German war machine, the elimination of Nazi tyranny over the oppressed peoples of Europe, and security for ourselves in a free world.

Your task will not be an easy one. Your enemy is well trained, well equipped and battle-hardened. He will fight savagely.

But this is the year 1944 ! Much has happened since the Nazi triumphs of 1940-41. The United Nations have inflicted upon the Germans great defeats, in open battle, man-to-man. Our air offensive has seriously reduced their strength in the air and their capacity to wage war on the ground. Our Home Fronts have given us an overwhelming superiority in weapons and munitions of war, and placed at our disposal great reserves of trained fighting men. The tide has turned ! The free men of the world are marching together to Victory !

I have full confidence in your courage, devotion to duty and skill in battle. We will accept nothing less than full Victory !

Good Luck ! And let us all beseech the blessing of Almighty God upon this great and noble undertaking.

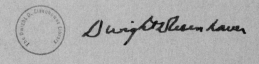

D-Day Speech given by Dwight Eisenhower from the Supreme Headquarters Allied Expeditionary Force in 1944. *Library of Congress.*

American Troops landing on Omaha Beach in
Normandy in 1944. *Library of Congress.*

Roosevelt, Churchill, and Stalin meeting at Yalta to finalize
plans to defeat Germany in February 1945. *Library of
Congress.*

# CHAPTER 10

# Roosevelt and the Isolationists

I have said this before, but I shall say it again and again and again:
Your boys are not going to be sent into any foreign wars.

—Franklin Delano Roosevelt, October 30, 1940

Chosen by George Washington for its tactical location between the South and the North, and for its accessibility to the sea via the Potomac River, the capital of the United States was founded on a parcel of land independent from any one state. With its low-profile skyline, Washington was a city of green parks and open spaces, grand buildings, historic landmarks, marbled monuments, and impressive museums. It surrounded a hub of power and diplomacy, commanding a political center stage for one of the most powerful nations in the world, representing all the democratic ideals in which the country had always taken pride. Politics was the capital's main industry.

Nearby, the White House, the private residence and office for every president since 1800, has an American flag flying whenever the president is in residence.

Inside, in dramatic fashion, President Franklin Roosevelt always appeared before the cameras in a seated position and covered his paralyzed legs with a blanket. He had told his press corps that he was never to be shown with a brace because it would diminish his image of competence. As newsreel cameras rolled, FDR sat before a radio microphone, giving "fireside chats," speaking to Americans.

Roosevelt came to power in the United States at almost the same time Hitler did in Germany. Americans looked on with horror as the German dictator crushed his domestic opposition, persecuted German Jews, supported a fascist uprising in Spain, reclaimed the Rhineland from France, and annexed Austria.

After losing more than 116,000 lives in the Great War, the United States continued to see events overseas as none of their business. Americans shrank the army, kept America out of tangled events overseas, limited immigration, and enacted a Neutrality Act barring arms sales to either side in any future war. Republicans were implacable isolationists, going along for the most part with public sentiment. But the president would make plans for a different production. He displayed unbounded optimism and self-confidence, refusing to surrender to his physical and political limitations with an uncanny ability to rally men and women to his cause. No other American would touch so many lives.

The president of the United States was a big man, huge-shouldered and long-armed. His graying hair was thin, little hollows dwelled on his massive temples, brown shadows sat under his deep, narrow-set eyes, and two big seams hooking down from his clear-cut nose made for grim parentheses around his mouth. He often looked tired, but weariness sat on him lightly, like a film of ash over a smoldering fire. Powerful, solid, imperturbable, he sat at his desk with an air of utter confidence. The crushing responsibilities of 1940 he wore as familiarly, as easily as his seersucker suit, buttoned into thick wrinkles over his paunch.

He too had been conscripted to draft a blueprint for an unpopular war. The president was working hard, incredibly hard. For hours sitting alone in the White House, eyes burning, legs cramping, he thought over and over, about domestic problems and world affairs. He knew he faced daunting decisions and uphill battles. Roosevelt was not without his critics.

Senator Joseph Nye suggested that Roosevelt had been watching events in Europe through partial eyes; the rise of Mussolini and the coming of the Third Reich, and in Asia, the emergence of a military society in Japan and territorial incursions in China. Correctly sensing that FDR would attempt to drag America into a foreign war, Nye and his isolationist cohorts pushed America's First Neutrality Act through Congress, and the United States was committed to remaining free of overseas imbroglios. While Nye made his case for American neutrality, there were other isolationists at large.

Father Charles E. Coughlin intimated that FDR was a puppet of a British-Zionist cabal, a theme that resonated in Hitler's speeches to the assembled crowds at Nuremberg. Born in Canada, and a Catholic priest, with a popular radio program receiving 80,000 letters a week in the late 1930s, for many years Coughlin had managed to keep his anti-Semitism muted while he was on the air. After his split with Roosevelt and with the rise of National Socialism and Fascism in Europe, however, he attacked Jews explicitly.

Some historians attribute this change to Coughlin taking advantage of rising anti-Semitism around the world in order to keep himself relevant. Coughlin publicly derided "international bankers," a phrase that most of his listeners understood to mean Jewish bankers. In the days and weeks after *Kristallnacht*, Coughlin defended the state-sponsored violence of the Nazi regime with an astonishingly misinformed argument that *Kristallnacht* was justified as retaliation for Jewish persecution of Christians.

As the tide rolled out and World War II unfolded, Roosevelt navigated his speeches through unsettling waters, steadfastly denying plans to bring America into foreign action: "Despite what happens in continents overseas, the United States of America shall and must remain . . . untangled and free."

The American audience of the mid-1930s made it evident that they would not attend the play counterpointing *Mein Kampf.* Why should they? Hitler was goose-stepping thousands of miles away, with an enormous expanse of water between the Nazi menace and America's shores.

Even after the Nazi invasion of Poland, Americans were convinced that the United States need not and should not join the show.

"It's over there," Roosevelt addressed his audience, "and we should not be involved in foreign affairs." Roosevelt's predecessor, Herbert

Hoover, supported this notion; Henry Ford vowed that he would not manufacture airplane engines for export to Britain; Colonel Charles Lindbergh assured his compatriots that America was safe from air attack.

Thousands upon thousands of times Franklin D. Roosevelt had flung up a long right arm, waving his hand or his hat to the cheers of voters. Over the course of thirty years he had mastered every trick; the engaging, nonchalant hand waggle, the last artful inflection of his voice; he was an expert in how to hit headlines in both afternoon and morning newspapers. As the presidential election campaign went into its final stretch, he took to the field as if 1940 were any year, as if the race were any race. His train moved with the exact precision that years of organization and the power of the presidency command. When the train stopped, a huge station crowd roared expectantly. As always, the president let them wait a few minutes. At last the door opened; the crowd bellowed. Out came a grinning porter to polish the brass work. Another minute, and the president made a carefully orchestrated appearance with a speech again timed for the afternoon papers.

Even with his reelection in doubt, FDR could not defer at least minimal substantive support for the last bastion of European defense against the Nazis. He exchanged a fleet of mothballed American destroyers for British naval bases in the Caribbean, passing this help off as "lend-lease" and immediately beneficial for America's economic and strategic interests. Trading destroyers suggested that the administration was not gearing up for a major involvement in a foreign war.

Many Americans began to question Roosevelt's narrative. Two days after the executive order authorizing the destroyers-for-bases swap, the America First Committee, with almost a million members and a leading and powerful noninterventionist pressure group against the United States entry into World War II, boycotted the European theater.

Charles Lindbergh's repeated visits to Germany and his visible presence on reviewing stands with Hitler and Göring painted him as a Nazi sympathizer. Others asserted that Lindbergh was actually an American espionage agent silently counting the Luftwaffe planes flying above his head and using his public stance as a cover for his intelligence activities.

If so, then Lindbergh did a superb job at appearing to be an isolationist. "Let us stop this hysterical chatter of invasion by the Nazis," Lindbergh said to admiring crowds at America First gatherings, implying that part of the public had been duped by the British, the Jews, and Roosevelt's inner circle into believing that a German conquest of the United States was imminent.

Meanwhile, backstage events tended to confirm Lindbergh's analysis that Roosevelt was under substantial pressure from the British to cast aside neutrality and enter the war on the Allied side.

In 1940, the president engaged in a rhetorical sleight of hand. Even as he insisted that America would remain free of involvement in affairs outside the Western Hemisphere, he planted the seed of an Axis threat to the United States. He reasoned that Hitler and his "bully boys" had plans for territorial expansion. Like Caesar and Napoleon before him, Hitler was driven to conquest. When the Nazi war machine moved west and the Benelux nations fell like dominoes, Roosevelt warned his countrymen that, left unchecked, Hitler's insatiable appetite would eventually lead him to cross the Atlantic, proclaiming, "They will, we know down in our hearts, enlarge their wild dream to encompass every human being and every mile of the earth's surface."

The leaders of the Third Reich assured anxious Americans that the conquest of the United States was not a part of their script, but to these sly protestations FDR responded, "History records that not long ago those same assurances were given to the people of Holland and Belgium and Norway. It can no longer be disputed that forces of evil . . . are bent on conquest of the world."

Most Americans realized that Neville Chamberlain was deceived at Munich, but there were other reasons to support the British, Roosevelt told campaign audiences that summer. Should the Nazis overrun the British Isles, *Festung Europa* (a term from Nazi propaganda, referring to Hitler's and the Wehrmacht's plans to fortify the whole of occupied Europe) would foreclose European markets to American goods and the Nazis would enjoy a slave labor work force against which American industry could not possibly compete.

Once the blitzkrieg came to an end and German propagandists like Lord Haw-Haw spoke of the Third Reich's awesome military force, FDR had more ammunition in his verbal arsenal to help the British. The same lightning attacks could move Nazis across the American continent in a matter of months and include a Japanese assault on the West Coast, with America divided down the middle. Still the American desire to avoid any involvement in war filled the papers.

# CHAPTER 11

# Churchill and Roosevelt Write the Script Backstage

———— ∝‰∞ ————

With dissenting critics suggesting what America's part in the war should in fact be, backstage Roosevelt collaborated on a script of British origin. The destroyers-for-bases exchange was a prologue, followed by the first peacetime draft in American history. The critical opening scene was lend-lease, and while Roosevelt would occupy center stage, it was Churchill who drafted the scenario. In truth, Churchill had little choice but to turn in his collaborator's direction.

Between the war's start and November 1940, the British government had purchased some $4.5 billion in armaments from the United States alone, so that its foreign exchange reserves had dwindled to a mere $2 billion. When the London Blitz began, Churchill wrote a personal letter to FDR, describing how serious survival was for Britain and urged the president to find means of transferring weapons and war matériel to Britain that would not deplete the Crown's exchequer. Receiving Churchill's plea while vacationing aboard the USS *Tuscaloosa*, Roosevelt gave a heartening reply: "There will be no bottlenecks in our determination to aid Great Britain."

While the bases-for-destroyers exchange had been mandated by a stroke of his pen, lend-lease would require the approval of a Congress where isolationist sentiments ran high. He called a press conference arguing for the extension of American-made equipment to "any country whose defense the president deems vital to the defense of the United States."

The president moved quickly and announced the revival, under the National Defense Act, of the Council of National Defense. He picked huge William Knudsen, Danish-born president of General Motors, as top coordinator. When he accepted the job, Big Bill Knudsen asked bluntly, "Who's boss?"

"I am," said Franklin Roosevelt.

Could any one man do it? Franklin Roosevelt knew he was director of the show and took the pulse of the nation.

Another presidential train raced south through the rich red and green foothills of Virginia. Inside, President Roosevelt made the last few changes in the speech of a day that sped into history. One hour before his train left Washington, Benito Mussolini had declared war on Great Britain and France. A light rain began as the train neared Charlottesville. Then, through the streets he drove to the Memorial Gymnasium of the University of Virginia, to don his cap and gown and face the graduating class to deliver his speech.

The president was specific in his promise of aid. "In our American unity . . . we will extend to the opponents of force the material resources of this nation." On that tenth day of June, 1940, he said with contempt in his voice, "the hand that held the dagger has struck it into the back of its neighbor." Ended was the myth of US neutrality: "Let us not hesitate. The whole of our spirit lies with those nations."

"WHOA! Whoa, Mr. President," cried the *Detroit News*, sensing in Franklin Roosevelt's non-belligerent intervention a pull toward war. Hundreds of letters approved the *St. Louis Post-Dispatch's* bitter declaration that the president, unless checked, would take the United States over the brink of war. Montana's isolationist Burton K. Wheeler in the Senate and Charles Lindbergh in the air both detected and resisted a drift toward total US war, but nearer the core of US fear and feeling was poet Edna St. Vincent Millay, writing in the *New York Times*: "Oh, build, assemble, transport, give, that England, France and we may live." Then night fell on France.

• • •

When the French capitulation came, Adolf Hitler actually snapped his fingers, chuckled, and did a little goose-step. Beaming with pleasure, the führer rolled into Berlin in his special antiaircraft train. Stepping onto the red-carpeted platform where Nazi bigwigs crowded to welcome him, he listened with frank delight to the metallic clamoring of bells, the roaring "Heil"s of Hitler Youth, the trumpeting blare of a Stormtroopers' brass band. With the savage chant of "Sieg Heil! Sieg Heil!" ringing in his ears, he entered his automobile and began a triumphal journey to the chancellery as crowds cheered and wept themselves into hysteria.

On either side, swastika banners covered the building fronts, garlands of flowers hung across the street on golden cords, bands thundered out continuously. The pavement beneath was a multicolored blanket of flowers strewn by white-bloused Hitler maidens.

• • •

The little oval room was hot. The score of frail, wobbly, gilt chairs were jammed close together on the deep scarlet carpet. Perspiring gently, the audience and distinguished guests sat still, in some nervousness. In the front row, not grinning, was big, jug-eared movie star Clark Gable in a chalk-stripe gray suit; his wife, Carole Lombard, in a funnel-like black hat with a veil, a simple black afternoon dress; Secretary of State Cordell Hull, as somber as his dark suit; and the president's mother, Sara Roosevelt, in a gray-blue evening gown.

On the desk, its top drilled for the wires, were seven microphones, two glasses of water, two sharp new pencils, a notepad, an open packet of Camels. The president came in five minutes before the broadcast on his small rubber-tired wheelchair. Mr. Roosevelt, in a dark blue serge suit, a black bow tie, was in high good humor. In the room's warmth he mopped his big, tanned face from time to time with a large white hand-kerchief. At 9:30 p.m. more than five hundred radio stations in the United States were tuned to his desk. Attendance at movies dropped sharply. In barrooms, farmhouses, trains, planes, and ships, people waited, listening. His words would mark a turning point in history. As he began his sixteenth fireside chat, the president spoke in simple terms, clearly, gravely.

He was deliberately trying to lead the nation as he had led it in 1933. Now he clarified a clear and imminent threat:

My friends,

We face this new crisis—this new threat to the security of our nation—with the same courage and realism. Never before since Jamestown and Plymouth Rock has our American civilization been in such danger as now. For, on September 27, 1940, by an agreement signed in Berlin, three powerful nations, two in Europe and one in Asia, joined themselves together in the threat that if the United States of America interfered with or blocked the expansion program of these three nations—a program aimed at world control—they would unite in ultimate action against the United States.

The Nazi masters of Germany have made it clear that they intend not only to dominate all life and thought in their own country, but also to enslave the whole of Europe, and then to use the resources of Europe to dominate the rest of the world.

In view of the nature of this undeniable threat, it can be asserted, properly and categorically, that the United States has no right or reason to encourage talk of peace, until the day shall come when there is a clear intention on the part of the aggressor nations to abandon all thought of dominating or conquering the world.

Instead, it was up to the United States to be the "great arsenal of democracy." Roosevelt concluded with a call to arms:

> As President of the United States I call for that national effort. I call for it in the name of this nation which we love and honor and which we are privileged and proud to serve. I call upon our people with absolute confidence that our common cause will greatly succeed.

*Arsenal of Democracy* was to become a slogan used by the president, promising to aid the United Kingdom with military supplies even if the United States refrained from fighting.

Franklin Roosevelt spoke as clearly as ever, but there was no lightness in his voice, no touch of humor. As he went on, his big head thrown back, his voice gained depth, strength, and emotion.

• • •

On the Fourth of July, as for 165 years past, fireworks softly looped and popped, ending with a bang or a whimper. The president, lounging in seersucker trousers, a blue, tieless shirt open at the collar, told reporters at Hyde Park he still hoped that the United States could stay out of the war, but he made it clear that his hope was not to be confused with belief.

For most of his life, FDR kept secrets. He loved keeping them, especially ones no one else knew, and nothing pleased him more than to sail north undetected to meet for the first time the prime minister of Great Britain on August 3, 1941. The White House Press Office fed a story that the president was just taking a few days off at sea to relax and take time to consider international hostilities. The presidential yacht, *Potomac*, sailed through the Cape Cod Canal, while the president was 250 miles away aboard the USS *Augusta*.

On a balmy, gray, wet afternoon, FDR met with Churchill for the first time aboard the USS *Augusta* anchored somewhere off the northeastern coast of the United States.

The cruiser *Augusta* with its large escort of other cruisers and destroyers, the British *Prince of Wales* with its own numerous escorts, together with a fleet large enough to fight a major sea battle if an enemy appeared, rendezvoused at the North Atlantic coast. The place was almost certainly Newfoundland. At the first meeting Mr. Churchill boarded the *Augusta,* the eight brass buttons on his blue uniform slightly marred by the gray marks where he had hastily brushed away the little mound of silver-gray cigar ash that collected on his stomach as he slouched down. Except on this Sunday, when the president crossed a short gangplank to attend services on the *Prince of Wales,* all the meetings took place on the *Augusta.* An officer present later reported that Churchill was much moved as the chaplains carried out the service when the British and American crews sang, "O God, Our Help in Ages Past." Churchill finally said, gruffly, "I'm not a religious man. But I thank God that such a man as you is the head of your government at a time like this." The chaplains led another song, "Onward, Christian Soldiers." The president and prime minister sang lustily, although their voices were drowned out by the drone of the patrol planes overhead. But as they measured their thoughts during the night, they drafted a plot in which one theme emerged loud and clear: in the face of tyranny, "they respect the right of all peoples to choose the form of government under which they will live."

The summit forged a draft for the war beginning with the joint endorsement of the Atlantic Charter, specifying British and American war aims as the liberation of Axis-enslaved nations, a pact to which the Soviet Union would become a signatory a few weeks thereafter. But, as Munich had demonstrated, pieces of paper were no substitute for action. Another act would have to be written, staged, and performed, if the American public was to be mobilized in support of alliance with Britain.

In the damp, disused, musty wharf shed in Rockland, Maine, fifty men stood or sat, impatient and chilled; newsmen, cameramen, radiomen, technicians, bottle-holders. They were the reception committee for Franklin Roosevelt, returning aboard the yacht *Potomac* from the greatest fishing trip that any president of the United States had ever undertaken. The United States, though not at war, had conferred through the head of its government with Great Britain, a nation at war, on how Nazi Germany was to be defeated, and had further agreed on control of the postwar world.

When Churchill returned to Great Britain, US flags waved in the shattered streets of London. News of his historic meeting with Roosevelt led to optimism. Later, at a crowded dinner of the White House Correspondents' Association, President Roosevelt spoke for thirty-four minutes and said, "I remember that, a quarter of a century ago . . . the German government received solemn assurances from their representatives in the United States that the people of America were disunited; that they cared more for peace at any price than for the preservation of ideals and freedom. . . . Let not dictators of Europe or Asia doubt our unanimity now." But Roosevelt still had not convinced his detractors. It was only a matter of time before he could step out of the circle of neutrality to reframe and commit to a script drafted on the USS *Augusta*.

What had passed in the long sessions when they dredged and searched each other's thinking only they knew in full. They did hatch plans, a draft of war aims and an invitation to Stalin to confer on Russia's war needs.

• • •

Germany overreached in September 1941. The American destroyer USS *Greer* was on a routine mail run to Iceland. In the cold clear skies, a British plane patrolled overhead, while under the surface of ink-blue waves, a Nazi U-boat quietly lurked, seeking British-flagged targets, but was again under injunction to avoid a skirmish with American ships. The plane spotted the U-boat and signaled ahead to the *Greer*. The U-boat attempted to avoid action with an unmarked British destroyer. Two hours after the initial sighting, with the *Greer* in hot pursuit, the German craft fired a torpedo past the destroyer, which, in turn, dropped depth charges on its attacker. Despite the efforts of the U-boat to disengage, the *Greer* continued anti-submarine maneuvers, clearly becoming the aggressor.

News reached Washington, and FDR initiated a "shoot on sight" policy for American lend-lease convoys and their escorts coming upon German warships. FDR accompanied the announcement of this provocative order with a disclaimer regarding the *Greer* incident's authenticity: "In spite of what Hitler's propaganda bureau has invented, and in spite of what any American obstructionist organization may prefer to believe, I tell you the blunt fact that the German submarine fired first upon this American destroyer without warning, and with deliberate design to sink her."

Not only was the attack of the *Greer* a valuable performance, it was entirely consistent with the script that FDR wanted to impress upon his American audience.

Feeling that it was just a matter of time before Europe would be in a crisis controlled by the Nazis, the president appealed to his countrymen that America should come to the aid of Britain, and insisted that anything contrary to this policy would be against his own core beliefs and America's ideals.

FDR was a willing accomplice in the *Greer* encounter and, far from being part of Hitler's grand design, this was a joint Anglo-American deception on the American public, a pretext that allowed FDR "to move to unrestricted convoying and to an unrestricted naval war at sea."

• • •

Less than two months after the *Greer* episode, the Nazis played a spontaneous role in moving the narrative line of Roosevelt's script along. On October 1941, a German U-boat torpedoed the USS *Reuben James*, and more than a hundred American seamen were sent to watery graves. The *Reuben James* lent textual support to FDR's reading of the *Greer* attack. It also gave rise to a popular song:

Have you heard of a ship called the good *Reuben James*?
Manned by hard-fighting men both of honor and fame,
She flew the stars and stripes of the land of the free,

But tonight she's in her grave on the bottom of the sea.
Tell me what were their names,
Tell me what were their names,
Did you have a friend on the good *Reuben James*?
What were their names?

This interventionist anthem was sung far and wide in the United States in the autumn of 1941, with its lyrics of destruction in individual terms, which brought the threat home to its listeners. Meanwhile, there was another voice sailing through American airwaves, on shortwave radio: an antagonist called Fred Kaltenbach.

# CHAPTER 12

# The Nazi Counter-Message
# to America

⟨⟨⟩⟩

On April Fool's Day 1940, the Third Reich, anticipating the problems that might emerge should America become an extraneous character in Hitler's carefully crafted script, transmitted broadcasts to the United States. Before the outbreak of war, the Columbia Broadcasting System issued official reports to the president about the "German Service" to North America. Its objective was not to win Americans over to the Nazi cause, but to raise doubts about the wisdom of helping the Allies.

With war declared in Europe, Radio Deutsche Europa Sender, Germany's international broadcasting facility known by its initials, DES, expanded its broadcasting time to North America from two to eleven hours of daily programming. Its outrageous spokesperson was compelled to support the German cause. Originally from Iowa, Fred W. Kaltenbach had taken a doctoral degree from the University of Berlin. Influenced by Roosevelt's media savviness, Kaltenbach took a page from FDR's radio book and structured his broadcasts as informal fireside chats. His topics, anything but intimate, were misinformed and misguided.

"Letters to Iowa" were directed at the American Midwest; they were in a simple and homey style. Germany's English-speaking propagandists began each program with "Greetings to my old friend, Harry in Iowa," then argued a case against President Franklin D. Roosevelt's reelection to a third term of office, and denounced the Lend-Lease Bill aiding Great Britain.

"It's a lost cause," Kaltenbach said. "It will only lead to an unnecessary war with Germany."

According to German intelligence, "British and French agents had met in Paris to plan to stage the subversive sinking of the American liners *Manhattan* and *Roosevelt*, with the intention of creating an international incident giving cause to war." Presupposing that the United States was looking for an excuse to enter the war, Kaltenbach manufactured Roosevelt's aims.

# CHAPTER 13

# FDR and a Platoon of Poets

—⊗⊗⊗—

Roosevelt knew he had to rebut Kaltenbach's nonsense and felt the broadcasts bordered on treason and abused the nation's principle of freedom of speech. He went to work polishing and rewriting his script, his message, his war. During the interwar era the United States failed to develop the rudiments of public information, propaganda, and impression management. Psychological warfare in the United States was in a fetal state when hostilities broke out.

American psychological warfare was improvised after the outbreak of war, and no peacetime agency existed that had preserved pertinent skills, trained expert personnel, or engaged in appropriate research and planning. During World War I, its direction was entrusted largely to men with experience furnishing news, opinions, advertisements, and entertainment to the home population, and their skills were inadequate. This characterization may seem inordinately harsh, but in fact, as America stood at the door of war in 1940, it had no outline for a script. FDR relied on himself and a few private individuals and organizations to "sell" his argument for American Allies' support.

It was not for lack of interest or energy that the president deferred to the isolationist establishment. Accusing the president that this was "his" war was frivolous at best, as he believed that German policy and action was a threat to freedom the world over. He recalled the propaganda abuses during the last war when President Wilson appointed George Creel, an investigative journalist, as the director of the Committee on Public Information. Creel's critics argued, "Creel's agency had succeeded too well in arousing intolerance and hysteria coupled with the militant spirit it sought." Then there was a more immediate problem. The isolationists had characterized FDR as a would-be dictator and a warmonger, and any suggestion that his administration was creating a propaganda unit could easily play into their hands.

After the United States entered the war, Roosevelt perhaps took too much time, was too cautious in assembling his scriptwriting team. Although isolationism could not withstand the Japanese assault on December 7, 1941, and the German/Italian declarations of war against America a few days later, the president knew that mobilizing public support for the war would become a crucial task throughout the conflict. He had to justify his military strategy. "Remember Pearl Harbor" offset the call for a "soft peace" with the Axis.

When news of war in Europe reverberated to the United States, President Roosevelt established the Office of Emergency Management as an overseeing body whose scope was to take responsibility for public information.

The OEM had a direct propaganda role, and in the summer of 1940, presidential assistant Lauchlin Currie suggested to FDR that the government sponsor a local defense committee to give citizens a vent for their energies and teach others by example. Days later, representatives visited the White House from an ad hoc body that had been created earlier within the ranks of the military to formulate a basic plan for a Public Relations Administration.

The plan, while calling for some type of morale-boosting agency, advocated caution, even secrecy, so as not to create public alarm about the imminence of American war involvement.

Roosevelt waited a full nine months before he created another propaganda body, and reasoned that, given its potentially controversial nature, the right man would have to be cast as its head.

He chose the Librarian of Congress and poet Archibald MacLeish to direct the reorganized unit. Indeed, as late as 1944, the Office of War Information (OWI), which was clearly a propaganda agency, steadfastly denied any functions apart from the dissemination of "information and the truth."

MacLeish became a key individual in the matrix for raising public morale and clarifying reasons behind America's entry into the war. His artistic abilities spanned several media and genres. Among other talents, he was a poet, playwright, journalist, and speechwriter.

MacLeish graduated from Harvard Law School, but after a short period as a working attorney he headed for the Paris of the 1920s, where he became an expatriate poet. By the 1930s, with social problems intensifying under the weight of the Great Depression, MacLeish returned to America and brought an abiding social concern to his artistic endeavors. Subsequently, he joined the staff of *Fortune* magazine and was then tapped by FDR to become the Librarian of Congress. Since 1800 the Librarian has been the custodian of over 50 million books, articles, newspapers, photographs, and oversees the Copyright Office. Today the LOC has more than 4.7 billion pages digitized in its research system. In the 1940s, the number of sources housed was still staggering, accommodating readers, researches, and scholars.

Taking a special interest in applying his talents to the production, and months before the Japanese strike at Pearl Harbor, MacLeish assigned noted radio dramatist Norman Corwin to write a radio script entitled *We Hold These Truths*, restating and rephrasing the Bill of Rights to commemorate its 150th anniversary.

The piece was originally intended as a powerful adjunct to Roosevelt's pro-intervention stance and was slated for broadcast over CBS on December 15, 1941. When war broke out, *We Hold These Truths* became a vehicle through which the administration underscored the conflict between representative democracy and totalitarian government. At the urging of the White House, the program was aired on four radio networks simultaneously. With sixty-three million listeners, Corwin was just as celebrated as FDR, winning the coveted Peabody Award for outstanding journalism.

With the New York Philharmonic Orchestra under the direction of Leopold Stokowski providing musical accompaniment, the roster of stars assembled to read from Corwin's script included show-business personalities Jimmy Stewart, Walter Brennan, Walter Huston, Lionel Barrymore, Edward G. Robinson, Rudy Vallee, Edward Arnold, and Orson Welles. They would contribute to the war effort throughout the duration of the conflict.

Sixty million Americans heard the broadcasts, the largest audience of any dramatic program in the history of radio. Climaxing in a special address from FDR himself, *We Hold These Truths* set a dramatic moral tone.

Public response to *We Hold These Truths* was so overwhelming that MacLeish asked the heads of the four participating networks to air a full thirteen-week series advancing the principles of *We Hold These Truths* with news from the front.

With Norman Corwin as director, the result was *This Is War!* For the next thirteen Saturday evenings, *This Is War!* audiences heard actors James Cagney, John Garfield, Robert Montgomery, Jimmy Stewart, and Douglas Fairbanks pay tribute to each branch of the American military. Throughout its run, *This Is War!* brought abstract concepts down to a level of personal freedoms. One episode narrated by James Cagney, "Smith Against the Axis," elaborated on two themes: the idea of the "little guy" and the image of the innocent child, the "kid," as the embodiment of Allied war motives, introducing Smith's son, Jimmy Smith, a fictional character representing the values of an ordinary American. Early in the script, Corwin's words, spoken by Cagney that night, included the emblematic passage:

He's what we are fighting for. So there will be a United States in thirty-five years for him to be president of. All over the world, the fight is freedom versus slavery. Smith against the Axis. Whatever your name is, whatever you do, you, Smith, the people, are everywhere. When a nation's soldier falls, there should be weeping in every town and village in America because they all fight for the same goal, for peace of mind and sweet sleep at night and for the future Jimmy Smiths of the world.

Couched in colloquial language, "Smith Against the Axis" distilled fundamental liberties into highly effective, personal terms, explaining to the Americans what they felt, or should feel, in their hearts and the basic principles of American government.

Another broadcast early in the war was the OWI-sponsored radio play *Listen to the People,* narrated and scripted by another respected poet, Stephen Vincent Benét. Again, two critical themes appeared in this piece: a call back to America's historical origins, with Benét's script alluding to Revolutionary War battles, and a rebuttal to Fred Kaltenbach's *Deutsche Kurzsender.* The purpose was to combat the idea that "democracy is a fake." While insisting that the American system of government was not fallible and Roosevelt's New Deal perfect, Benét allowed:

Sure, there were lots of things we didn't like about the Triple A— at first. But we've worked it out with our government over ten years now and they've listened to what we've said. We've got Pearl Harbor written down in our hearts. We're not a special class or a special interest. We're part of the something that's bigger than any of us. It's called the United States, Adolf.

At a time when the forces were suffering reversals in the field, an allowance for error added credibility to the Allied script.

All of the separate strands still required working into a unified fabric, and in Roosevelt's State of the Union address, MacLeish wove them together. Lacking a script that motivated the Germans compared to Hitler's *Mein Kampf,* MacLeish wrote an address for FDR that charted an entire information campaign for months:

We are fighting, as our fathers have fought, to uphold the doctrine that all men are equal in the sight of God. Those on the other side are striving to destroy this deep belief and to create a world in their own image—a world of tyranny and cruelty and serfdom. This is the conflict that day and night now pervades our lives. No compromise can end that conflict. There never has been, there never can be, successful compromise between good and evil. Only total victory can reward the champions of tolerance, and decency, and freedom, and faith.

MacLeish parsed Roosevelt's speech into organizing themes: demands for unprecedented effort and individual sacrifice; an understanding of the Hitler script of global domination; international order guaranteed in the world by a United Nations after the war; and above all, the fight for freedom.

These goals chosen by MacLeish were embodied in the "Four Freedoms" enunciated by President Wilson during World War I, pointing to the desire to:

create a new world, of people who, in terms of the Four Freedoms, are not afraid, are not hungry, are free to live and to think and to worship as they please. The Four Freedoms and the charter of the United Nations lay the basis for the definition of this cause [of which] the basic belief is a belief not in races and not in political units, but in humanity; a cause of which the program and the ultimate purpose is to sweep the world clean of mass fear and mass want, creating instead and at last a human world dedicated to humanity.

Advocating the principle of equality, MacLeish would be more than just a refutation by those intent on shredding the Allied script for World War II; it would be a central rallying cry that would push the narrative line toward the final aim of victory.

Absolutely essential was conveying an image of America as an ethnic, racial, and class mosaic that formed a whole. When the OWI was founded, MacLeish was eminently aware of the propaganda potential that social inequality and disharmony might afford. If America was to play the role called for in the emerging Allied war script, these divisions could not be simply ignored; they would have to be transformed into a source of strength.

This imperative informed an OWI inspired by MacLeish with a recommendation to the mass media, which read, in part: "We must emphasise that this country is a melting pot, a nation of many races and creeds who have demonstrated that they can live together and progress. The typical war worker as portrayed in films might be a Chinaman, a Negro, a Greek, a Pole, a man from the grain belt, the mountains, the slums, from Park Avenue or a park bench."

While Germany discriminated against any dissenters protesting the national will of the Fatherland, condemning Jews and Poles to a landscape of concentration camps, the leadership in America aimed to preserve its founding values: freedom, endowed by the Creator, in the pursuit of happiness as the inalienable right for every American.

As unity became inseparable from victory in the OWI's depiction of America and its cause, disunity became synonymous with defeat, and those uttering divisive words became fools manipulated by the enemy. By confronting the criticism of American integration propaganda that Kaltenbach and his staff had organized, the OWI reinforced the unity theme, and such criticism could now be unmasked and identified as a weapon of psychological warfare.

With the OWI's notable effectiveness, Roosevelt became more comfortable and did something that would prove to be of enduring significance. He established yet another body, the Coordinator of Information (COI), around a specific individual, William "Wild Bill" Donovan. Shortly thereafter, Donovan's office subsumed the COI's Foreign Information Service into its ranks and became the Office of Strategic Services (OSS), the immediate predecessor of the Central Intelligence Agency (CIA). Donovan's unit had more latitude in carrying out its mission, one that Donovan would create, especially when the OSS began to work with the British.

A graduate of Columbia Law School, Donovan became an influential Wall Street lawyer, and in World War I he earned a Medal of Honor for bravery under fire. With a rich and daring imagination, he was solely responsible for the organization of a centralized intelligence program and quickly cultivated a close relationship with Winston Churchill and Stewart Menzies, head of the British Secret Service, learning much about psychological warfare and spycraft. In so doing, he established close ties with a group that sparked his creativity, and led him toward black propaganda, which he intended to use to help win the war. That group was the Political Warfare Executive, known as the PWE, the clandestine British body that had been put in place to produce and disseminate both white and black propaganda, with the goal to target enemy morale.

In June 1942, Milton Eisenhower, the brother of military commander Dwight, convinced Roosevelt to clear the decks of myriad agencies performing propaganda duties and unite under the Office of War Information. It was charged with supervising the release of war news, meeting requests for publicity campaigns from other government departments, and constructing policy guidelines for the mass media regarding their portrayal of the war to the public.

Four individuals were placed in command of the new super-agency: Elmer Davis, a CBS radio commentator, experienced journalist, and Roosevelt confidant, was named director; Milton Eisenhower handled the administrative end; publisher Gardner Cowles Jr. was assigned the post of director of the OWI's domestic branch; and Archibald MacLeish developed long-range strategy and would work closely with playwright Robert Sherwood in actually writing scripts for OWI and OWI-sponsored films and radio shows. In the end, the central division of duties was between the OWI, handling white propaganda, and Donovan's OSS, dealing with black.

The team embarked on lengthy discussions hatching elaborate plans for black and white propaganda. Bogus radio stations and leaflets were still favored instruments, while Donovan intended to expand their role in cooperation with the Brits.

Donovan worked closely with Eisenhower, and was briefed on all aspects of the war. One report meant for the president came to their office from Churchill, an account from an inside operative that shook him to his core.

It read:

Despite Nazi attempts to keep secret the *Einsatzgruppen* (Special Action Squads) extermination of the Jewish people, news of mass murders has been filtered into Britain by an underground resistance group reporting unimaginable atrocities in Poland and Russia. Whole districts are being exterminated and "scores of thousands" of executions in cold blood are being carried out by mobile killing units. The mass exterminations are well organized. Once rounded up with the help of police and collaborators, people are marched, following signs pointing to "resettlement centers" located on the outskirts of cities and towns. Reaching the destination, they are shot.

The *London Times* had run an eyewitness account that they managed to obtain through an intelligence operative from MI6:

We were instructed to drive the truck outside of town. On the way there, we came across Jews carrying baggage, walking on foot, in the same direction we were traveling. There were whole families. The farther we drove, the denser the columns became. They were led past a number of different areas, and at each designated place they had to leave their luggage, then their coats, shoes, garments, and underwear, valuables. Despite the efforts of the Sonderkommandos, who aid in the killing process at work camps, some were left alive. After they left the area, the soldiers were given schnapps to help anesthetize the horror of their work. The squads, apparently anxious to get back to their quarters to continue drinking, had left too expeditiously to shovel the earth properly.

This alphabet of organizations created by the president was dedicated to the eradication of horror and terror any way they could. It was part of the American script.

But it was the Nazi script that had dominated the war in its early years. Could America and Britain find a way to bring the reality of the front lines to the home front, with eyewitness accounts exceeding the work conjured up by propaganda poets?

# CHAPTER 14

# The American "Patriotic" Press Responds!

—⚬∞∞⚬—

As events escalated in Europe, William S. Paley, head of CBS, saw an opportunity on the war horizon. A broadcasting pioneer, he had harnessed the potential reach of broadcasting, being responsible for growing the Columbia Broadcasting System from a small chain of radio stations into one of the world's dominant communication empires.

When war clouds darkened over Europe in the late 1930s, Paley recognized Americans' desire for news coverage of the coming war and built the CBS news division into a powerful force. During World War II, he would serve in the psychological warfare branch of the Office of War Information, holding the rank of colonel.

Having for some time cherished the notion of transforming the CBS news department into a *New York Times* on radio, Paley's interest went beyond journalism; he believed that the news must play an active part in world affairs. Paley saw with crystal clarity the value of describing the potentially cataclysmic course of events in Europe and incorporated into this reportage the use of explicitly dramatic techniques.

In March 1937, CBS aired *The Fall of the City* on its radio broadcast network. Written by Archibald MacLeish, the script was based on events from the Spanish Civil War in which troops from the Italian and German armies joined Franco's Fascists to crush the legitimate Republican government.

Other CBS presentations made more oblique references to the Axis threat. When Orson Welles's *Mercury Theater of the Air* broadcast an updated version of H. G. Wells's *War of the Worlds* in 1938, many Americans believed that the armies invading East Windsor, New Jersey, were not composed of Martians, but of Nazis in advanced flying machines. While disclaimers framed the show, Paley's organization did nothing to dissuade its listeners from drawing analogies of this sort. But it was real, accurate, on-the-scene, eyewitness reporting that became a priority for the news division.

Paley cast an entirely new type of player that would emerge onto the stage of World War II. It was the war correspondent (or warco) who would now function as a narrator. The seminal warco, who virtually defined the role, was indeed the man he had encouraged, CBS's London correspondent Edward R. Murrow. In 1937, Murrow was the primary CBS correspondent in Europe, but as Hitler's script began to unfold, Paley sent some extraordinarily talented journalists to join him, including William L. Shirer and Eric Sevareid. CBS initiated a daily *World News Roundup*, with news from Europe prominently featured. Station managers interrupted regularly scheduled programs with special news bulletins in the months that followed, and when the Nazis unleashed their blitzkrieg against the Poles, CBS went to round-the-clock reportage of the war. Largely because of these changes, a *Fortune* magazine survey conducted in 1939 reported that more Americans were getting their news via the airwaves than from newspapers and believed radio news to be more accurate and reliable than print.

When the bombing of London began in 1940, the public's admiration for radio news only increased and, in the British capital, Ed Murrow transformed radio news broadcasting into an institution and an art form.

At age thirty-two, Murrow tackled extraordinarily demanding tasks. He was without fear. During the height of the Blitz, he roamed London's streets in a small open car and never sought protection in an air-raid shelter. His broadcasts were honest. Despite his personal sympathy for the Allied cause, he refused to place the British evacuation at Dunkirk in a positive light and was unsparing in his description of the horrors of modern warfare. A brilliant wordsmith, Edward Murrow constructed a vivid canvas:

> This is London. As some of you may have heard, when I was talking from Trafalgar Square shortly before midnight tonight, the London sirens sounded for the third time in twenty-four hours and the after-theater crowds in Piccadilly were startled by the roar of British anti-aircraft guns not far away. Screaming bombs were dropped as well as firebombs on the London area. From a rooftop I watched the skies over London assume a vivid red glow that changed to bright yellow as flames spread from a small area beneath. Pink smoke overwhelmed the flames, and the crisscrossing of searchlight beams over the fire provided one of the most extraordinary spectacles London has ever seen. Over the flames a German bomber hovered, roaming noisily. Rooftops for miles around were illuminated. The dome of Saint Paul's Cathedral, one of London's highest landmarks, was thrown into sharp relief. The all-clear signal was sounded in central London before the flames were completely extinguished.

It was from Murrow that Americans got a dramatic account of what Hitler might have in store for America as a sequel to the drama performed in Britain.

CBS was part of the patriotic response, to advance the promise and purpose by radio, as dramatic witness as news unfolded, becoming the front-runner of on-the-spot news airing to living rooms across America.

CHAPTER 15

# War Comes to America's
# Movie Theaters

———— ✺ ————

While there was a strong documentary film tradition in Europe
by the time of the war's outbreak—an obvious example being
the work of Leni Riefenstahl—the form itself actually originated in
the United States with Robert Flaherty and his best-known movie,
*Nanook of the North*, a film about a family's struggle in the freezing
climate of northern Quebec. The documentary filmmakers working
in the United States made several contributions to the future American
script for World War II, in thematic as well as technological terms,
which would help future filmmakers adapt to shooting documentaries
with wartime messages.

On a technical basis, Flaherty developed cold-resistant camera grease
that enabled him to shoot footage in Arctic climes, and, in fact, both
16-mm film and what would become the "combat" camera were prod-
ucts of America in the 1920s. Early documentary film directors provided
a pool of experienced talent and a set of working techniques that served
both government-sponsored and private wartime film productions.

Most World War II films were made under the official home front
umbrella. In *Ring of Steel*, a film produced by the Army Signal Corps

about America's military history and the courage and attributes of the American soldier, Spencer Tracy becomes an eternal citizen-soldier crossing decades. In this work, with the first scene showing Tracy firing "the shot heard round the world" at Concord, he then marches into a succession of historical epochs through a series of dissolves: "Marching, I made America great. South to the Rio Grande, I made America free. I built America with Kit Carson and Davey Crockett. In the Civil War I was Blue and I was Gray. I fought the tribes with Custer. Wherever I was needed, whenever called, I came through."

When World War II began, Americans had little information about wartime functions, what was needed to prepare for war and, if necessary, to fight, and there was a lack of understanding as to why the world was at war. Roosevelt's creation of the OWI helped clarify these reasons and dispel American apathy toward the war. Films such as *Bomber, Tanks,* and *Troop Train* advanced this cause. In *Bomber,* narrator-writer Carl Sandburg harnessed the engines of a B-26 to drive the nation's past into the present: "The B-26 bomber lives and breathes the spirit of America. The engines are John Henry on one wing, Paul Bunyan on the other. Here is America's strong heart, keen, aware, alive, and honest! Bombers for a new day!"

While the moguls of Tinseltown had no reservations about exploring the causes of and creating films essentially for box-office profit, with homegrown themes, in the early days of the isolationist/interventionist debate many in the industry remained neutral. In fact, well-known examples of Hollywood's output in the late 1930s like *The Road Back* and *They Gave Him a Gun* evinced a pacifism that could be interpreted as a tacit endorsement of the isolationist argument, while even *Gone with the Wind* appeared to suggest that the cost of the Civil War was greater than the benefit of keeping the Union together. Most 1930s films about the contemporary military were essentially mindless pap; one might point to works like *Navy Blue and Gold, Wings over Honolulu,* and *The Singing Marine.*

Why in the years leading up to Pearl Harbor was Hollywood so slow on the uptake in dealing with the conflict? One powerful explanatory factor was the position taken by the Hays Office. Headed by William H. Hays, this quasi-public body set standards and regulated the content of films released to American movie theaters. Following the protocol of the BBC, even though it was not news reporting, its chief praised Hollywood power players for steering clear of propagandistic films in an annual report from his organization dated March 1938:

> In a period in which propaganda has largely reduced the artistic and entertainment validity of the screen in many other cultures, it is pleasant to report that American motion pictures continue to be free from any but the highest possible entertainment purpose. The industry has resisted and must continue to resist the lure of propaganda in that sinister sense persistently urged upon it by extremist groups. The function of the entertainment screen is to entertain. There is no other criterion. Only those who have a self-ish purpose to serve can cry out against such a policy. There is no place in motion pictures for self-serving propaganda. Propaganda as entertainment would be neither honest salesmanship nor honest showmanship.

Beyond propaganda, beneath the Hays Office veneer of film as good, clean fun was a darker consideration. As late as 1940, MGM, Paramount, and Twentieth Century Fox still enjoyed a major outlet for their movies in the Third Reich, a market that would be quickly closed to them should American films begin to show Germany in a negative light. Radio networks could afford to take potshots at the Nazis; their overheads were low and their range of distribution limited to the domestic market. Movie producers, on the other hand, had a good deal more to lose financially.

One studio, Warner Brothers, ignored the commercial fodder, pushed aside Hays Office guidelines, and produced accurate movies about Nazism in the late 1930s, even before Hitler's invasion of Poland.

By the late 1930s, Warner Bros. Pictures had become more anti-Nazi than any other major Hollywood studio. It banned Nazi newsreels from its theaters, and produced Hollywood's first wholeheartedly anti-Nazi film, *Confessions of a Nazi Spy* (1939), with Edward G. Robinson and George Sanders, made in an era when movies were more liable to avoid political controversy than court it. By showing the inner working of espionage in "safe" America, the film countered Nazi ideology and aimed to keep America safe. It was banned in Germany, and while at first it did poorly at the domestic box office, it was voted best film by the National Board of Review. Rereleased in 1940 with scenes describing the invasions of Norway and the Netherlands that had taken place since the films initial release, the film gained further attention.

Even Groucho Marx raised his glass—and for once not his eyebrows—at an anti-Nazi luncheon, to praise a front office he usually trashed: "I want to propose a toast to Warners—the only studio with any guts."

According to studio chief Jack L. Warner, and documented in the studio's archives, the reason for the anti-Nazi activism was as much personal as political. In his memoir, *My First Hundred Years in Hollywood*, Warner recalls how, in 1936, he learned the sickening news that Joe Kauffman, "our Warner Brothers man in Germany, had been murdered by Nazi bullies in Berlin. Like many an outnumbered Jew, he was trapped in an alley. They hit him with fists and clubs, and kicked the life out of him with their boots, and left him lying there."

Warner closed down the studio's German distribution branch and became committed to the war effort.

Having made a name for their social conscience pictures of the 1930s, Warner Brothers made films not only to entertain but to support the country's political and military efforts, exposing the horrors of Nazi Germany. It was the first studio to warn the world about the Third Reich. When America entered the war, the studio offered its resources to President Roosevelt and went on to make fiercely patriotic movies, chief among them the enduring masterpiece *Casablanca*.

In the beginning of the propaganda process, director Walter Wanger's 1938 *Blockade*, starring Madeleine Carroll and Henry Fonda, presented a fictionalized account of the Fascist destruction of republican Spain, with German Stukas dive-bombing civilians. The plot tackles a subject Hollywood had refused to touch, resulting in pressure on the producer to leave the film unreleased. Ultimately it was recognized with Oscar nominations for its script and score.

Much the same theme as that of *Confessions of a Nazi Spy* was found in another Warner Brothers production, *Foreign Correspondent*, in which actor Joel McCrea and director Alfred Hitchcock unmasked a fictional British organization, the United Peace Party, as a Nazi espionage front.

Director Howard Hawks teamed up with writer John Huston to make *Sergeant York*, based on a true story. The film's eponymous character, played by Gary Cooper, is a rowdy backwoodsman who becomes a pacifist after a spiritual epiphany. Reluctant to heed the call of conscription in the American army of World War I, York then put aside his conscientious objections when his comrades fall before a German machine gun nest—he picks up his gun, and personally dispatches or captures the bulk of an enemy battalion.

As the war progressed, major studio heads jumped onto the movie wagon. One film produced by Metro-Goldwyn-Mayer took all the awards. *Mrs. Miniver* was a portrayal of a British family ravaged by the war, while retaining its grace and integrity. By 1942, films with wartime themes outnumbered all others. Hollywood became a wartime production plant and a source of directorial talent that would be called upon by government information agencies for documentary and training films, including filmmakers John Ford and Frank Capra, whose *Why We Fight* series would soon become its centerpiece, crafting the best-directed documentaries with messages that would profoundly impact an audience.

At the behest of Army Chief of Staff General George C. Marshall, a group of Hollywood motion picture producers and directors assembled to prepare a series of orientation films that would explain the cardinal motives and objectives behind armed opposition to the Axis for audiences comprised of newly inducted servicemen. Capra led the team. Eventually, the films proved so compellingly effective that the target audience was expanded to include civilians, and the OWI released them for non-theatrical distribution to schools, war plants, and civic and fraternal organizations across America.

*Why We Fight* was a purely American interpretation of the war, its themes extrapolated from FDR's 1942 State of the Union message. As the war played in the European theater, the United States entertainment industry was a principal contributor to the Allied war script. While it was their British mentors who truly understood the scope of black activities, even in black radio propaganda the Americans became a prominent player. But it was in white propaganda for domestic audiences that America's information and entertainment partnership left an indelible imprint.

Capra was one of the country's most noted and revered filmmakers, and the series he oversaw faced tough challenges: convincing a recently noninterventionist nation of the need to become involved in the war and ally with the Soviets, among other things. Into many of the films Capra spliced examples from twenty years of the Axis powers' propaganda footage, re-contextualizing it so it promoted the cause of the Allies.

According to Professor Thomas Bohn, author of a compelling book, *Mass Media*, Capra was charged with the task of "maintaining morale and instilling loyalty and discipline" into the civilian army "to make war on professional enemies."

The director assembled a team and produced the entire series in less than three years. The overall style was based on the principle of blending existing and seemingly unrelated visuals of documentary footage and creating a coherent, compelling unity through careful editing and the addition of effective narration and stirring music.

This is not to say, of course, that Capra's *Why We Fight* series were the only dramas in play. Two works composed prior to America's entry into the war that had significant impact were Charlie Chaplin's *The Great Dictator* and Bertolt Brecht's play *The Resistible Rise of Arturo Ui*, the latter only staged a few years later. In each, the main figures in the Nazi leadership were portrayed as gangsters who performed roles concealing hidden motives. Chaplin's and Brecht's renditions of the Nazi rise to power presented the sweep of these historical events in outlandishly, bitingly satirical ways.

The *Why We Fight* films played to millions of people, becoming by some distance the most widely seen and comprehensive OWI white propaganda productions of the war. Paradoxically, this expansion encountered opposition from Hollywood and the government's own Bureau of Motion Pictures on the grounds that it unfairly competed against war films made under private aegis. It required President Roosevelt's personal intervention to secure a general release for the first film, *Prelude to War.*

Apart from having been commissioned as a major in the United States Army, very little in Capra's background indicated that he would become a passionate spokesman for America's motives and aims in World War II. A self-made man from humble origins who had worked his way up the Hollywood success ladder, Capra openly disdained documentary cinema, what he called "ash-can films made by kooks with long hair." In the run-up to the war, his own portfolio as a Hollywood director consisted exclusively of romantic comedies and idealistic fables—*It Happened One Night, You Can't Take It with You, Meet John Doe, Mr. Deeds Goes to Town,* and *Mr. Smith Goes to Washington.*

Ironically, it was Capra's apolitical idealism that qualified him for the task to which he had been appointed; he could be counted on to tell the story of *Why We Fight* without any obvious motive, and he was in step with mainstream public attitudes toward the war. In approaching his job, Capra was not working with a blank slate in terms of gearing his *Why We Fight* reels to the deeply held convictions of the American public.

Capra's product consisted of seven separate productions released over two years. All of the films followed chronologically the events of the war. Released in 1943, *Prelude to War* introduced the series and reviewed the war's background with the Italian conquest of Ethiopia. It was followed in that same year by *The Nazi Strike,* which concentrated upon Hitler's invasion of Poland, and *Divide and Conquer,* which recounted the German path through Western Europe. Shortly thereafter, *The Battle of Britain, The Battle of Russia,* and *The Battle of China* traced the Axis onslaught in each of these theaters. The last film in the series, *War Comes to America,* finished in 1945 and took a step back, recalling the isolationist/interventionist debate prior to the war. The film ended with blazing footage of Pearl Harbor.

The fact that Americans were spared the ravages of wartime destruction made the need for a series acutely compelling. American understanding of the legitimacy of the war was weakened by geographical and cultural distance, far removed from the places of death and destruction, lacking an authentic sense of immediate danger experienced by the British, Russians, and French. Americans experienced the war on a secondhand basis. It required the talents of a skilled communicator like Capra to bring the war home to America. Later he would say of the *Why We Fight* project: "Here was the world stage, here were the actors . . . here were the stories, and I told them dramatically. You had the world's greatest heroes and the world's greatest villains competing. You had a chance to dramatize it with film."

As technical compositions, the *Why We Fight* films were masterful. Their vivid and powerful combination of newsreel footage, staged reenactments, stirring musical accompaniment, and graphic animation—unified through an impassioned narrative spoken by actor Walter Huston, couched in simple, colloquial terms—had an overwhelming impact on viewers. Taking a page from German documentary makers, Capra emphasized the visual facets of the film and subordinated the verbal elements.

Diverse events gave the *Why We Fight* series its punch, the presentation of the enemy's aggression as part of a single, diabolical plot, a "script" that pivoted upon the conquest of the United States. With the benefit of hindsight, Capra wove together the far-flung machinations of the Axis into a single fabric, a swastika whose threatening arms pointed directly at America.

The series hammered home the point that conspiracy threaded together each act of enemy aggression. Huston's voice intones the lesson that during the mid-1930s, "It was impossible to convince a farm boy from Iowa, or a driver of a London bus, or a waiter in a Paris café that he should go to war because of a mud hut in Manchuria." From these modest beginnings, Capra would remind his audiences of conflicts in other European countries that had been outside the interest and attention of the man-in-the-street. While the Axis armies spread across Europe like wildfire, this was no random pattern. Each episode was a scene of a carefully scripted play that would have the destruction of the American way of life as its climax and complete world domination by a monolithic dictatorship as its terminal tableau.

From Capra's standpoint, the Nazi threat to America was not confined to the political, national, or economic sphere. It was cultural, even spiritual in thrust and aimed directly at those values and institutions that Americans cherished most dearly: church and family. Thus, in *Prelude to War*, Hitler cements his stranglehold on the German nation by supplanting Christianity with his own version of pre-Christian "Messiahship." In the most disturbing and graphic terms available, the sequence ends with the replacement of the cross on the wall of a German church by a swastika. Curiously, although Capra and his associates may not have been able to envisage the enormity of the Nazi campaign against the Jews, as the magnitude of the Holocaust became plain only at the war's end, the *Why We Fight* series contains scant reference to those acts of anti-Semitism in the Third Reich. While the filmmakers did not play to deep-seated religious prejudices among American audiences, by concentrating on Nazism as anti-Christian with little mention of its anti-Jewish thrust, the series may have deferred to a longstanding bias against Jews within American society.

The Nazi design, in Capra's exposure, was not limited to the destruction of the Christian faith but also aimed at another pillar of American life, the family. Capra foretold the destruction of the family that would occur if the Nazis were allowed to carry out their scheme for worldwide conquest. Through skillful cutting, Capra showed a group of babies in a Nazi hospital transformed through the magic of cinematic dissolves into a column of Hitler Youth and then into a line of Stormtroopers. German footage of Nazi officials in the schools of the Third Reich played into

Capra's hands. Stated in no uncertain terms, while John Q. Public's happiest hours were spent watching his children grow, these moments were contrasted with German children carrying artillery shells and sporting gas masks under the eyes of goose-stepping tutors.

Most notably in *Divide and Conquer*, but evident elsewhere in the series as well, Capra and his colleagues used German newsreel footage to give American audiences a sobering portrait of the Nazis at work. Capra had seen Riefenstahl's *Triumph of the Will*, and he freely borrowed several of the Nazi filmmaker's dynamic editing techniques, such as rapid-fire cutting and the radical reduction of spoken narrative.

In *Divide and Conquer*, Capra underscored the mechanical efficiency of the Wehrmacht by including footage of a mock assault upon a Czech castle laid out to resemble a key fortress that the Germans were to over-run. The sequence served to lend the Nazi military a machine-like visage and to re-enforce Capra's broad point that each episode in the Axis expansion was but one component of a preset design for global domination.

The defining character trait in the aggregate German military personality was sheer, unadulterated cruelty. Nazi newsreel directors furnished Capra with all the material that he needed to drive home this point, such as footage of Stukas bombing cities with no regard for civilian life. When Nazi Propaganda Ministry material proved insufficient for Capra's purposes, the director simply turned to animated recreations of German iniquity carefully matted out at the Walt Disney Studio. Much was made of the fact that even after Dutch leaders had agreed to surrender Rotterdam to the Germans on the latter's terms, the Nazis still assaulted the city in one of the most ruthless exhibitions of destruction by the Luftwaffe in action.

*Why We Fight* did not pretend to be a sharply honed analysis of enemy motives; its purpose was to express the fundamental conflict at hand, without shades of gray, but in stark black and white.

The narrative that had been written by Frank Capra explained the underlying need to stop the Axis juggernaut and imposed a unified meaning on the disparate events that made up the Second World War.

This, in turn, helped justify Allied plans for the postwar world to audiences who saw the series before or after the signing of peace treaties with Germany and Japan.

In *The Battle of Britain* and *The Battle of Russia*, Capra and his scriptwriters confronted a far more difficult task than merely portraying the enemy as evil incarnate. One of the facets of American public opinion the Nazis exploited before and after the entrance of the United States into the war was the notion that Britain and the Soviet Union were unworthy allies. German propagandists presented shortwave radio listeners in America with an image of the British as haughty aristocrats. According to the Nazi propaganda line, these elites had manipulated the Roosevelt administration in an effort to enlist Americans in a war to preserve privilege and empire. Capra took dead aim. Turning aside all differences between Britain and America, Capra gave his audiences images of ordinary Britons battling valiantly against the Luftwaffe Blitz. No taint of upper-class snobbery or condescension existed in the scenes of London under fire. The survivors of the Blitz were simply courageous men, women, and children displaying a spirit that their American counterparts could well admire.

A shared language and culture helped Capra to make his case for the British as being "just like us," but when he turned to the Russians, the challenge became substantially greater. Contrary to the opinion that America was on the same side as a godless communist dictatorship arguably no better than Nazi Germany, Capra showed the Russians as a courageous people combating the scourge of Nazism. The Nazi-Soviet Pact of 1939 was transmuted by Capra's writers into a clever, time-buying ruse by the Kremlin, while the Soviet invasion of Eastern Poland was portrayed as a rescue mission rather than a rapacious division of spoils. As for the word "communist," *The Battle of Russia* contains not a single instance of its usage. Lenin makes a cameo appearance in the film and is labeled as the leader of the Russian Revolution, while Stalin is seen in an equally fleeting glimpse, with no hint of the purges of the 1930s. The focus again is on the man in the street taken collectively and comprising a "Great People," with liturgical music in the background to complement the Eastern Orthodox tradition of Mother Russia.

• • •

Perhaps the most perplexing question that Capra and his associates faced centered on a paradox. If the American way of life was so superior to that of the totalitarian dictatorships the United States and its allies now faced, then why wasn't the war's outcome a foregone conclusion?

The American public had heeded the arguments of the isolationists and saw Hitler and Mussolini as amusing figures engaged in a foreign-language play that could not open on American shores. The most intriguing national character delineated in the *Why We Fight* series was that of the American people. Capra was intent upon reminding Americans that they had inadvertently played a role in the conflict that they faced. America was engaged in a life-and-death struggle with the Axis not because of the interventionist policies of the Roosevelt administration, but because of the muddleheaded isolationism of the late 1930s that had inhibited America and other freedom-loving nations from nipping Nazism, Fascism, and Japanese Militarism in the bud. As the entire imbroglio of the *Why We Fight* series suggested, America should have responded to the Japanese conquest of Manchuria in 1931, but it had not, and so the Japanese felt free to move on to further adventures.

The failure to act in this instance, most particularly the ineffectual response of the League of Nations, had doomed the Wilsonian notion of collective security, had stimulated Japan and her European cohorts to further aggression, and had inured the Western democracies to onslaughts upon freedom. Reaching the Italian conquest of Ethiopia in 1936, narrator Huston said in *Prelude to War*, "Yes, we were a nation that wanted peace. But we hadn't learned that peace for us depends on peace for all. . . . Correctly interpreting our attitude, the aggressors were all the surer that they could get what they wanted."

The litany of American complacency, narrowness, and naïveté rose to a crescendo in *Why We Fight* as the appeasement at Munich was reached and the United States continued to encourage aggression through the passing of neutrality laws. From a dramaturgical perspective, the United States had played the fool long before it became the hero that would oppose the Axis villain. Listening to the blandishments of the isolationists, Americans had erroneously concluded that events abroad had no connection whatsoever to their own lives. The basic error they had made, Capra reminded them, was to think of freedom as being somehow divisible, rather than realizing that early Axis assaults on freedom were frontal attacks on human liberty as one integral whole.

Not only was *Why We Fight* a powerful rendition of the causes of World War II, it was also a primer on the demands of a postwar peace. If the Axis powers were able to threaten the United States, then another conspiracy of evil might well do the same in the future, once the war had been won.

• • •

In making peace settlement plans, officials of the Roosevelt administration were guided by lessons learned between the wars, and of paramount importance was the need for strong collective security organizations. It is evident that the series was in league with the Roosevelt administration. But there was another lesson from the 1930s that Capra wanted to impress upon the mind of the American public.

A mood of national confidence stood in sharp contrast to the erosion of the American spirit during the Depression. The war seemed to provide concrete evidence that all the doubts about the American character of the 1930s had been misplaced. Better still, not only had America been proven right, her antagonists had been proven wrong in their evaluation of the American spirit. During the war itself, FDR often tried to rouse radio listeners by reminding them of Axis charges that "we have grown fat, flabby, and lazy, and that we are doomed." Of course, Roosevelt would continue to refute this evaluation by stating, "those who say that know nothing of America." Thus, the war not only demonstrated that

America still had the stuff, it did so in a way that directly countered the charge that the American era had come and gone.

This theme became most prominent in analyses of the war issued in the months after VE Day. One *New York Times* editorial had begun with the observation that Axis leaders had assumed that "the United States is a country of softhearted fools that can be insulted with impunity and defeated with ease on the battlefield."

Aided by the dramatic presentation of the war served up by Capra, Corwin, and their colleagues during the conflict, World War II became a watershed event in the evolution of the American character and psyche. On one side was a past of weakness and frivolity, of cynicism and social division. On the other side was an inspiring presence of determination, strength, and common purpose. In an issue of the *New York Times Magazine* published shortly after the war's end, Hal Borland presented a piece entitled "We Find Ourselves," in which he described a basic transformation of the American sense of purpose. Since Pearl Harbor, Borland observed, Americans had begun "reappraising values and finding the fundamentals beneath the fluff." He continued:

> For years we were told repeatedly that the tough fiber that went into the making of America . . . had gone soft. We were living on our fat, spending the inheritance of a more sturdy past. Now we know this was not true; and there is a deep and abiding satisfaction in that knowledge. When the test came, we did not back away. . . . Thrown back on our resources, we are finding that our moral fiber is still around. From the war emerged a cleaner, tougher, better breed of man.

Thus, in the interpretation of the war put forth by the media-government machine during the conflict, not only were the Axis powers defeated, not only was the future secured, but also America itself had undergone a spiritual transformation. Presented as a morality play to the American people by the propagandists of World War II, the victory became proof positive of a spiritual renewal. The war became a kind of secular myth, replete with the language of myth, and so, when the troops returned home, they were heroes returning in the most archetypal sense of that term.

World War II developed its own spiritual significance, iconography, its pantheon of saints and demons. In short, it was largely because of the work of individuals like Capra that the war became more than simply a political triumph for the Allies; it also became the moral basis for the affirmation of the American spirit on the front lines.

# CHAPTER 16

# On the Road with Wild Bill Donovan

———— ∞∞ ————

In the early days of the war, Wild Bill Donovan had gone to London as a special envoy. Meeting Hugh Dalton and other Electra House and SO 1 staff members, he toured British black radio propaganda operations, including the transmitting center for the Free German Station and the German Revolution Station at Woburn Abbey. Donovan was suitably impressed by this display of British propaganda ingenuity.

In his report to the president, the chief of the Office of Strategic Services (OSS) noted that British morale remained high despite nearly nine months of Luftwaffe pounding. After a behind-the-scenes look at PWE's Gustav Siegfried Eins operation, he advised FDR that "radio is the most powerful weapon in psychological warfare." Although the Office of War Information had staked its claim to white radio propaganda, OSS's niche would be in the black game.

The Americans were amateurs. It was through Dalton, Delmer, and Howe that Donovan and an OSS cadre were schooled in the black arts. The first American venture into the field was code-named Operation Muzak, and listeners believed that it was an undistinguished musical entertainment station in the Reich. Donovan contacted the J. Walter

Thompson Agency to negotiate wage rates with members of the Musicians' Union. To the band, Donovan added skilled composers and accomplished performers to the cast; these included Kurt Weill of *The Threepenny Opera*, Grete Stuckgold, Sig Arno, Lotte Lenya, and Marlene Dietrich.

Apart from their talent, Donovan found actors with perfect enunciation. The reason for this goes to the heart of the scheme. Favorite American standards would be translated into German and arranged to suit German tastes. In most cases, the resultant recordings would be faithful translations of the original, but in some instances (about 10 percent of broadcast times) what German audiences heard was a version of the original doctored to include an implicit antiwar message. A black slave lament, "Nobody Knows the Trouble I've Seen," was revised so that the trouble stemmed from wartime conditions. Because the propaganda message was carried through a musical vehicle, precise pronunciation was required for the new lyrics to register against orchestral accompaniment.

OSS personnel, heartened by the ease with which they had entered the black game, sought to copy the British and produce scripted shows along the lines of Gustav Siegfried Eins. For a time OSS hired Hollywood "story idea men" and Broadway advertising campaign planners to develop scripts. Although there were several exceptions, they failed for the most part. It was finally necessary to let the black radio teams, made up of men who were thoroughly conversant with German and Germany, do their own interpretation.

Eventually OSS's black radio operatives mastered the art of deception. But for much of the war's duration, until its European climax, D-Day, with less time in the game, less contact with German culture, and fewer POWs available to provide speakers and touches that would lend their shows credibility, the United States trailed its senior partner in the performance of black business.

# ACT IV

# Before the Final Curtain

———— ⊶∞∞⊷ ————

*In commensurate dramatic form, the play continues and moves toward its climax. A major conflict occurs offstage in the winter of 1942–1943, set on the frozen ground of Stalingrad. The drama takes a turn. Edward R. Murrow continues his on-the-scenes reports of the London Blitz. D-Day sets the stage for the play's finale, and there is grand, theatrical subterfuge along the way, notably with the case of "The Man Who Never Was," but even with near-fatal miscues and rehearsals—the twin debacles of Slapton Sands and the DD amphibious tanks—the war becomes an American show. Then Stalingrad compels a revision to the script, an allied production for D-Day goes into rehearsal, and as the production approaches its climax the Americans move decisively into the realms of black propaganda with Radio Annie.*

# CHAPTER 17

# The Allies Launch a Crusade

Drama has become one of the principal vehicles of information, one of the prevailing methods of "thinking" about life and its situations.

—Martin Esslin, *The Field of Drama*

The actor is engaged in dramatic action when he or she sometimes disguises those parts of the activity that convey desired information.

—Jerold Heiss, *The Social Psychology of Interaction*

The planning of D-Day was an enormous production, but in time it was scripted and soon in play. As Supreme Allied Commander Dwight D. Eisenhower would label it, the liberation of Western Europe that began on D-Day was a crusade, a knightly quest with overtones of Christian redemption. Collectively, the "Yanks" and "Tommies" who landed on Normandy's beaches were analogous to St. Columba sailing from the West to restore Christianity to a European continent that had descended into paganism.

With D-Day, the Allies would assume total control of the writing of the World War II script. The version of the war that Hitler and Goebbels attempted to project as reality in the minds of their followers and adversaries was entirely discredited by events after D-Day and became the equivalent of a false folio. When the Normandy invasion unit reached its destination, it was apparent that critical elements of Nazi stagecraft were constructed from cardboard, there was no Great Atlantic Wall, and that *Festung Europa* was, at best, a papier-mâché barrier.

• • •

While miscues were hallmarks of Allied operations throughout the war, nowhere were such discrepancies and conflicts over script interpretation more apparent than in the events surrounding D-Day. The Allied engagement on June 7, 1944, was loaded with unplanned departures and deviations from the show that FDR, Churchill, and their field "directors" Eisenhower and Montgomery had written.

By the time that the Allied forces reached Paris, there were events taking place off stage. Goebbels was compelled by some such events to amend Hitler's script and change the führer's part from an infallible savior into a compassionate but doomed martyr.

• • •

Before the play's climax there was one last dramatic turning point of World War II. It was staged eighteen months earlier, six thousand miles away in the Soviet city of Stalingrad, when the perspective was enlarged and dramatic economy was no longer a possible mode of presentation. Stalin and the Red Army took over the scriptwriting role. From Stalingrad onward, the war in Eastern Europe changed from a German romance into a patriotic Soviet anthem.

One hundred and seventy-five million Russian faces were drawn. It was not terror that made their lips tight, their eyes tired; not despair, not resignation. It was the awful waiting. When would the glorious Red Armies win? For years they had watched tanks clanking through the streets, and outside the villages had seen the parachutes pouring down like crazy cotton snowflakes. They had accumulated tremendous faith in this power, but this power had now been pushed back deep into Russia. When would the marshals, who wore gold stars studded with diamonds, show their worth to the men who had never had any badge but mud? When would winter come? It would make the difference.

After they had violated and then altogether broken their nonaggression pact with Stalin, the Germans launched their second and supposedly final attack on Moscow. A Berlin military spokesmen called it a "do-or-die" drive.

It was commanded by Field Marshal Fedor von Bock, a gaunt, steely general who lectured his men about the glory of dying for the Fatherland. His approaches to Moscow made a first-class military cemetery. The land was mostly flat, some of it gently rolling terrain, decorated with superb internal communications, railroads, truck highways, and numberless small roads; it favored the defender. Moscow was teeming with buses, trucks, and cars available for urgent transport. The city itself was a death trap. It was huge, a maze of irregularly winding streets, and remarkably self-sufficient. But Moscow's greatest death-dealing weapon was its life. Moscow's eight million had a stern order from their government: "To retreat one more step is a crime none shall forgive. Stop the enemy. Beat him out of his positions. This is an order which is not to be broken."

As the government moved back from its hideaway in Samara, the Russians told the world their story of the Battle of Moscow. An overwhelming German offensive, begun on October 2, had cracked the city's defenses wide open. On October 15 and 16, the Russians had considered the capital lost; then came the organization of fresh reserves and civilian defenders. On November 16, Field Marshal von Bock, indifferent to the cost in blood, flung his armored divisions against Moscow for a second time.

By December 6, the cold of winter hit his soldiers and the Russians counterattacked. By the final week, Bock's northern army was driven back; his southern army was withdrawing rapidly under a ferocious hammering. The Soviet cavalry was harassing the Germans in retreat. Since November 16, said the Russians, 85,000 Germans had been killed. Further south, in Ukraine, Marshal Timoshenko was driving the

Germans back from the oil of the Caucasus. Around Leningrad, red banners moved forward, too. An offensive for the relief of the city was under way. It was too early to assess the action. Perhaps the Germans were withdrawing to a line, well prepared in their rear, where they might rest through the frightening winter cold.

At the very least, it was a Russian success, for the German retreat was costly. In Moscow's snow-clad streets there were celebrating infantrymen in fleece-lined leather coats and yellow fur hoods. Provincial troops in worn quilted jackets and spiked woolen forage caps. In the street, a grinning, drink-happy young man suddenly seized *New York Times* correspondent Cyrus Sulzberger by the arm and exclaimed in wonderment: "It is Moscow! Here we are still in Moscow!"

It was a scant two months and two weeks since Adolf Hitler had announced to the German nation, "I say that this enemy is already smashed and will never rise again."

# CHAPTER 18

# Stalingrad Compels a Revision of the Nazi Script

——⚬⚬⚬——

aving stopped short of the gates of Moscow in the winter of 1941–42, the once-invincible German Wehrmacht suffered the same fate that Napoleon's forces had more than a century before. A combination of Red counteroffensives and the Russian winter caused crucial delays in the implementation of Hitler's plans. Taking over the Eastern Front production, the führer ordered army groups in the southern sector to spare no effort in their renewed drive to capture the strategic Soviet transport link at Stalingrad.

Stalingrad would be framed by Goebbels with almost mythic legend, by elevating his propaganda machine to the status of a Nordic concept called Ragnarök: an essential turning of events in Norse mythology when the world would be refreshed by a great battle. The German Valkyrie would finally defeat the Russian forces of evil. But it did not play out. A million-man Red Army surrounded the German Sixth, and, despite Hitler's orders to hold out to the last, at least one hundred thousand of Von Paulus's army surrendered to Marshal Zukhov's troops in February 1943.

As it became evident that Von Paulus could not take Stalingrad, Goebbels realized that some dramatic explanation was required. In the account given to the German people, Stalingrad had not fallen because the German führer, unwilling to repeat a "Verdun," wanted to save German lives. The seeming failure to make progress was a reflection of Hitler's humanitarianism.

As November wore on into December, this thin and nearly transparent narrative device collapsed under the weight of Stalin's counterassault. On his own initiative Goebbels took a bold stroke to redeem the debacle at Stalingrad; he personally revamped the entire Nazi war script. He released a special communiqué, the only Nazi press release of the entire war dedicated to a German military defeat. In it, he transformed the German Hitler's control over the destiny of the nation into an act of heroism and public mourning.

There was a change as to how the German foot soldier was portrayed in Nazi newsreel footage from the Eastern Front. Soft-focus German cinematic accounts of the triumphs in the West were summarily replaced by sharply etched realism. Corpses, enemy and German, now littered the frames of Nazi documentaries. German lads in uniforms had become grizzled veterans in a rat's war. Even dead civilians were captured by the camera in the frozen wastes.

An urgent need for sacrifice and the consequences of defeat for the German public were underscored. Clearly, the propaganda minister had turned the German anxiety level up several notches, using the pretext of heroic military sacrifice by the German foot soldier to drive home the premise of what waited for the civilian population at the hands of the Reds.

Putting forth the theme that an unstoppable German military under the command of an infallible führer would quickly vanquish its enemies and fulfill the *Mein Kampf* script, Nazi propaganda's changes after Stalingrad were far too abrupt to be easily digested by the German public. German defeats in the field reached Germany, if only through Allied propaganda. Goebbels miscalculated and underestimated the existing anxiety level when he tried to ratchet it up through the theme of heroic sacrifice.

On the front lines, however, the message was different. Sacrifice was emphasized, but news of how bad things had become at home was withheld from the German military man in the field. Goebbels sent a phalanx of speakers to German towns warning the local citizenry not to mention war damage and death in letters sent to the troops. For both groups, there was a unifying, revised script that Goebbels drafted for Hitler: an attempt to humanize the leader in Germany as a suffering and compassionate genius who wrestled with fate. It was a hard sell.

As German casualties mounted, Goebbels became a proponent of an all-out battle to the death against the Allied forces. He took to the microphone to motivate and incite Germans. Speaking from the Sports Palace in Berlin he did all he could to inspire support for a total war effort. If Germany was destined to lose the war, he reasoned with a sad premonition, it was fitting that the German nation be obliterated.

If Hitler was no longer infallible, then the claim that he was the sole author of the World War II script could no longer be maintained. Instead, scenes were taking place on stage that did not play well. From here, it was a relatively short leap toward the actual situation; the Allies were now wielding the pen and writing the final pages of the war.

As the war's end approached, the Nazis tried desperately to persuade America, Britain, and France that they were in the wrong show. Goebbels's last-ditch propaganda stroke was a retreat to the historical past. In the summer of 1943, Goebbels supervised one final Nazi cinematic extravaganza. *Kolberg* was an unsettling parallel of Germany's real situation. Describing the efforts of the citizens of Kolberg to resist Napoleon's armies in the early nineteenth century, Goebbels personally wrote the decisive line to the citizen-troops: "Better to be buried under the ruins than to capitulate."

What boggles the mind about *Kolberg* is Goebbels's willingness to deplete German military resources for the purposes of making the film. Nearly two hundred thousand troops were diverted from the front to serve as cast members in battle scenes directed by Veit Harlan, who had studied under Max Reinhardt, and was an actor and director who made some of the Third Reich's loudest, most colorful and expensive films. Earlier in his career, he was spotted by Joseph Goebbels. He had been married to—but divorced from—a Jewish cabaret singer and film actress who died in Auschwitz. Defense industries were ordered to make ten thousand period costumes while German soldiers froze in the snow for want of winter coats.

As the work's director would later attest, during the production of *Kolberg* a law of madness prevailed. The historical film begins as the Napoleonic Wars are ending and the *Befreiungskriefe* [War of Liberation] begins. The citizens in the city of Kolberg are taught the importance of a citizen army, and can be saved only by one leader.

Hitler and Goebbels were obsessed with the idea that the film could be more useful than even a victory in Russia. Never art, Goebbels's cinematic propaganda had descended still another rank; it was an artifact, a talisman meant to keep the furies of Goebbels's fertile imagination at bay. Weeks after *Kolberg*'s premiere in war-ravaged Berlin, the real Kolberg fell to the Red Army. Days later, Goebbels attached a personalized addendum to the script he had written; he took his own life without recording an exit in the last stage direction.

Now the scene was set for one of those great occasions on which war hinges. Preparations had long been under way for four men, one of whom became another member of the play-writing team. They were the spokesmen and the symbols of the most powerful nations on earth. They had made an appointment with one another. They were four men on the stage of destiny.

# Behind the Scenes

———— ∞∞∞ ————

Adolf Hitler had always regarded the German-Soviet nonaggression pact as a temporary tactical strategy. His plan for defeating the Soviet Union and securing prime land within Soviet borders for long-term German settlement had been core policy of the Nazi movement.

Academic historians contributing to the Holocaust Encyclopedia document that German military and police authorities intended to wage a war of annihilation against the Communist state and the Jews of the Soviet Union, whom they characterized as the "racial basis" of the Soviet state. Einsatzgruppen, mobile killing units, operated in Ukraine and behind the front lines to physically annihilate Jews, Communists, and any dissenters deemed to be dangerous to the establishment of long-term German rule. With full fighting strength, German forces invaded the Soviet Union on June 22, 1941, less than two years after the German-Soviet pact was signed.

For months, the Soviet leadership had refused to heed warnings from the Western powers of the German military build-up along its western border. Stalin had focused upon a centralized state with an autocratic rule, to achieve a form of government transitioning from Marxism to Communism.

Nazism and Stalinism were similar in one respect. Both leaders ruled with utter ruthlessness, using terror as a key weapon in securing and maintaining their status. In order to maintain his own grip on absolute power, Stalin was obliged to remove to the Gulag (an acronym in Russian for the "Main Camp Administration") millions of his own countrymen, from peasants to the bourgeoisie. The Cheka, his secret police force, would dispatch anyone who did not fit into Stalin's strategy to forced labor camps in Siberia or to unmarked graves.

Where Hitler publicized his dreams of a thousand-year Reich and a dominant master race, Stalin promoted agrarian reforms and the redistribution of land for a collective people. The Soviet Republic aimed to infuse its populace with a renewed sense of national pride and confidence and was bent on rapid industrialization.

Comrade Stalin owed an explanation to his countrymen when, early one Sunday morning, Russians woke up to learn that Hitler had invaded their country. After Germany's perfidious assault, it was a challenge to explain why he had promoted the pact in the first place.

On radio, Stalin addressed his fellow comrades in patriarchal tones: "Comrades, citizens, brothers and sisters, men of our army and navy, women of our nation! I am addressing you as my friends. . . . A grave danger hangs over our country. . . . Germany has suddenly and treacherously violated the treaty between us."

Pausing for a glass of tea, he questioned in what way he could have rejected Hitler's nonaggression proposal. Had he been duped? Did he wish to become neutral, believing he would gain territory from satellite states by doing so? He reasoned to his people, "I think not a single peace-loving state could have declined an agreement with a neighboring state."

Russian radio now promptly began promoting Stalin's newest party line: "The people of the Soviet Union are now fighting a great patriotic war in defense of our country, and extend their ardent greetings to the American people on the occasion of their glorious national Independence Day holiday. It is altogether fitting on this occasion for the American and Russian people to clasp hands more firmly."

The sleeping bear had been stunned. Germany was on the march on land and in the air; battles and sieges brought unimaginable suffering and an appalling death toll. The fierce blows came again and again. Planes targeted Soviet communications networks, while other bombers blitzed cities. Engineers built bridges, infantry advanced fluidly as the first silent snowflake fell on Moscow.

As Hitler moved towards the city, the eyes of the United States turned towards the White House. In answer to that mute demand, the president announced that everything possible was being done to send materials to aid Russians in their brave defense. The Russian army was far from defeated. There was still optimism. With Nazi troops battering the last hundred miles towards Moscow, Russia's situation grew ever more desperate. Adolf Hitler appeared to be beating the last heavily equipped army that opposed him on the continent of Europe.

Yet after months of fighting, the German army was exhausted. They had expected a rapid Soviet collapse, so the German generals had failed to prepare their troops for winter warfare. On December 6, 1941, Stalin mobilized the Soviet Union and launched a major counter-attack driving the Germans back from Russia in chaos. Joseph Stalin had shuffled his High Command, serving notice that his country was by no means defeated.

In Germany, civilians went to their cinemas and saw newsreels of the Russian front. They saw carloads of woolen socks and great overcoats rolling to the front through the snow-covered countryside. Winter had come. In the far north, it had come with sub-zero weather that froze gun barrels, rendering them inoperative. Winter had come with a great fog, silent and cold, wind howling through the forests, along with blankets of snow, damp and heavy as wet cotton.

But Russia's greatest weapon, through intemperate weather, was its people. To retreat defied national character, and soldiers and civilian defenders fought on the front lines with fresh reserves.

The waging of their Great Patriotic War was placed on the marquee, as the Soviet Union, having suffered through savage battles at the hands of the Nazi war machine, played a decisive role in defeating Germany. For all the vast cost in lives lost it was ultimately a mighty Russian success; red banners moved forward, the Nazis were in retreat.

Germany breaking its treaty with Russia was in many ways fortuitous for the Allied cause: the resolute defiance of the Soviet Union played a vital role in helping the Allies win the war. In a popular notion, one endorsed by Britain and the United States, the European theater was won first on the beaches of Normandy and then through the destructive power of the relentless Allied advance through French towns and into Germany, with battles shaped by the willfulness and wiliness of Roosevelt and Eisenhower, and the bulldog courage of Winston Churchill. The truth was of course far more complex. The Russians played a significant role in defeating the Nazis and bringing to an end the greatest, most brutal conflict thus far in human history, and in so doing suffered 95 percent of the military casualties of all the major powers in the Grand Alliance.

# CHAPTER 19

# The Tehran Conference

—∞∞∞—

The tide had turned for the Soviets with the Battle of Stalingrad, and as the war continued, Joseph Stalin left one stage for another.

Even if Churchill mistrusted the General Secretary of the Communist Party's Central Committee, Stalin was invited to participate in the major Allied conferences, including those in Tehran and Yalta. His iron will and deft political skills enabled him to play the loyal ally while never abandoning his vision of an expanded postwar Soviet empire. Without revealing his long-range plans, he joined Roosevelt and Churchill for the conference in Tehran.

It is easy to visualize a meeting of men, from points very far apart in time and space and ideology, sitting down for the first time to discuss the future of the world. In the background was a vast panorama of battle, the pounding of the Red Armies driving the Nazis out of Russia, the roar of German cities going up in smoke, that fire of Anglo-American guns blasting the road to Rome. As war scripters, Franklin Roosevelt, Joseph Stalin, and Winston Churchill were acutely conscious of the drama Adolf Hitler had put into play, his stunning performance in his own theater. But no longer. Now three leaders who had in this war been cast as the most unlikely allies were gathering to draft a version of the conflict's final act.

For a military strategy against Germany, they each made a number of important decisions including ones concerning the post-World War II era, but most notably focused on the next, final phases of the war. They discussed the terms under which the British and Americans committed to launching Operation Overlord, the invasion of northern France, to be executed by May of 1944. The Soviets, who had long been pushing the Allies to open a second front, agreed to launch another major offensive on the Eastern Front that would divert German troops away from the Allied campaign in northern France.

This could not take place until a basis of agreement was reached and a dramatic notification sent to the world that the directors of this war were resolute and would in partnership devise a strategy for victory.

It was a memorable scene. The stage was smaller, the dialogue private and informal. The president and the prime minister expressed their plan clearly. Stalin for all his reputation as a man of mystery was by no means a man of silence. He had the blunt decisiveness of a Marxist leader who was never contradicted, but was steadfast and stubborn with his own agenda.

Even physically these main characters were a study in contrast. The round cherubic countenance of the Briton differed as sharply from the square, pock-marked visage of the Georgian as it did from the smiling oval face of the American. Stalin smoked his pipe in contemplation, with a cool watchful glance under the brush of his steel hair.

• • •

After a photo opportunity performing before the cameras and for each other, the president's eyes were slightly quizzical. Making large gestures, with his long cigarette-holder carefully positioned as to make a statement, he appeared more casual and at ease than the others, but his unquenchable curiosity and stagecraft made him just as much a performer as Stalin. Churchill listened intently, slumped in his chair. He chewed his Montecristo, his ever-present stage prop.

They were the men directing stellar events in the tremendous drama of war and peace. They were alike in the power they wielded with massive self-confidence. They had assumed extraordinary powers to draft secret plans and decisions, to impose military censorship. Total war had applied its own rules, its own unities. Thus, as leaders and writers of this drama, they met on a wartime stage as equals in a way that would never have been possible in peacetime.

The quest for peace and order was the reality overshadowing all lesser considerations. They had to construct a final act under a diplomatic umbrella in which all problems, while arguable, were solvable. Coming together from points so far apart, shaped by personal experiences and systems of life so different, driven together only by the attack of a common enemy, they carried with them old suspicions and reservations, barriers to agreement. Together they drafted a concluding framework to win the war. All representatives of national interests, they were convinced that the cooperation they sought was a title that at last might be authentically called "Peace in our Time."

• • •

To have listened to Stalin talking of Lenin, and of himself as the successor to the founder of the Soviet State, was to understand that he considered himself a chosen instrument of history. He banished the Old Bolsheviks in favor of heroes of imperial history because he believed that Russia had once been and could be again the greatest power in the world, and Stalin thought of himself as a towering figure of that greatness.

The president's sense of history was strong. Long before the war, from the beginning of his administration in fact, he thought of himself as head of a small company of American chief executives destined to defend value and principle. Perhaps any premonition of immortality came from his triumph over his physical disability, or perhaps from the crisis in which he was induced into office. The role he felt elected to fill became not simply one in an American play but one performed on the international stage.

Churchill, the triumphant Conservative who restored the prestige of the British Empire, had a greater sense of mission and destiny than

Franklin Roosevelt. Certainly he was attracted by large ideas and global plans. Still, there were imponderable factors, the impressions they made, the impact of mind and manner upon each other. The prime minister and the president were already friends. Churchill often pondered aloud on the fate that pushed the president, Stalin, and himself into a relationship that none of them could have foreseen before the war began. It struck him as extraordinary that such an odd assortment should be cast on the same stage to play out and ultimately resolve conflict and crises.

It was extraordinary that their personalities should be so important to the fate of the world. It was extraordinary that so much depended on how they got together in historic parlay. They had become not merely the instruments of great forces, the symbols of their nations, but the ultimate dramaturges, the writers of the war's final, decisive scenes.

# CHAPTER 20

# A D-Day Production

The director collaborates with the playwright, actors, and designers to create on stage a carefully selected imitation of life, a special mirror. The director works with the actor and designers to interpret the playwright's world, characters, and events.

—M. S. Barranger, *Theater: A Way of Seeing*

Franklin D. Roosevelt, as commander in chief of the United States Armed Forces, played an active and decisive role in determining strategy. In his ongoing discussions with British Prime Minister Winston Churchill and with the American Joint Chiefs of Staff, he steadily promoted an invasion which by his reckoning constituted the final pages of his script.

Across the Atlantic, around the table in the library in a country house somewhere in England, sat a small group of men, lounging in comfortable chairs, smoking, talking quietly. Eisenhower was at the head of the table. Grouped around him were the leaders of his team; his deputy, Air Chief Marshal Tedder; Admiral Sir Bertram Ramsay; General Sir Bernard Law Montgomery, the tactical Air Force (ground support) chief; Air Chief Marshal Leigh-Mallory; Lieutenant General Walter Bedell Smith, the supreme commander's pale, hardworking chief of staff. Into the room came three men, the weather experts. They gave their report: what the weather was likely to do in the next few hours; probable conditions for sailors and airmen; a general forecast for the next fifty hours. Quiet, stocky Admiral Ramsay spoke first. He gave his estimate of what the naval forces could do under those conditions. Cool, incisive Leigh-Mallory summed up the airmen's point of view. Monty said, in effect, "Well, if the navy can get us in, and the air can give us cover, let's go."

Somebody asked the head weatherman about conditions. He stared intently at the table and finally said, "If I answered that I wouldn't be a meteorologist; I'd be a guesser."

Everyone laughed. It was no time for guessing. At last General Eisenhower crisply summarized the situation. He pointed out that there were many factors in favor of the operation. He spoke also of the possible fatal effects of delay, notably the problem of security and the morale of troops already aboard ship, poised and ready. Finally he said what all were waiting to hear: "In view of all these factors, I think we had better go ahead."

The die was cast. The meeting had taken just half an hour. With one characteristically casual sentence, General Eisenhower loosed the fateful storm that would thunder over Europe until Nazi Germany was down. Similar conferences had been held twice a day for three days. On the preceding Saturday the operation had been ordered, then cancelled again almost immediately when the weather took a sudden turn for the worse. That, even the calm Tedder admitted, had been "pretty nerve-racking," but this time there would be no turning back. The decision to invade had been made at 4:00 a.m.

The master of this titanic effort was a generally affable, obviously brainy Midwestern American. As a professional soldier, he was distinctly the command-and-staff rather than the warrior type. Ike Eisenhower never took a platoon or a company into battle. He had no specific battle experience remotely comparable to that of Britain's generals Montgomery and Alexander, or such US generals as Bradley and Patton. A rollicking, better-than-average graduate of West Point, Ike was speedily marked down as an expert training officer, a fact which cost him his chance for combat duty in World War I.

Through the peacetime interlude, Eisenhower had worked hard at home and abroad, most notably as Douglas MacArthur's technical adviser in the Philippines. He had acquired as solid a military background as a US officer could get. He had diligently cultivated his chief virtues of smartness, judgment, a concern for fine detail, and a marked ability to make people work for him. He was definitely one of the army's coming men; there was no reason to believe that he was particularly startled by any of the promotions that in thirty-five months boosted him from lieutenant colonel to full general.

A strict disciplinarian with the troop formations under his command, Eisenhower was a bear on uniform neatness, a bug on such items of military smartness as saluting. Once in Eighth Air Force headquarters he took General "Tooey" Spaatz down because West Pointer Spaatz, steeped in the Air Force ways of offhand efficiency, had banned saluting in the corridors as a damned nuisance.

D-Day found Ike Eisenhower in one of his worst moods. The supreme commander had little to do but wait in galling idleness before the vast fleets of landing craft and gliders could put their troops ashore and some vestige of order could begin to appear out of the vast amphibious chaos. At such times Eisenhower's carefully controlled temper bent under the strain; he hated uncertainty. All he could do now was to pace around headquarters, scribbling memos to himself. One of his self-memos could stand as a masterpiece of military understatement: "Now I'd like a few reports."

For this crisis in his life, Ike kept himself in excellent physical trim. The magnitude of the gamble did not outwardly affect him. His health was robust, his sleep undisturbed. His chief recreation, in the days when he still had occasional free evenings, was a session of bridge, at which he was ruthlessly expert. In the weeks just before D-Day, he usually began his day at the stereotyped US military hour of 5:00 a.m.

Eisenhower lived with his close personal friend and naval aide, Commander Harry Butcher, peacetime CBS vice president, and his orderly, Sergeant "Micky" McKeogh, onetime bellboy at New York's Plaza Hotel, in an unpretentious eight-room cottage near headquarters.

Commander Butcher's role had puzzled many civilians, although veteran officers understood it well. As a general moved up in the military scale, he become surrounded with a loneliness not unlike that which enfolds the master of a ship at sea. No matter how close and amiable relations with his staff may have been, the general was set apart, behind an invisible wall of rank and responsibility. If he was not to be completely alone on his side of the wall, he had to have a special sort of confidant. This person was a congenial friend, understanding and totally discreet, with whom the general could talk with utmost freedom.

Some thirty hours before H-Hour, as General Eisenhower made the final decision, as the moon, the tide, the carefully calculated weather forecasts were favorable. At night, while his staff got out the orders, the general walked alone on the crunching cinder path near his headquarters tent. Deep within himself he wrestled with the feeling he called "boiling over." His fingers rubbed the lucky coins he had rubbed before the invasions of North Africa and Sicily. Now began the taut moments that came to every commander after the battle order has been given, and there was no turning back. Twenty-four hours were left to bid his battle teams a last Godspeed. In the morning Eisenhower stood at an English quayside, chinning in his friendly Kansas way with embarking Tommies.

In the afternoon he called newsmen into his trailer tent, told them of the great decision. He slouched in his chair, grinned lopsidedly, chain-smoked cigarettes, wisecracked a bit, once leaped like an uncoiled spring to exclaim, "The sun is out!" All evening his khaki staff car, marked with the four red stars, rolled across the sleeping countryside as he visited his units. He joked with one youngster about his haircut. He asked a boy who had been a Dakota farmer how much wheat he had grown per acre.

Night cloaked the countryside and the airdromes were humming with preparation when he gave his last "good luck." From the rooftop of an ivied English mansion he watched the cavalcade of planes roaring across the sky, toward France.

Two documents were written by General Eisenhower in the days before the actual invasion at Normandy. He had to follow a script and not appear to be improvising. The first is comparatively well known and was delivered as a glorified "pep talk" to the troops by Ike on June 5, 1944:

> You are about to embark upon the Great Crusade toward which we have striven these many months. The eyes of the world are upon you. The hopes and prayers of liberty-loving people every-where march with you. In company with our brave Allies and brothers-in-arms on other fronts, you will bring about the destruction of the German war machine, the elimination of Nazi tyranny over the oppressed peoples of Europe, and security for ourselves in a free world. Have full confidence in your courage, devotion to duty, and skill in battle. We will accept nothing less than full victory!

This, of course, was a rousing send-off, and, listening to it, Allied soldiers must have felt justified in their perception that their command-ers had pored over all the contingencies so that full victory was assured.

Had they been privy to another narrative that Eisenhower had writ-ten to accompany prospective events on Normandy's beaches, this com-forting perception would have been shattered. The unread note Ike carried in his pocket read:

> Our landings in the Cherbourg-Havre area have failed to gain a satisfactory foothold and I have withdrawn the troops. My deci-sion to attack at this time and place was based on the best infor-mation available. The troops, the air, and the navy did all that bravery and devotion to duty could do. If any blame or fault attaches to the attempt, it is mine alone.

Moreover, had they been aware of the myriad miscues that took place in the preparations for the assault on Normandy, the troops would have become even more concerned.

Precisely where an Allied invasion force would land in France was in the hands of American and British scriptwriters. There were at last three options: an assault in southern France; a landing in Normandy; or an amphibious operation breaking the heart of Germany's Great Atlantic Wall at Pas-de-Calais. The first alternative was implemented, but it could only be a sideshow, since moving on Germany from southern France would require Allied forces to move thousands of miles with commensurate logistical problems. By contrast, Calais would place an Allied army just a few hundred miles from the Reich itself, but it would be risky given the resistance it was likely to encounter from Germany's 15th Army, concentrated near the fortress.

The German General Staff was aware of the choices facing its adversaries, but as long as the Allied Supreme Command maintained absolute secrecy, it had no way of determining which route the Allies would take. In their preparation for D-Day, only a handful of security-cleared individuals on the Allied side were aware of the plan. Called "Bigot," these informed individuals were kept under close scrutiny, not because of the threat of a conscious security leak, but to prevent them from being captured and interrogated by the Nazis.

On D-Day itself, the rehearsals, and the deception long crafted and planned, were reinforced as American and British aircraft dropped tons of metallic strips over the Calais area and Allied ships set vessel hulls adrift. These objects appeared to be actual planes and ships on Nazi radar, and, on the morning of June 6, 1944, the Germans were confident that they had anticipated the Allied plans, that the invasion would come at Calais.

The commander of a US base in England said to his airmen, "May I have your attention, please? This is what we have been waiting for. This is invasion morning." His young men went out to their planes and up into the Channel dawn. On invasion day, sunrise came at 5:47 a.m. and high tide at 10:33 a.m.; the landings on the beaches were made between 6:00 and 8:25 a.m.

The Germans were caught napping. According to Admiral Sir Bertram Ramsay, Allied Naval Commander, the Allies had expected to lose 10 percent of their landing craft. Instead, they got through virtually intact. Closely timed bombardment by warships and planes put enough coastal defense guns out of action to make landings possible in most places without heavy casualties. By landing on a ninety-mile stretch of Normandy, the Allies placed two major ports, Cherbourg and Le Havre, in danger. If they extended their assaults in either direction, they would gain at least one of them. Meantime, the Allies poured men, supplies, tanks, and big guns onto the beaches. By the first nightfall they commanded, in one sector alone, by German admission, about ten miles of once-fashionable beaches from Trouville to Villers-sur-Mer, including Deauville.

In the carriers the paratroops dozed, or pretended to. They were the army's elite, the tough boys, lean, wiry men clad in green camouflaged battle dress, faces stained with cocoa and linseed oil: "We'll have something to eat if our rations run out." Near midnight the first planes reached their objective. Men snapped their ripcords over static lines, and waited, crouching. The command came, and they leaped. White, yellow, and red parachutes blossomed in the night. Men by the thousands, weapons by the thousands, floated down upon captive France.

Battleships, cruisers, destroyers stood off the coast, wrapped themselves in smoke screens, and hurled steel from 640 guns. Never before, not at Tarawa or Kwajalein or Salerno, had a target been subjected to such overwhelming bombardment from air and sea. Some fifteen minutes after a rosy sun lifted over the pastures of Normandy, khaki-clad US and British troops began to pour ashore. On the way to the boats in England some of them had picked flowers, stuck them in their gun muzzles. At the boats they got the last miscellaneous tokens of the supply service care: seven sticks of chewing gum, emergency rations, insecticide powder, cigarettes, a tin of canned heat, water-purification tablets, chewing tobacco, one razor blade, twelve seasickness pills, two vomit bags, which many of them used. On the beaches, the landing craft disgorged, riflemen deployed. By ten thirty in the morning, bulldozers were carving out temporary airstrips. England was tied to the invasion coast at last. The crusade was on, and at day's end the boats that had landed the greatest amphibious force in history began ferrying the wounded and the dead back to England.

The Germans had been divided in their view about where a second front would open. The majority of the General Staff were convinced that a landing at Pas-de-Calais was the most likely course. Uncharacteristically, Hitler himself correctly outguessed the professional soldiers under his command, believing that a Normandy assault was in the offing. From the Allied perspective, an advantage could be gained by exploiting these diverse perceptions of how the last act in the Allied show would unfold. Secrecy about the real plan for D-Day was not enough to gain this advantage. True to the drama, some form of illusion had to mislead the enemy. Such deceptions had been under way for some time.

On an April morning in 1943, a fisherman spotted the corpse of a British soldier floating in the sea off the coast of Spain, placing in motion one of the most successful British disinformation plans during World War II. Part of Operation Barclay, a widespread deception to misinform the Axis powers about the invasion of Italy from North Africa, Operation Mincemeat fooled Nazi espionage chiefs, sent German troops racing in the wrong direction, and saved thousands of lives by deploying a secret agent who was unique in one crucial respect: he was dead. His mission: to convince the Germans that instead of attacking Sicily, the Allied armies would invade Greece.

The brainchild of an eccentric RAF officer, Charles Cholmondeley, and a brilliant barrister, Ewen Montagu, the great deception involved an extraordinary cast of characters: a famous forensic pathologist; a beautiful secret service secretary; a submarine captain; three novelists; an irascible admiral who loved fly-fishing; and a dead Welshman. Using fraud and imagination, Winston Churchill's team of spies spun a web of deceit so elaborate and so convincing that they began to believe it themselves. From a windowless basement beneath Whitehall, the hoax traveled from London to Spain to Germany.

After obtaining a dead "man without a name" body from a London coroner, they set about creating an entirely new personality for the dead man, whom they designated William Martin, a major in the Royal Marines. They gave the dead man a father, a fiancée, and a back story. The body was dropped into the sea from a Royal Navy submarine and then floated toward the coast of Spain. Montagu and Cholmondeley had a specific target in mind: Adolf Clauss, a German spy operating in the port of Huelva on Spain's south coast who was known to be efficient, and extraordinarily gullible. About the dead man's person were false identity cards, faked personal letters, receipts, bills, photographs, and chained to his wrist a briefcase with a packet of secret documents. Among them was a top-secret classified letter from Sir Archibald Nye, then vice chief of the Imperial General Staff in the War Office, to General Sir Harold Alexander, the British commander in North Africa under American General Dwight D. Eisenhower, identifying Greece and Sardinia for invasion by the Allies. These precious documents quickly made their way into German hands and by May 1943, Hitler had taken measures by sending his troops to fortify their position in Sardinia, Corsica, and Greece, and further ordered two additional panzer divisions to prepare to move from Russia to Greece. Two months later, the Allies stormed into Sicily with hardly any resistance from German and Italian defenders, whose eyes were turned northward to Sardinia.

Operation Mincemeat worked. German troops were deployed to the wrong place; thousands of British, Canadian, and American lives were saved; Mussolini was deposed; and the course of World War II was changed. After the war, a successful film was produced, *The Man Who Never Was,* documenting the incident.

More recently, the Allies had staged a fake D-Day invasion show for the benefit of the Germans. Allied air and naval power concentrated its might on Pas-de-Calais, docking areas were established at Dover, the most suitable port of embarkation for an armada destined for Calais, and Allied organizational charts included a phantom First United States Army Group and a British Fourth Army aimed at the fortified shores around Calais.

Believing the deception, the Germans gave the command to Field Marshall Erwin Rommel, who would have to repulse the Allies at Calais. Widely known as the "Desert Fox," Rommel, as it turned out, would soon take part in another subplot when he became a participant in the German attempt to assassinate the führer.

The Normandy poppies were pale with dust. In the fair fields where the tide had rolled, the ground was littered with the debris of battle: tanks, jeeps, rifles, ration tins, bulldozers, first-aid kits, canteens. Everywhere lay the dead, weltering in the waves along the shore, lying heaped in ditches, sprawling on the beaches. Here and there in trees hung the shattered bodies of paratroopers. In field hospitals, the wounded lay.

One paratroop lieutenant survived to return and tell how the Germans "were machine-gunning us all the way down. It was unlike any movie I had ever seen. Could I have been in live action with no cameras filming me?" Another officer told of seeing German tracers ripping through other men's parachutes as they descended. In one plane, a soldier laden with his ninety pounds of equipment got momentarily stuck in the door. A 20-mm shell hit him in the belly. Fuse caps in his pockets began to go off. Part of the wounded man's load was TNT. Before this human bomb could explode, his mates behind him pushed him out. The last they saw of him, his parachute had opened and he was drifting to earth in a shroud of bursting flame.

On the beach itself were great tripods of steel rails, braced steel fences, all of them ingeniously mined. The demolition units went to work clearing paths while German shells fell among them and German machine gunners, hidden in tunnels and six-foot-thick concrete pillboxes, raked them. An assault engineer said, "We had to work with water up to our necks, sometimes higher. Snipers were nipping us off. As I was working with two blokes on a tough bit of element, I suddenly found myself working alone. My two pals just gurgled and disappeared under the water."

After eleven days of fighting in Normandy, Lieutenant General Omar Bradley announced his casualties to date: 3,283 Americans dead, 12,600 wounded. Although the Allies' move to envelop, capture, and develop Cherbourg as a port was plainly behind schedule, the campaign was running smoothly, overcoming great handicaps. Said Bradley, "The Germans have lost their last chance to drive us into the sea." At a crossroads near Barneville, not far from Cherbourg, stood five German MPs waiting to direct traffic. The traffic that came was American. Captured, the MPs conceded they were probably the most surprised men in the entire German Army of Occupation.

The battle for Cherbourg opened on a clear, cool, summery day. Leaflets had warned the battered Cherbourg garrison to surrender or die. They were ignored. Nazi officers had orders to shoot any man who attempted to retreat or give up. Before the last push began, the German positions were methodically bombed for eighty minutes. The bombers' targets were close enough to the US lines to make sweating doughboys hug their ditches and curse in exasperated admiration.

For three days the Americans closed their ring, always moving closer, taking cover skillfully, using their superiority in air and artillery without mercy. The Germans fought back savagely with heavy coast-defense guns, field artillery, and multiple-barreled *Nebelwerfers,* whose incendiary rocket projectiles sailed through the air with an unearthly noise, described by one reporter as "something like a titanic horse whinnying." As troops pushed ahead into the city, German detachments fell back in desperate street fighting. Some of the small harbor fortifications leveled their antiaircraft guns to fire at the incoming Americans. In a few hours the German resistance had been cut into pockets, no longer under centralized control.

Even though Eisenhower felt that Normandy was the right choice for the starting point of a second front, his British counterpart, Field Marshal Montgomery, had strong misgivings. In the field marshal's view, miles of beach front would be required to land a force of one hundred thousand men initially and create port facilities that could supply an even larger contingent. The Normandy landing zone was but half that breadth. These directorial disputes were quiet while Allied soldiers and seamen had assumed their leaders were united.

# CHAPTER 21

# Miscues and Misinterpretations
# of the Allied Script

⸺ ∞ ⸺

Indeed, a litany of miscues and misreadings plagued the Allies as they planned the invasion. The air bombardment of German fortifications at Normandy was relatively ineffective, the bulk of the tonnage falling well behind the enemy's front lines. Concurrently, the naval broadsides that were supposed to complete the job of softening up the Nazi resistance failed in their mission, most of the shells falling thousands of yards short of the mark. The bulk of German defensive positions were intact when American, British, and Canadian troops stormed ashore.

But far more intriguing than these routine, prosaic military failures were two episodes that have never been fully recognized in accounts of the crusade in Europe: the unacknowledged disaster at Slapton Sands weeks before the D-Day landings; and the fiasco of dual-drive (DD) amphibious tanks on D-Day itself.

In 1944, the 4th American Infantry Division joined with other units in an immense rehearsal for D-Day under the rubric of Operation Tiger. Some two hundred ships took part in the exercises near Devon, and every effort was taken to make the war game as realistic as possible, with mock enemy counterattacks.

As the ships approached the beaches to discharge their complements of infantry, there was an unexpected and abrupt shift from rehearsal to actual performance by the Germans in nine sleek German E-boats. Dispatched from Cherbourg, the E-boats fired torpedoes at the armada, sinking two LST landing craft and leaving some 749 American soldiers and sailors dead on the beaches. Though their guns were loaded with live ammunition, American gunners were inhibited from firing on the E-boats, believing them to be part of the rehearsal.

What marked Slapton Sands was not what took place that particular day, but how the Allies dealt with its aftermath. Releasing the true story of the incident would have been a blow to morale. Consequently, word of the fiasco was systematically blotted from official records. The bodies of the fallen troops were secretly buried in a mass grave on the Devon farm of Mr. Nolan Tope. The wounded were quarantined. As for the families of those who died that day, news of the deaths was delayed for six weeks, then the relatives were informed by the US War Department that the men had been killed valiantly in the initial assault on the Normandy shore. Only after the Axis surrender did the details of the Slapton Sands flop emerge.

The second incident happened on D-Day itself. Months before, Allied engineers met with top American and British commanders and showed them blueprints for a tank that could operate as both a standard land vehicle and as an amphibious craft. It was a remarkable machine that could shift from a standard automotive drive to a makeshift propeller with an extended collar to keep waves from inundating its topside hatches. Of British design and American manufacture, the DDs were approved by General George C. Marshall, and, following a brief and calm ride in a DD prototype, General Eisenhower added his imprimatur to the project.

Prime Minister Churchill had no reason not to believe that this secret weapon would greatly facilitate the coming amphibious assault on Nazi-occupied France, allowing armored units to precede infantrymen onto the beachheads for the first time in history. A production run was ordered, and 32 DD tanks were worked into the Supreme Command's D-Day strategy.

Some on the Allied side were skeptical about claims that had been made on the DDs' behalf. They included the British Admiralty and American tank veterans assigned to the 741st and 743rd tank battalions. Their doubts were heightened when a planned DD exercise was canceled because the waters in which they were to "swim" were too choppy. Matters were complicated further when Army General Omar Bradley insisted that commanders from his branch determine the exact position at which the DDs would become ocean-borne when they were discharged from navy vessels. This suggestion ran into a stonewall of service rivalry.

Apart from inherent design problems, the DDs' performance on D-Day was determined by nature. The waters off the Normandy coast were so turbulent that the entire operation was reviewed on June 5 with an eye toward delay. With improved weather, the invasion was rescheduled and the order was given, but rough waters blasted the DDs apart. Fears of DDs running aground prompted the navy to lower gangplanks for the DDs several thousand yards farther out into the water. Of the thirty-two DD tanks in the Allied invasion force, three could not be launched owing to technical problems, two reached Omaha Beach, and twenty-seven dropped like stones to the bottom of the sea, sending their crews to their watery graves.

What is of interest about the DD tank folly was the manner in which it was handled by Allied public relations officers. No mention of the fiasco was made in press releases distributed after D-Day, and no effort was made to recover the bodies of the tank crewmen who died as a result of this failure in staging apparatus. Forty years later, a recovery attempt was initiated. It failed, and the unofficial record of the incident closed.

· · ·

The war remained the most extensively reported in history. Indeed, without war correspondents bringing news from the front lines, many of the conflict's dramatic nuances would never have been given full play.

Wartime reporting and wartime publishing were not without limitations, official silence and censorship were imposed, and very often battles were shrouded in a veil of misinformation. There was a lot of news to report, and correspondents became adept at circumventing censorship rules. American newspapers could not show dead soldiers, or people weeping. The British press could not publish any image of war dead or badly injured soldiers.

They wore military uniforms and a helmet. Just below the shoulder and across the sleeve, was a "correspondent" patch signifying courage under fire. They were not shy of exposing wartime atrocities, such as those that took place in the Czech town of Lidice where on June 10, 1942, the Germans destroyed the small village, killing every adult male, and some fifty-two women and children, its residents forever blotted from memory; or the expanding concentration camp horror made known fully at the end of the war. They filed reports of the enactment of German policy against the Jews, of the events of *Kristallnacht* in 1938, and in November 1942, Heinrich Himmler's systematic slaughter of Poles beginning with a process of rounding up Jews, of cattle train transport in which half the victims died, the extermination camps at Treblinka, Sobibor, and Belżec, the selection of Jews for forced labor with others slated for liquidation, despite German efforts to conceal the crime.

The *New York Times* had over a million words a day flooding in by radio, teletype, or wire, with an average of 125,000 words in every weekday edition. Controversy arose when publisher Arthur Sulzberger of the *Times*, who was conflicted about his own Jewishness, took great pains to ensure that anti-Semites would not be able to identify the *Times* as a paper controlled by Jewish interests.

Susan Tifft and Alex Jones wrote in *The Trust*, their history of the *Times*, that Sulzberger missed an opportunity to use the considerable power of the paper to focus a spotlight "on one of the greatest crimes the world had ever known." Articles about the murder of Jews rarely made it to page one, relegated instead to the back pages, only appearing now and then in diluted and fractured form. As a newspaper publisher, Sulzberger might have taken more of a stand, just as the Warner brothers as filmmakers had done against the Nazi tyranny and astonishing systematic elimination of the Jewish people in Europe.

The narrative moved from crisis and uncertainty through a tense period in 1942 and 1943 toward a rush to victory when a stubborn defense was more costly and longer-lasting than the public had expected. But correspondents wanted to soften the grim reports of war and death and rewrite the story with an emphasis on virtue and triumph. It is all the more remarkable that an editor of the *Times*, Robert Duffus, would write in 1940 after the British evacuation of Dunkirk, "It is the great tradition of democracy. It is the future. It is victory."

At the war's outset, some 735 men and women were drafted into the military to serve as war correspondents for the three major wire services, United Press, the Associated Press, and Hearst's International News Service. Within months, however, enlistees would outnumber conscripts. When Allied forces reached Paris, the number of warcos stationed in the French capital nearly matched men in uniform. The Paris-based cast would soon be filing three million words a week along with thirty-five thousand still pictures and a hundred thousand feet of newsreel footage. The best of their group had been given the opportunity to comment upon the proceedings of D-Day in an American radio broadcast that lasted nearly sixteen hours.

An award winning American journalist, Ernie Pyle was a correspondent for the Scripps-Howard newspaper chain, earning deep respect and affectionate acclaim for his accounts of American soldiers, writing about ordinary men who became extraordinary people during World War II. He was an average, down-to-earth guy, writing poetic prose and lasting descriptions about the battlefields where he left his own footprint.

He began to cover the war with the Allied invasion of North Africa in the autumn of 1942. At that time, his syndicated daily columns appeared in forty-two newspapers that had an aggregate circulation of around 3.5 million readers. By the time Pyle was killed in Okinawa by a Japanese machine-gunner, 393 daily newspapers and 297 weeklies with a total of thirteen million readers were running his reports. In less than three years Pyle became the most-read newspaper columnist in history.

He won the Pulitzer Prize for journalism in 1944 and was considered the nation's number one correspondent that same year.

What set Pyle apart from his colleagues? Most of his readers could not escape the illusion that he was a personal friend of theirs. Reducing the complexities of battle into simple, colloquial language, Pyle spoke to his readers in their own terms.

His bond with his readers gave him credibility as a cultural authority, that is, as an observer who could be relied upon to translate foreign scenes and ways into American terms. Pyle's accuracy gave an understanding of what the GI's role in the war was all about. He did not hesitate to spell out how the "folks" back home should view those fighting on their behalf, as individuals and neighbors whose accomplishments were to endure the unendurable. Pyle did not think of himself as a journalist, but as a letter-writer creating an epistolary account of the action around him. He limited his reportage to what he could actually see. Pyle was labeled the "GI's Boswell," the diarist of the common foot soldier; he took the greater narrative that leadership advanced to the average reader, in his own style, in his own way.

Perhaps the finest piece of writing sent stateside was Pyle's account of D-Day:

> I took a walk along the historic coast of Normandy in the country of France. It was a lovely day for strolling along the seashore. Men were sleeping on the sand, some of them sleeping forever. Men were floating in the water, but they didn't know they were in the water, for they were dead.

One is struck by the effects that its author achieved through the unexpected, the incongruous, the "all-too-human," and the tragicomic aspects of the invasion. Pyle noted that one soldier had a banjo slung over his shoulder when he hit Omaha Beach on H-Hour, while another appeared to have lost a tennis racket that Pyle discovered on the sands of Normandy. In perhaps the most effective passage, Pyle found a Bible on the beach with a soldier's name on its inner jacket. As he told his readers, he picked the Bible up and carried it for a half mile or so, then put it back on the beach: "I don't know why I picked it up or why I put it down again."

For Pyle, there was nothing noble about the war, no matter how noble it might be made to seem. He thought of war as an unalleviated misfortune, and his foot soldiers were capable of performing terrible acts under the pressure of wartime conditions. As for the patriotic stripe that was an obligatory feature of OWI "information," Pyle asserted that, while huddling with infantrymen before a battle, he never heard anybody say anything patriotic, the way the storybooks had people talking.

# CHAPTER 22

# Operation Joker

———∞∞∞———

The battle was won, but the drama was not over. It was time for the last performances to ensure a complete and unqualified victory in Europe. Americans branched out to become an equal partner with the British in black radio propaganda. Prior to D-Day, the Americans had scored some minor successes with Operation Muzak, but could not match the British counter-scripts sent to the Reich through Gustav Siegfried Eins and Soldatensender Calais.

Wild Bill Donovan was determined to become a full player with the British in the black radio game, and, in the months following D-Day, the OSS achieved his aim. On July 20, 1944, an attempt was made on Hitler's life by a group of German General Staff conspirators that included career soldier General Ludwig Beck. Beck's role in the failed assassination came to light. He was arrested by the Gestapo, and he committed suicide shortly thereafter, but rumors persisted within Germany that Beck had escaped his captors and was alive. The OSS learned of these rumors from interviews with German POWs and soon recognized that the stories could serve as the basis for what would be code-named Operation Joker.

To give their scheme credibility, OSS teams scoured libraries for the biographical details of Beck's life. While no recordings of his voice were available, they did discover discs and tapes of other General Staff members, Rommel, Keitel, and Doenitz, which enabled them to construct a profile of the idiom common to German officers of Beck's stature.

Among the German POWs held by the Allies was a major whose speaking voice and mannerisms closely approximated those of General Keitel. Better still, the major had served on the General Staff and knew Beck. The man who would become Beck's voice was persuaded to play this part in exchange for special treatment, as were other POWs.

With the show's elements assembled, "General Beck" went on the air in August 1944. An announcer exhorted listeners to the shortwave transmission band to stay tuned for a special broadcast from an unidentified, clandestine site within Germany (the real location being in Allied-held France). General Beck was invited to the microphone at the appointed hour.

Without any apology, he described his involvement in and motives for the attempt on the führer's life. It was Hitler who had personally led Germany and its military into crushing defeats. To substantiate this, Beck ticked off all of the times that Hitler had insisted upon playing the role of Supreme Field Commander, the abandonment of Operation Sea Lion, the decision to invade the USSR, the irrational command to hold the group at Stalingrad to the last. The transmission closed with an old German adage: "The individual may perish, but Germany must live." The message was clearly that Hitler must go, by whatever means possible.

Precisely what impact Operation Joker had upon its intended audience cannot be determined. We do know that the Nazis feared the potential influence of Operation Joker; for almost two weeks after the Beck broadcast, German transmitters jammed the 282-meter band upon which his voice had been heard.

When the talented British newsman-turned-producer Sefton Delmer praised the Beck script as a well-written piece and beautifully spoken work, the OSS was heartened and expanded their black radio activities, creating a series of clandestine transmissions known as Operation Annie, a station that like the others that had preceded it, achieved legendary status in subversive broadcasting history.

When a Luxembourg radio station used by the Gestapo fell into Allied hands, the swastikas, posters, and items of symbolic paraphernalia that the Gestapo had left behind remained in place. Donovan's OSS staff reasoned that the black radio crew taking over the location could, if needed, flourish in the actual set.

The voice of the effective black radio station, Radio Annie, broadcasting from the studio in Electra House, was not a Nazi nor even a German POW, but Lieutenant Frank Benno, a patriotic German from the Rhineland who immigrated to America before the war and saw a life-and-death conflict for his former homeland. He had a warm, rich, slightly husky, middle-aged Rhinelander's voice, invoking confidence.

With some crucial exceptions, the trust that his audience placed in Frank was justified. Most of the content consisted of accurate reports of war damage inflicted by the Allies on the German military and behind the front. This information was far more accurate than the heavily censored damage reports issued by the German ministry.

Damage accounts were scripted as if they had been constructed from onsite observations and with close scrutiny of aerial reconnaissance cross-referenced by street maps, telephone directories, and death notices in local German newspapers.

Delmer and his team would not let up until a German surrender was secured, the script complete, the play over. One Radio Annie segment that the OSS crew incorporated into its broadcasts to the beleaguered Wehrmacht with few amendments was authentic advice to his troops issued concurrently by Field Marshal Model, a member of the German High Command. To the panzer grenadier calling vainly for ammunition, Model gave advice on how to wash woolen underwear without soap. To the tank driver searching for safety from the airplanes swooping from the skies, the good field marshal spoke of the duty of every soldier to worship the führer and, time permitting, to respect his own mother. To the infantrymen, Model offered an elaborate recipe for making sawdust and potato sausages into a delicious ragout.

Where Gustav Siegfried Eins had used the off-color appeal of salacious material, Annie enlarged and held its Wehrmacht audience by
reporting German football scores before they were available through
Nazi-controlled information channels. Apart from home news, Radio
Annie freely included items about scandals revolving around key party
and SS officials, reporting that "jolly" Hermann Göring had entered an
Institute for Fat Research, and that finding adequate sustenance was no
problem for those at the top of the Nazi pyramid.

In Annie's final days, a change occurred that had been delayed until
the Allies had exploited the full strategic potential of black propaganda.
Code-named Operation Intruder, it required a transition to tactical
propaganda, with completely false information regarding the movement
of Allied and Nazi troops for the masterful template that had been used
for the D-Day invasion.

In some instances, Allied troops were reported to be more advanced
than they really were. In others, the Allies had encountered phony setbacks, leaving the false impression that certain sectors were free for
German military operations, and playing a part in traps set for Nazi
military units.

The director of Britain's Political War Executive initially rejected this
approach since it was too vulnerable to verification and would under-
mine other types of black and white propaganda aimed at Germany, but
General Eisenhower supported Operation Intruder when American and
British troops stood poised for the final assault upon the Reich. Although
some success came from radio's tactical usage, including a German infantry battalion stumbling into mass capture when it moved on the basis of
Annie's false assurances, the station's last week was dedicated to another
form of propaganda that had played a limited part in British and
American black propaganda for German consumption. It made a call for
German citizens to openly revolt against the Hitler regime.

It was only in April 1945 that PWE-OSS launched its drive to get
German citizens into direct sabotage on a mass basis in an effort to bring
the war to a swifter conclusion. Annie was a significant instrument on
this front. The radio broadcast of April 4, 1945, included a special

announcement addressed to "New Germany" groups in Osnabrück, Hanover, and other German cities.

These groups were, in fact, creations of the OSS and did not, at least initially, have real counterparts. Phrased cryptically to give the impression that a code was in use, specific instructions were issued about prospective sabotage by New Germany contingents. Hence, for the benefit of the New Germany cadres in Stuttgart, Radio Annie transmitted the following:

> The SS has plans to destroy the last water and power installations. The Attack Division must prevent every piece of party sabotage under any conditions. It must be explained to your fellow citizens that the enemy is not dependent upon our water systems and that party sabotage only leads to damage to the Germans.

Two days later, Annie raised the stakes. Specific information to New Germany groups was augmented by a call addressed to all civilians who had been eavesdropping on Annie, as well as to remnants of ·the Wehrmacht. On that day, Annie began to cash in her credibility chips. All of the accurate news broadcast over the station was now used as a platform to bolster its claims to authenticity and authority:

> In our nightly broadcasts we have given our listeners the truth, because we believe that the truth is the only reliable signpost to a better future. Our single purpose was to be faithful, faithful to the future of Germany. In this, the hour of our greatest need, we have come to know that our duty to Germany demands that we do more than speak the truth. Today we know that this hopeless war is lost. The time for decision has definitely arrived, and nothing remains but the choice between destruction or peace.

Operation Annie's strategic mission was to generate distrust for the Nazi leadership among troops and increase their reliance on news reports emanating from the station. Her tactical mission was to then use her reputation for truthfulness to lure listeners into a military ambush and so hasten Allied victory.

During the remainder of the year, Radio Annie scripted reports of sabotage by New Germany groups, incidents in which revolutionaries had been discovered and executed by the SS/Gestapo. It called for New Germany followers to scratch out the second, fourth, and fifth letters of the Nazi Party acronym, NSDAP, leaving only "ND"—*Neues Deutschland*—to signify their handiwork and presence in public places. At the end of the month, Annie, like SGE before her, lost credibility, and the station experienced a faked raid by Nazi die-hards, the staged event being transmitted over the air.

In terms of listenership, Radio Annie did develop a large and loyal following. Interviews with German POWs indicated that about half of the Wehrmacht troops within the station's reach listened to Annie. For many Germans, Annie and her sister stations were the only available sources of news about the war as it was unfolding, and this clearly helped to attract and keep large audiences for their transmissions. While some soldiers and civilians within that audience may have guessed at Annie's real nature, many were convinced that the station was the work of revolutionaries inside Germany. As Allied forces drove deeper into Germany, they began to see NSDAP signs reworked according to radio instructions and actually discovered some real, active New Germany groups.

The final stages of the black radio game concentrated on a single message. The black mask was dropped, and all stations now openly revealed they were controlled by the Allies. Black propaganda turned white. The last message sent out to Germany via these channels centered on a single theme: the Allied demand for immediate, unconditional surrender; this surrender, they emphasized, would not mean the destruction of Germany or the enslavement of the German people.

# Chapter 23

# The Beginning of the End

———— ❦ ————

The Allied invasion of Europe played until the final curtain fell on Poland, just where it had all begun with an out-of-town opening. World War II began and would end in Poland. The Warsaw Uprising began on August 1, 1944, a story not often told. On that date, the Polish underground, the Armia Krajowa (Home Army), aware that the Soviet army had reached the eastern bank of the Vistula River, sought to liberate Warsaw, much as the French resistance had freed Paris when the Allied armies fanned out across France.

The Poles didn't know that the British and Americans, having made a secret postwar pact with Russia in Tehran, would not intervene. Stalin rewrote the final script. Because the Soviets did not want an armed and victorious Polish noncommunist military force, they halted their offensive and let the city be destroyed by the Germans. The Soviets remained on the eastern bank of the river and provided no assistance or aid to the uprising. Instead, they gave the Germans free reign. During the ensuing sixty-three days, it is estimated that 250,000 perished in the ruins of Warsaw. Eventually, the Home Army, including men, women, and children, surrendered. After the Germans forced all the surviving civilian population to leave the city, Hitler ordered that any buildings left standing be dynamited. After Warsaw was reduced to rubble and the Germans were defeated, the Russians entered.

The year saw the end of the war both in Europe and the Pacific. In Europe, US troops beat back the enemy's last massive counterattack in the Battle of the Bulge, after which Allied armies moved into the enemy heartland on all fronts. The size and scope of the Nazi thrust into the Bulge made it imperative for Allied forces to keep the breakthrough point as narrow as possible, thus making it more difficult for the Germans to push enough supplies and reinforcements through the bottleneck to keep their offensive rolling.

The Allies managed to hold on to both positions, and the attacking German troops were so effectively contained that most of them were eventually killed or captured.

• • •

In this, the last year of his life, Franklin Roosevelt was just beginning his fourth term in office. The nation was hearing persistent rumors that the president was seriously ill, but these reports were discounted by the White House, and in February, President Roosevelt undertook an arduous trip to Yalta to confer with Stalin and Churchill on the postwar partition of Germany. Two months later, on April 12, 1945, he suffered a fatal hemorrhage and the office passed to Vice President Harry S Truman, a onetime railroad timekeeper and haberdasher from Missouri who had served two terms in the US Senate and created a nationwide reputation as chairman of a Senate committee investigating the war effort.

• • •

The final act began in Normandy and ended with the tragic discovery of the Holocaust victims by Allied forces and the trial of Nazi war criminals at Nuremberg in 1945.

Before the end, a drama was borrowed from the structure of the Elizabethan Romance, a masque in which the central characters of the play are resurrected and the moral lessons of the drama are brought into sharp focus.

Well before the war was over, and before the Allied invasion of Normandy, teams of American and British propagandists were busily composing tributes on the assumption that victory was at hand.

But the drama was not over just yet. For his second conference of the Big Three—the first was at Tehran in 1943—and his ninth with his collaborator Winston Churchill, the president departed from Washington shortly after his inauguration. He appeared at Malta on a spotless US battleship wearing an old-fashioned tweed cap. There he was met by Winston Churchill.

The president and prime minister then boarded planes for a night flight to a secret Crimean airport and their meeting with Joseph Stalin at Yalta. The Germans had wrecked the little city so badly that Russian workmen had to rush temporary restorations for the Big Three staffs. The white stone palace where President Roosevelt stayed was built in 1911 for the last of the Romanovs. As at Tehran, the eight days at Yalta were not all work. Roosevelt and Churchill talked, ate, and drank together before Marshal Stalin joined them. Then, between working sessions, came the toasts. One of Stalin's toasts named the gathering for history: "The Crimea Conference."

When he returned, the president spent afternoons in Warm Springs to recover from his long trip. He felt he had written the final act of the war, but there were still scenes to play out. Bad weather had held up the plane which brought the president's daily mail from Washington, so it was late that morning before Mr. Roosevelt got down to work.

He sat beside the fireplace in the cozy, cluttered living room of the cottage at Warm Springs, the Little White House, while his secretary helped him sort through the mail. At one end of the room his cousins Laura Delano and Margaret Suckley sat chatting. There were a lot of things to sign, several State Department nominations, some postmasters' appointments, some citations for the Legion of Merit, the bill to extend the life of the Commodity Credit Corp. When he got to the bill, Franklin Roosevelt grinned at Bill Hassett, spoke the words that always made his secretary smile back: "Here's where I make a law."

Mrs. Elizabeth Shoumatoff, a portrait painter, came in. She had once done a portrait of Franklin Roosevelt and was now anxious to do another. She had driven down from her Long Island home several days before and had been making sketches. Hassett gingerly collected the papers, letting the president's signatures dry. "Don't mind me," Hassett remarked. "I'm waiting for my laundry to dry."

The president laughed. Mrs. Shoumatoff remembered afterward, "He was so spirited." Mr. Hassett left, leaving a stack of state papers within easy reach of the president's chair. The artist sketched while the president unconcernedly shuffled his papers.

Utter weariness had kept him close to the cottage since he had arrived less than two weeks before. He had seen few people, but this afternoon he was going to a barbecue. In the evening, the polio patients at his beloved Warm Springs Foundation were going to give a variety show for him. He was looking forward to both affairs. Miss Suckley glanced his way. He had suddenly slumped sideways in his chair and, alarmed, she ran across the room to him.

She heard him mutter: "I have a terrific headache." The women were upset at what they saw. The president fainted. They called his valet. Big Arthur Prettyman, veteran of twenty years in the navy, was accustomed to helping the crippled president around. With the help of "Joe," a Filipino mess boy, he lifted the unconscious man in his arms and carried him into the bedroom. There, in the small, plain room with its paneled walls and scatter rugs and the picture of a ship and a ticking brass chronometer, doctors found the stricken president. They untied his tie, took off his gray suit, and put pajamas on him. But there was little they or anyone else could do. He had suffered a massive cerebral hemorrhage. They could only wait and pray.

The shadows of the pines grew longer. In the bedroom of the Little White House one of the physicians looked at the time. It was 3:35 p.m. At that moment, death had come to Franklin Delano Roosevelt, director, producer of a theater of war he never wanted to script.

Mrs. Roosevelt, as guest of honor, arrived at the Sulgrave Club tea for the benefit of Washington's children's clinics "with a very light heart."

She had heard from Warm Springs that the president had eaten a good breakfast and was feeling fine. The anxiety that she had borne so long was eased a little.

She sat next to Mrs. Woodrow Wilson. Soon afterward, she was told that she was wanted on the telephone. Mrs. Roosevelt rose and left the room. She returned after a few moments to apologize for leaving "in this way" and rode back to the White House. In her sitting room on the second floor, surrounded by hundreds of cherished photographs of her family and friends, she faced Stephen Early and Vice Admiral Ross T. McIntire, the president's personal physician. "The president," said Early, "has slipped away."

"I am just as sorry for the people of the country and the world," Mrs. Roosevelt said after a moment, "than I am for us." Steve Early telephoned Mr. Truman. Soon the vice president came up to the sitting room. "The president has passed away," Mrs. Roosevelt told him.

When Harry Truman choked, "What can I do?" she answered, "Tell us what we can do. Is there any way we can help you?"

Later, she changed to a black dress and strode with her usual determined gait to the waiting limousine and went to the airport to fly to Georgia. In the dark morning hours, Eleanor Roosevelt walked into the little white cottage on Pine Mountain. Silent and alone, she went to her husband. A short time afterward, a train rolled through the dark hills of Virginia into the nation's capital at last and toward the end of Eleanor Roosevelt's longest day.

The news had come to people in the hot soft light of the afternoon, in taxicabs, along the streets, in offices, bars, and factories. In a Cleveland barbershop, sixty-year-old Sam Katz was giving a customer a shave when the radio stabbed out the news. Sam Katz walked over to the water cooler, took a long, slow drink, sat and stared into space for nearly ten minutes. Finally he got up and painted a sign on his window: ROOSEVELT IS DEAD. Then he finished the shave.

Everywhere, to almost everyone, the news came with the force of a personal shock. A woman in Detroit said, "It doesn't seem possible. It seems to me that he will be back on the radio tomorrow, reassuring us all that it was just a mistake."

It was the same through that evening, and the next day, and the next; the hand-lettered signs in the windows of stores: CLOSED OUT OF REVERENCE FOR FDR; the unbroken, eighty-five-hour dirge on the nation's radio; the tributes of typical Americans in the death-notice columns of their newspapers. Said one: "A Soldier Died Today."

A great president who scripted World War II, with the help of his dear friend and co-collaborator, was gone, but not before he had done all he possibly could to make the world a foundation for democracy. His tomorrows were no more, but his yesterdays remained.

In Washington's hush, every sound was audible, fluttering birds nesting in new-leafed shade trees; the soft, rhythmic scuffing of massed, marching men; the clattering exhaust of armored scout cars moving past, and the beat of muffled drums. As Franklin Roosevelt's flag-draped coffin passed slowly by on its black caisson, the hoofbeats of the white horses, the grind of iron-rimmed wheels on pavement overrode all other sounds. Men stood bareheaded. An elderly black woman sat weeping on the curb, rocking and crying: "Oh, he's gone. He's gone forever. I loved him so. He's never coming back."

At last, the caisson ground up the graveled White House drive. The coffin was carried out of sight into the executive mansion. It was put in the East Room. Franklin Roosevelt's wheelchair stood near the wall. The warm, flower-scented room was filled with Franklin Roosevelt's family and friends, the top men of the United States, representatives of the foreign world, the new president, Harry Truman, the cabinet, Britain's future prime minister, Anthony Eden, Russia's Andrei Gromyko. The pianist struck a chord, the mourners stood to sing the hymn, "Eternal Father, Strong to Save."

Mrs. Roosevelt listened, pale but dry-eyed, beside her son, Brigadier General Elliott Roosevelt, and her daughter, Mrs. Anna Roosevelt Boettiger, but many near her could not control themselves. Harry Hopkins, who had hurried east from the Mayo Clinic, stood almost fainting beside his chair, white as death and racked by sobs.

That night, aboard his special train again, the president took one last journey to Hyde Park. In the green-hedged garden of the ancestral home, two carloads of flowers lay heaped beside the open grave. The Reverend George W. Anthony, a white-haired clergyman, spoke at the Episcopal burial service. "We commit his body to the ground; earth to earth, dust to dust. Blessed are the dead who die in the Lord. Lord have mercy on us. Christ, have mercy on us."

A squad of West Point cadets raised rifles at the graveside, fired a volley, then another and another. A bugle sounded the long notes of taps. The gray-clad cadets swung smartly away. The crowd slowly scattered. After a while Eleanor Roosevelt walked back through a wide opening in the hedge. She stood alone, silently watching the workmen shoveling soil into her husband's grave. Then, silent and alone, she walked away again. On her black dress she wore the small pearl fleur-de-lis, which he had given her as a wedding present.

Down from the walls of the oval White House study came Franklin Roosevelt's Currier & Ives prints, his ship's clock. After the final packing was done, there were a thousand boxes and bundles in all, secured by secret servicemen.

White House office workers and servants came to Mrs. Roosevelt's upstairs study to say good-bye. She thanked them, her voice warm, her face strained. In the early evening, she put on her coat and hat. Past the White House rooms, past where she walked, the outlines of vanished pictures showed on bare walls. Two black limousines took Mrs. Roosevelt and her family out through the gate in a drizzling rain, headed for the Union Station. That night in Manhattan the usual knot of reporters awaited her. She spoke only four words. "The story," she said, "is over."

In a few breathless days, the US people got an idea of how their new president would carry on with the script. He did not need to polish, nor rewrite. The scenario had long been established and staged, and it was only for the new president to follow, until the final curtain fell.

Harry Truman was quick, decisive, and seemed to have a talent for working hard without getting confused or losing his temper.

Within a few days US citizens grew accustomed to pictures of Harry Truman's neat, compact figure striding briskly across the street from Blair House and up the gray, curving driveway into the executive offices at the White House. Once, when traffic halted to let the president pass, a cab driver yelled, "Good luck, Harry!" Harry Truman grinned and waved.

In the White House he upset the whole routine. An inordinately early riser, he was at his desk at eight thirty, and began his day's appointments promptly at nine thirty. No matter how crowded the list, he kept the schedule running on time, a feat that the loquacious Franklin Roosevelt had seldom been able to do. One thing Harry Truman could not quite get used to: the office comforts of being president. He had presented to Eleanor Roosevelt the desk at which the late president had worked, and for himself had taken the old, dark red mahogany desk which had been used by presidents Theodore Roosevelt, Taft, Wilson, Harding, Coolidge, and Hoover.

On the desk was a little oak plaque with three black buttons on it to summon secretaries and stenographers, but whenever Harry Truman wanted a stenographer he would jump up, rush to the door and say, "Look, I want to dictate a few letters," and his work began.

Assuming his role as custodian of the final script, Truman kept a front row seat as American divisions hammered the bulge flat. Along a forty-mile front east of the Ardennes, some ten US divisions were clawing their way through the saw-toothed tank traps, over the concrete pillboxes of the Siegfried Line. The snow that had blinded them during the German breakthrough, the ice that had immobilized their trucks, turned into deep slush and mud through which they slid and slithered.

At SHAEF (Supreme Headquarters Allied Expeditionary Force), correspondents were telling another anecdote about unpredictable Lieutenant General George S. Patton. An Allied officer had asked Supreme Commander Dwight Eisenhower where in Germany Patton might be. Ike's reply: "Hell, I don't know. I haven't heard from him for three hours."

Patton had always been the most colorful soldier in the US Army. A cavalryman loyal to Pancho Villa, he earned the title of "Old Blood and Guts" for his aggressive bravery. A strutting, hard-talking, no-nonsense general, his uniform fitting his design, and his strategy adapting to his own improvised script, always smart, intelligent, and sometimes non-conforming to the army's way of doing battle. But all in all, following the production plan Eisenhower had crafted, he was unfailingly loyal.

George Patton was sitting in his headquarters, his highly polished cavalry boots cocked on the glass top of his desk, his long-fingered hands relaxed in his lap. He listened now and then over his command radio to battle reports. Willie, the general's white bull terrier, snuffled sleepily on the rug. Patton had reason for calm and happy reflection. He was having the time of his action-choked forty-year career. Some of Patton's men were fighting less than 180 miles from Berlin. The Germans seemed to be scattering before his attacks. They had reason to fear him. The Germans had always put more men and guns opposite Patton's outfits. Now there were fewer German men and guns, and now Patton was playing his favorite role.

He was the swift, slashing halfback of Coach Eisenhower's team. George Smith Patton Jr. was fast becoming a leading player. The US public, always more interested in the ball-carrier than in the blockers who opened a hole for him, liked Patton's flourishes, his flamboyance, his victories; and in slim, big-chested Patton, hero-worshipping Americans had a candidate to fit the mass idea of what a Hero General should be, the colorful swashbuckler, the wild-riding charger, the hell-for-leather Man of Action, above all, the Winner. He was a dazzling mixture.

The oldest field commander of any Allied army in Europe (he reached sixty on Armistice Day of 1945), Patton was still a tiger in action. On the field he could rawhide a private or a lesser general with a flow of profanity that was perhaps the richest in all the hard-swearing US armies. A moment later he could be gently lifting a wounded man from a tank, calming him with soothing words. Patton the general was also Patton the actor. Showmanship was instinctive in him, and he fitted his act to his audience's mood. His greeting to a black battalion arriving at his battlefront was: "I don't give a damn what color you are so long as you get out there and kill those sons-of-bitches in the green suits." A favorite story with his officers was how the general stopped the rain after the Rundstedt breakout. Rundstedt's offensive was blessed by soupy days at its start. No planes flew. Tank men, called on to drive eighty miles in a night, could not find the enemy in the endless drizzle. By the third day Patton called in one of his chaplains. The reported conversation:

> Patton: I want a prayer to stop this rain. If we got a couple of clear days we could get in there and kill a couple of hundred thousand of those krauts.
>
> Chaplain: Well, sir, it's not exactly in the realm of theology to pray for something that would help to kill fellow men.
>
> Patton: What the hell are you, a theologian or an officer of the US Third Army? I want that prayer.

The General got his prayer; it was printed on thousands of small cards with Patton's Christmas greeting on the reverse side. On the fifth day of rain it was distributed to the troops. On the seventh day the sun shone.

• • •

Terror came on the cold wet wind of Russian guns sounding. Panic came on the heels of the milling, stumbling horde of refugees. Berlin, at last, was a battle zone. The city had not been captured by a foreign invader since its citizens came out and welcomed Napoleon's troops with open arms.

Now German radio spewed an endless stream of threats to traitors, cowards, shirkers, defeatists. All army "stragglers" and all males over thirteen were ordered to report for duty.

The defense of the city was laid out. Even the zoo was fortified. Streetcars stopped running. Food rations were stretched for an extra week and the potato ration was cut, yet the panic and terror seemed somehow to be kept in bounds. Berlin and the rest of uninvaded Germany were carrying on the fight.

Hitler took to the airwaves. His voice sounded weak, as if it was being nursed along. "The National Socialist State, our two-thousand-year-old civilization, can neither be replaced by Bolshevism nor by democratic-plutocratic ideology. This nation and its leading men are unshakable in their will and unswerving in their fanatical determination to fight this war to a successful conclusion."

His voice gained a full-throated resonance as in the past and had a high hypnotic timbre: "I am at present speaking less frequently, not because I do not want to speak but because my work leaves little time for speeches. I have not been sleeping. I promise solemnly to the Almighty that the hour will strike when victory will come to the Greater German Reich." This was the old shrill cry; it was unmistakably Hitler. The pages of Hitler's script had failed and faded, no longer an indelible blueprint for a thousand years, but a soggy, unreadable ledger, with tear-flecked blood running down its pages, smearing a vision that had once been clear and ambitious, running and falling into a pool of stagnant, muddy water.

The German Supreme Command held a conference in a little bomb-proof room deep in the earth under the Berlin chancellery. The last pages of the play were written. The decisive briefing that determined the fate of all Germans began at three o'clock on the afternoon of April 22 and lasted until nearly eight o'clock that evening. At this briefing Adolf Hitler declared that he wanted to die in Berlin.

He repeated this ten or twenty times in various phrases. "I will fall here," or "I will fall before the chancellery," or "I must die here in Berlin." He reasoned that the cause was irretrievably lost, in complete contrast to his former command, "We will fight to the last tip of the German Reich." Hitler himself was generally composed. Each time he got angry or excited he would quickly regain control of himself. His face was flushed and red, however, and he paced the floor almost constantly, walking back and forth, sometimes smacking his fist into his hand. Of all the participants at all the conferences, the führer was generally the one who kept his nerves best under control, but in defeat, no longer.

The really crucial, fateful decision took place in the late afternoon. It lasted only about fifteen minutes. Present were Hitler, his personal representative, Martin Bormann, Field Marshal Wilhelm Keitel, and

Colonel General Alfred Jodl. All others were sent away, except two stenographers. Hitler again expressed his determination to stay in Berlin
and said he wanted to die there. Keitel, Jodl, and Bormann all came out
strongly against Hitler. Jodl declared firmly that he, personally, would
not stay in Berlin; he thought it was a mousetrap, and his job was to lead
the troops. The führer was by now rather vague and uncertain, giving no
direct orders, apparently preoccupied with the prospect of his own
imminent death. Jodl interjected that Germany still had some armies
capable of action. Perhaps, said Jodl, these armies could change the
course of events around Berlin.

Hitler evinced little interest. He just shrugged. The artillery fire on
the chancellery was increasing, and even deep down in the cellar the
generals felt tremors shaking the building. Hitler's secretary and staff
members were ordered to leave Berlin with stenographic reports. That
was the last plane and these were the last people to leave Berlin. The
conference finally broke up in a spirit of indecision. Hitler had written
the final lines.

Though every Berliner must have known in his heart that the mam-
moth march of Red Army power could not be stopped, thousands of
Berliners, men and boys, poorly-clothed, poorly-armed, even hundreds
of women, went to the fields and forests at the edges of the city to man
the trenches, pillboxes, anti-tank ditches, and enormous numbers of
antiaircraft emplacements, dug-in tanks, and machine guns.

Then, from the wall of smoke on the close horizon, broke the first
bolts of doom. Russian shells and rockets showered, then poured over
them. After them came the Red Army tanks. Thus, in a seventy-mile arc
of flame and steel, the soldiers of Red Marshal Georgy Zhukov came up
to the outskirts of the Nazi capital.

In five days they had fought through five defense belts, smashing
down a great concentration of enemy tanks in what may have been the
war's last battle. The millions of Berliners who could not fight milled
about in panic. They fought each other to get on the last trains to anywhere. They massed in the air-raid shelters, choked the Untergrundbahn
platforms and tracks. Stunned, they huddled wherever they could find

shelter and waited for the end. No words to read, no plays to follow, no battleground to fight, no speech to applaud, no music to play, no hope to fulfill, no dreams to dream.

• • •

Berlin posters cried fifty-sixth birthday greetings to the führer: "Our walls may crumble but our hearts stay firm." Tiredly, Propaganda Minister Joseph Goebbels eulogized, "Even the greatest of leaders of history will be faced with occasional setbacks." Discreetly the radio did not play the refrain, "Today Germany, tomorrow the world!" Instead it broadcast a Handel concerto. On his fifty-sixth birthday Adolf Hitler spoke not a word. Cried the BBC, "Yes, flags out on Hitler's birthday. Flags out, at half-staff! It might be his last."

Ten days later, on April 30, 1945, Hitler and his longtime mistress, Eva Braun, committed suicide in his Berlin bunker.

Berlin's end came sixteen days after the armies of marshals Zhukov and Konev lunged for the Nazi capital, twelve days after they reached its streets. The date was May 2, 3:00 p.m. Moscow time. It had almost ended sooner. In the gloomy dawn of May Day, a German colonel bearing a huge white flag appeared at a ruined side street held by the Russians. "Will the Soviet Command receive emissaries to discuss negotiations?" he asked. Red Army Major Belousov agreed and walked with the Germans toward their lines. A shot rang out. Belousov dropped with a Nazi sniper's bullet through his head.

The raging Russians answered with the greatest artillery barrage they had yet let loose on the capital, continuing without letup through the day, the night, and the next morning; then the German commander, Nazi Artillery General Kurt Webling, came with a white flag and did his surrendering within the Soviet lines.

At the end, the small German town of Torgau was almost deserted. Soviet Marshal Konev's artillery had battered it from across the Elbe. Two infantry and one armored division of the US First Army pulled up alongside a narrow tributary. The following morning a patrol from the

US 69th Division, dispatched to direct surrendering German soldiers in the rear, rolled beyond its officially prescribed radius of action and found itself in Torgau. The patrol consisted of four Yanks in a jeep: Second Lieutenant William Robertson and three enlisted men.

The Russians on the other side of the Elbe sent up colored flares, the prearranged signal to designate friendly forces. Robertson had no flares. He took a bedsheet from a house, broke into a pharmacy, found mercurochrome and blue ink, made a crude representation of a US flag and waved it from the tower of an ancient castle. The Russians, who had been tricked by the Germans waving US flags, sent over a volley of anti-tank shells.

Then Robertson decided on bold action. He and his men strode confidently out into the open, toward a bridge partially blown up by the Germans, whose twisted girders offered a precarious footway across the river. The Russians decided that only Americans would do such a thing. In the center, only a few feet over the swift-running water, the men of Eisenhower and Stalin met. Robertson slapped a Russian on the back and cried: "Hello, *tovarish*!"

It was real at last. Moscow fired its maximum salute of twenty-four salvos from 324 guns; Joseph Stalin, Winston Churchill, and Harry Truman issued resounding statements. A Red Army lieutenant, rising in the midst of joyous celebration, said, "My dear, quiet please. Today is the most happy day of our life, just as Stalingrad was the unhappiest when we thought there was nothing left to do for our country but die. But now, my dear, we have the most crazy of our life. You must pardon I don't speak the right English, but we are very happy so we drink a toast. Long live Roosevelt!" A comrade whispered Harry Truman's name; the speaker looked at him blankly and went on: "Long live Roosevelt! Long live Stalin! Long live our two great armies."

The Berlin that surrendered was the pounded corpse of a city. Wrote a Soviet correspondent,

> Ruins, craters, smashed guns, tramcars riddled with holes, half-demolished trenches, heaps of spent cartridge shells, fresh graves,

corpses still awaiting burial, masses of white flags, crowds of glum and hungry inhabitants lie before our eyes. The Tiergarten is burning. The Reichstag is smoking. Hitler's Berlin residence is also burning. The windows are blocked with heaps of books, and machine guns stick out between them.

With a fallen Berlin, the war effectively over, CBS officials had asked Norman Corwin to prepare a radio script, a few words. Corwin wrote *On a Note of Triumph*, a victory message, beginning with the injunction, "Take a bow, little guy." In the last, dramatic broadcast Corwin was guardedly hopeful when on May 26, 1945, he marked the defeat of Germany. It's among Corwin's most powerful writing, a summary of his views on war and peace. He expressed in the last stanza:

Take a bow, little guy.
Free men have done it again.
The common man proved tougher and smarter
Than the brown-shirt bully boys
And the little man of the fascist countries.
As in the Battle of Marathon 2,500 years so,
The enemies of freedom have been defeated.
But the little guy wants to know if it will all happen again.
We learned something in this war . . .

Corwin concluded that the war has proved the truth of liberal internationalism. He ended the show with an admonition:

That man unto his fellow man shall be a friend. Forever.

# CHAPTER 24

# The End of the Beginning

———◈———

In London, there was a landscape of fallen buildings that had been reduced to rubble, and immense yellow cranes began shoving and lifting splintered bricks, shattered windows, and broken doors high into the air, calling cards left by German bombers during the Battle of Britain. So many of London's buildings had been destroyed. The giant cranes were in the process of putting Humpty Dumpty back together again; their jagged silhouettes and powerful, swinging arms shadowed an unwelcomed past. There had been so much destruction, of cities, of the human spirit.

During the war, London had been relentlessly bombed by airplanes and flying bombs. Thousands of people were injured or killed, and the city was devastated. Night after night they slept in air-raid shelters underground, and when morning came, some stumbled from their shelters, walked over all the craters in the ground, and picked their way over the debris from buildings that had crashed. The fires were smoldering, the noise had stopped, and people went to their shops. They confirmed, "London can take it." They came through the war in the only way they knew how: staying the course, without complaint, sturdy and firm, a proud people, standing in a proud realm.

St. Paul's Cathedral, which had been hit by an incendiary bomb, had survived the assault and still stood. There were some flowers gathered around a few marble steps under a charred dome. On the side, a work-man had carved *1914–1918*; dates intended as a reminder of what was called the Great War, and now dates had been added, *1939–1945*. Gentlemen took off their hats when they passed, even if they were on the top deck of a bus. A curtain call, a final bow to the war to end all wars.

There were music-hall songs that began playing over the radio. Vera Lynn took to the stage singing "When the Lights Go on Again (All Over the World)." Lots of soldiers returned from battle, still in uniform, and hanging on to their arms were "khaki-whacki girls." That's what they were called; pretty girls, looking at their men in admiration. The lights in London were on, and the rebuilding process began.

Like a long-deferred spring, victory in the European Theater came at last, in its own sweet time. Gone were the films, the propaganda, the rousing speeches, the banners, the battlefields of death and desolation. The impressions of victory became a sweeping blur. For most people, the war in Europe ended not when they heard the hoarse voice of the radio, nor when they saw paper blizzards falling between skyscrapers, but when they took their first breath of freedom, slowly, silently, by degrees, some-where in each man's and each woman's heart.

Before the July 1945 election that Churchill would lose, the *Times* published an editorial suggesting that the prime minister as a nonparti-san world leader step down and retire gracefully.

"Mr. Editor," Churchill replied, "I leave when the pub closes."

Churchill, the scriptwriter—steadfast in his refusal to consider defeat, surrender, or compromise, who had inspired British resistance especially during the early days of the war when Britain stood alone among European countries in its active opposition to Adolf Hitler—had lost his co-authors.

In 1945, a new cast was performing in the theater of War. Without Hitler and Roosevelt, Joseph Stalin became antagonist, and Harry Truman, long an understudy to Franklin Roosevelt, joined the cast.

Churchill, Stalin, and Truman met in Potsdam to discuss their roles. When Churchill flew to Germany, the devastated areas of the northwest-ern region of the country unrolled before him. Over the wastes of Berlin, over the roofless houses and the crumbling church towers, his plane banked and circled. On land, US, British, and Russian guards lined the roads from the airfield; a cavalcade of cars rolled behind motorcycle escorts to the thickly guarded compound, to a refurbished castle once owned by Kaiser Wilhelm, where Churchill and two new cast members were listed in the program.

Before the stage on the castle grounds, the Russians had dressed a courtyard with red flowers in the shape of a huge red star. The leaders of the United States, Great Britain, and the Soviet Union, who, despite their differences, had played in the same theater of war, and remained allies throughout most of the conflict, would never meet again collectively to discuss cooperation in postwar reconstruction.

Inside the home of Crown Prince Wilhelm Hohenzollern, where the meeting began, was a dark-paneled room overlaid with a red and purple Oriental rug and a twelve-foot circular table. Here they would decide the fate of nations. In the rococo rooms, the Great Emperor Frederick had played his flute, while in its gardens, he schemed to confuse and divide his enemies. Stalin could easily play this role.

He mugged for the cameras and showed off his stock of English phrases: "So what?" and "You said it," then to confirm his proficiency, "The toilet is over there," and "What the hell is going on here?"

Harry Truman and Joseph Stalin got on strikingly well. Stalin's dislike of Winston Churchill had been obvious ever since their meeting in Malta.

Churchill had always known how disingenuous the Soviet dictator was, serving his own ends. Stalin's dislike of Churchill's long-winded speeches was never more apparent. When Churchill voiced a detailed bill of complaint against Russian plundering in southeastern Europe, Stalin was merely quiet. Truman sprang up saying that he had investigated and found the British charges to be inaccurate but would investigate further. Stalin twinkled and pointedly replied, "I will believe the Americans."

Now a modest player, the Missourian played his role. One evening at dinner, Joseph Stalin turned up in a fawn-colored uniform with scarlet epaulets and the big Gold Star of a Hero of the Soviet Union. Not to be outdone, or upstaged, Churchill, who had seen and envied Stalin's fawn outfit at Yalta, remembered that as Lord Warden of the Cinque Ports, he was himself entitled to wear a fawn-colored uniform. So he did. Truman, new to the theatrics, just wore a brown business suit.

After dinner, Sergeant Eugene List of the US Army arranged a concert for Stalin: some Tchaikovsky, three Shostakovich preludes, folk songs of the Volga, the Caucasus, and the steppes. Stalin shook List's hand, drank a toast to him, and asked for more. Churchill, well-rehearsed and briefed on Truman and his musical ability, asked the president to play *The Missouri Waltz,* which he did happily. Then, glowing with camaraderie and his own bourbon, Truman played a minuet in G. Stalin was enthusiastic.

The study in contrasts ended with a round of vodka.

• • •

The actual capitulation of the German armies was a confused and checkered operation. The first large-scale surrender was made to Britain's Field Marshall Montgomery in northern Germany on May 4. Three days later General Jodl unconditionally surrendered the entire German military force to General Eisenhower. But Stalin insisted that a formal signing should be staged in Berlin. Accordingly, a third acknowledgement of defeat was signed in the presence of General Zhukov at his field headquarters near Berlin on May 9.

At the war's end, Dwight Eisenhower was appalled at the extent of the carnage. Flying into Russia, in 1945, he did not find a house standing between the western borders of the country and the area around Moscow. Famed Russian General Marshal Zhukov told him, "So many numbers of women, children, and old men were killed that the Russian Government will never be able to estimate the total."

Stalin also had the blood of countless Russians on his hands because in the years preceding World War II his purges of anyone who did not fit his plan for a new Russia led to the death and starvation of millions. Soviet Ukraine, Soviet Belarus, and Leningrad were territories where the Stalinist regime had in the previous eight years starved and shot some four million people. Then add the Nazi invasion, when some 14 million civilians were killed with 60 percent of Soviet households losing at least one member of their family.

The Soviets fought valiantly, and the sacrifices of the Soviet triumph led to the rewriting of the script, which would continue into a cold conflict.

All the bordering countries liberated by the Soviets had communist governance imposed on them, especially Poland, East Germany, and Hungary. They were established because historically, Russia had no secure border, no mountains or deserts, no rivers or oceans to separate her from potential warlike neighbors. As countries became consolidated into the Russian political landscape, the Soviets wanted to push the border as far away from Moscow as they could. The Red Army had conquered the territory at a great cost, and Stalin was not willing to withdraw. The Yalta Agreement between FDR, Churchill, and Stalin established the spheres of influence that each of the Allied countries would have, and these satellite countries all fell under Soviet dominion.

With a different view of governance, the Communist Party was supported by a Marxist ideology, so that Russian doctrine continued as a mission to export the revolution to other countries and to prevent a unified Germany from being a threat to the Soviet Union ever again.

• • •

While yellow crocuses bloomed in Hyde Park, Britain counted up the two thousand days and nights the War had played. Two thousand performances of invasion-threats, blitz, bombs, immense suffering, and imperturbable defiance in the face of near-defeat. For most of that time, Britons had stared into the hollow eyes of disaster and death; it had never occurred to them to give up. Now the unseasonably warm winds brought not only the scents of fresh soil and flowers, but also the sense of long-deferred victory. There were no special celebrations. But Britons attended to sundry matters. The House of Commons passed a bill making rear lights compulsory on bicycles because during wartime, more people had been killed by traffic on surrounding country roads than by falling bombs.

On Victory in Europe Day—May 7, 1945—Churchill broadcast to his nation that Germany had surrendered. Afterward, Churchill told a huge crowd at Whitehall, "This is your victory." The people shouted back, "No, it is yours." They had in so many ways taken part in the show, the script, the battles, the performance. Then Churchill conducted them in the singing of "Land of Hope and Glory."

As Europe celebrated peace at the end of the six-year drama, Churchill was concerned that the performance would soon be interrupted before the last act was finished. He anticipated that the Red Army would ignore previously agreed frontiers and agreements in Europe, and rewrite the play with Russia taking a leading role.

Churchill wrote a subplot and, if it had played, Operation Unthinkable would have begun on July 1, 1945, with a sudden attack against the Allied Soviet troops stationed in Germany in order to carry out the script of Britain and the United States. The plan was rejected by the British Chiefs of Staff as militarily unfeasible.

With victory assured in Europe, the British government scheduled the nation's first general election in ten years. Churchill, who had led the British through five years of crises, offered to continue as a leader of a coalition.

But the opposition Labour Party, led by Major Clement Richard Attlee, a colorless, self-effacing, somewhat chilly little man who walked with a shuffle, refused the offer and campaigned vigorously against Churchill on a platform calling for immediate peacetime social reforms. At the Big Three Conference he looked, critics said, like Churchill's butler.

At the "Win with Winnie" rehearsal, the annual conference of the Conservative Party in London, Churchill made his entrance with the grandeur of royalty. The delegates waved agenda sheets in well-bred excitement and burst into a politically modulated "For He's a Jolly Good Fellow." Rosy-cheeked and beaming in a tailcoat and striped trousers, "Winnie" waved back. Then he launched into his speech, a masterly mixture of lofty patriotism and adroit politics. It was well-brushed and well-tailored, with well-timed metaphors: "We held aloft the flaming torch of freedom when all around the night was black as jet." By the time he reached his glowing finish, the leader had shown how he proposed to win the election. It sounded like a foolproof formula: "We have to carry on. We have to get our dear country on the move again and into full swing." But they were airy phases and windy platitudes. He was not reelected to serve. Many reasons have been given, key among them being that a desire for postwar reform was widespread among the population and the man who had led Britain in war was not the man to lead the nation in peace. In the minds of some, it was a forgotten lapse of appreciation to a man they had loved so much.

· · ·

To the palace the prime minister came to give King George VI a first-hand review of current events. There he waited for the election count. Next day, when the curtain came down, he went back to Buckingham Palace to resign and hand over to the king the seals of office. His Majesty offered him the Order of the Garter. Churchill refused the dignity. An hour later he issued a statement: "I have laid down the charge which was placed upon me in darkest times. I regret I have not been permitted to finish my work. It only remains for me to express to the British people, for whom I have acted in these perilous times, my profound gratitude for the unflinching and unswerving support which they have given me during my task and for the many expressions of kindness which they have shown towards me."

In defeat, there was no one could take from Winston Churchill a simple but undeniable the truth: seldom had so many owed so much to one man.

During his intermission, he won the Nobel Prize for literature, and soon roared back to power as prime minister.

• • •

Another play called *The Cold War* would soon premiere. The world would never be the same, but four men, leaders of four countries, would be remembered, each in their own way, writing a script for political theater, with a theme of national will, while spinning history.

# Invaluable Sources

⁕

*Citizen Soldiers: The U.S. Army from the Normandy Beaches to the Bulge to the Surrender of Germany* by Stephen Ambrose (New York: Simon and Schuster, 1998). A skillful blending of eyewitness accounts in World War II, combining history and journalism.

*All the President's Spin* by Ben Fritz, Bryan Keefer, and Brendan Nyhan (New York: Touchstone, 2004). The authors reduce George W. Bush's truth in media to a national debate on spin.

*Churchill and Secret Service* by David Stafford (New York: Overlook, 1997). Stafford compellingly details Sir Winston's ongoing fascination with spies, national intelligence, and secret warfare.

*Overlord, D-Day and the Battle for Normandy* by Max Hastings (New York: Simon and Schuster, 1984). Concentrating upon the Normandy Invasion, this popular book from a fine writer is a worthy addition to any military historian's library.

*The World at War, 1939–1945* by Max Hastings (New York: New York Times Books, 2012). A stunning single-volume history of the entire WWII conflict with striking detailed stories.

*The Nazi Dictatorship: Problems and Perspectives of Interpretation* by Ian Kershaw (London: Hodder Arnold, 1985). An academic classic, this is an erudite study of the Nazi dictatorship and the psychology used in the Third Reich. Updated as recently as 2000, but not meant for the general public.

*The Second World War* by John Keegan (New York: Penguin, 1989). Keegan's title focuses on war production, occupation, bombing, resistance, and espionage.

*The Rise and Fall of the Third Reich* by William Shirer (New York: Simon and Schuster, 1990). Shirer's monumental study of Hitler's German Empire has been acclaimed since its initial publication in 1960.

*D-Day, June 6, 1944: The Climactic Battle of World War II* by Stephen Ambrose (New York: Simon and Schuster, 1994). The classic and best-selling account of the day that changed the world.

*To Win the Peace: British Propaganda in the United States During World War II* by Susan Brewer (Ithaca, NY: Cornell University Press, 1977). Brewer writes about Britain's efforts to influence an American public to enter the war.

*Selling War: The British Propaganda Campaign against American "Neutrality" in World War II* by Nicholas Cull (New York: Oxford University Press, 1996). A scholarly analysis of America's isolationism and the ensuing propagandistic efforts by the United Kingdom to bring the American public around to their side.

*Black Boomerang* by Sefton Delmer (London: Secker and Warburg, 1962). Sefton Delmer, a London journalist, recounts in a memoir his contribution to the "black propaganda" radio stations organized to disseminate information to Germany in World War II.

*The History of Broadcasting in the United Kingdom. Volume III: The War of Words* by Asa Briggs (London: Oxford University Press, 1995). The third part of a five-volume history of broadcasting in the UK. Together with other volumes, the work is an authoritative account of the rise of broadcasting in the UK.

*The Intelligence and Deception of the D-Day Invasion* by Jock Haswell (London: B.T. Batsford, 1979). Author Haswell, who has written about British wartime intelligence, describes in detail the events of D-Day.

*Radio Goes to War: The Cultural Politics* of *Propaganda During World War II* by Gerd Horten (Berkeley: University of California Press, 2002). By focusing on the medium of radio during World War II, Horten provides a window into radio broadcasting and its impact on American domestic life during World War II.

*Bloodlands* by Timothy Snyder (New York: Basic Books, 2010). An important work of European history focusing on Hitler and Stalin; a stunning work of scholarship exploring mass killings in the twentieth century with powerful storytelling.

*The Collaboration: Hollywood's Pact with Hitler* by Ben Urwant (Cambridge, MA: Belknap Press, 2013.) An examination of the collaborative arrangement that remained in place through the 1930s, as Hollywood studios met regularly with the German consul in Los Angeles and would at times adapt subject matter and distribution according to the wishes of the German government.

*TIME Capsules: The Editors of Time, Inc. 1937–1945* (New York: TIME, 1967). A series of volumes condensed from the contents of *TIME*, the weekly news magazine.

# Bibliography

Abbazia, Patrick. *Mr. Roosevelt's Navy: The Little War of the United States Atlantic Fleet, 1939–1942 Part I*. New York: Columbia, 1972.

Abel, Theodore. "The Patterns of a Successful Political Movement," *American Social Review* 2, no. 3 (June 1937).

Albert, Ernst. "The Press in Nazi Germany," *Contemporary Review*, no. 447 (December 1938).

Alexander, Charles C. *Nationalism in American Thought*. Chicago: Rand McNally, 1969.

Arndt, K., and K.F. Reamers. *Albert Speer Speaks About Architecture and Dramatic Techniques of the National Socialist Self-Portrait*. Gottingen, West Germany: Institute for Scientific Film, 1975.

Arnoff, Joel. "Relations in Public: Micro-studies of the Public Order," *Sociological Quarterly* 14, no. 1 (Winter 1973).

Artaud, Antonin. *The Theater and Its Double*. New York: Grove Press, 1958.

Balfour, Michael. *Liberation*. Alexandria, VA: Time-Life Books, 1978.

Baream, Richard Meran. *Non-Fiction Film: A Critical History*. New York: E.P. Dutton, 1973.

Barnouw, Erik. *Radio Drama in Action: Twenty-Five Plays of a Changing World*. New York: Farrar and Rinehart, 1945.

Barranger, M.S. *Theater: A Way of Seeing*. Belmont, CA: Wadsworth Publishing, 1991.

Barry, Jackson G. *Dramatic Structure: The Shaping of Experience*. Berkeley: University of California Press; 1970.

Bauman, Benjamin. "George Herbert Mead and Luigi Pirandello; Some Parallels Between the Theoretic and Artistic Presentation of the Social Role Concept," *Social Research* 34, no. 3 (August 1967).

Becker, Howard. "The Nature and Consequences of Black Propaganda," *American Sociological Review* (April 14, 1949).

Bentley, Eric. *The Brecht Commentaries*. New York: Grove Press, 1987.

Berger, Peter L., and Thomas Luckman. *The Social Construction of Reality*. Englewood Cliffs, NJ: Prentice-Hall, 1966.

Biel, Richard. *The Emergence of a Dramaturgic Model: A Case Study*. PhD diss., City University of New York, 1971.

Bittner, Egon. "Radicalism and the Organization of Radical movements," *American Sociological Review* 28, no. 6 (December 1961).

Blumenson, Martin. *Liberation*. Alexandria, VA: Time-Life Books, 1978.

Blumer, Herbert. *Symbolic Interactionism: Perspective and Method*. Englewood Cliffs, NJ: Prentice-Hill, 1969.

———. "Action vs. Interaction," *Society* 9, no. 6 (April 1972).

Borland, Hal. "A Far Thought by Humans," *Saturday Review* (October 30, 1943).

Bradby, David, and John McCormick. *People's Theater*. London: Croom Helm, 1978.

Brenner, Hildegard. *The Cultural Policy of National Socialism*. Hamburg: Rowohlt Taschenbuchverlag, 1963.

Brisset, Dennis, and Charles Edgley (eds.). *Life as Theater: A Dramaturgical Sourcebook*. New York: Aldine de Gruyter, 1990.

Brockett, Oscar. *History of the Theatre*. New York: Holt, Rinehart & Winston, 1984.

———. *The Essential Theatre*. New York: Holt, Rinehart & Winston, 1985.

Brook, Peter. *The Empty Space*. New York: Athenaeum, 1968.

Brown, Anthony C. (ed.). *The Secret War Report of the O.S.S.* New York: Berkley Publishing, 1982.

Brown, Richard Harvey. *A Poetic for Sociology*. Cambridge: Cambridge University Press, 1977.

Bullock, A., and O. Stallybrass (eds). *The Harper Dictionary of Modern Thought*. New York: Harper & Row, 1977.

Burke, Kenneth. *A Grammar of Motives*. New York: Prentice-Hall, 1952.

———. *Permanence and Change*. Chicago: Bobbs-Merrill, 1965.

———. "Dramatism," *Encyclopedia of the Social Sciences*. New York: MacMillan and Free Press, 1968.

Burns, Elizabeth. *Theatricality: A Study of Convention in the Theater and in Social Life*. New York: Harper & Row, 1972.

Cantwell, John D. *Images of War—British Posters 1939–45*. London: Her Majesty's Stationery Office, 1989.

Capra, Frank. *The Name Above the Title*. New York: Macmillan, 1971.

Ceplair, Larry, and Steven Englund. *The Inquisition in Hollywood*. Garden City, NY: Doubleday Press, 1980.

Chapman, Ivan. "Social Interaction versus the Appearance of Social Interaction," *International Review of History and Political Science* 11, no. 2 (May 1974).

*Chronicle of the French Revolution 1788–1799*. London: Chronicle Publications, 1989.

Churchill, Douglas W. "Hollywood's Censor Is All the World," *New York Times*, March 29, 1936.

Churchill, Winston S. *The Second World War, vol. IV: The Hinge of Fate*. Boston: Houghton Mifflin, 1953.

Cochran, Larry. *Portrait and Story: Dramaturgical Approaches to the Study of Persons*. New York: Greenwood Press, 1986.

Cohen, Robert. *Theater*. Mountain View, CA: Mayfield Publishing, 1988.

Colgan, Christine Ann. *Warner Brothers' Crusade Against the Third Reich: A Study of Anti-Nazi Activism and Film Production 1933 to 1941*. University of Southern California, Dissertation, 1985.

Collier, Richard. *The Warcos: The War Correspondents of World War II*. London: Weidenfeld & Nicolson, 1989.

Combs, Jonathan E., and William Mansfield. *Drama in Life: The Uses of Communication in Society*. New York: Hastings House, 1976.

Conot, Robert E. *Justice at Nuremberg*. New York: HarperCollins, 1983.

Cooley, Charles Horton. *Human Nature and the Social Order*. New York: Scribner's, 1902.

Coser, Lewis A. *The Functions of Social Conflict*. Glencoe, IL: Free Press, 1956.

Cragan, John F., and Donald C. Shields. "Foreign Policy Dramas," *Quarterly Journal of Speech* 68, no. 3 (October 1977).

*Daily Express*. London, March 1940.

Dallek, Robert. *Franklin D. Roosevelt and American Foreign Policy*. New York: Oxford University Press, 1979.

Dalton, Hugh. *The Fateful Years*. London: Fredrick Miller, 1957.

Davie, Michael. *The Diaries of Evelyn Waugh*. Boston: Little, Brown & Company, 1976.

Denzin, Norman K. "Symbolic Interaction and Ethnomethodology," *Understanding Everyday Life*. Edited by Jack D. Douglas. Chicago: Aldine Press, 1970.

Dewey, Richard. "The Theatrical Analogy Reconsidered," *American Sociologist* 4, no. 4 (November 1969).

Dick, Bernard F. *The Star-Spangled Screen — The American World War II Film*. Lexington: University of Kentucky Press, 1985.

Donald, Ralph R. *Hollywood & World War II: Enlisting Feature Films as Propaganda*. Dissertation, University of Massachusetts–Amherst, 1987.

Doob, Leonard W. *Public Opinion and Propaganda*. Hamden, CT: Archon Books, 1966.

Dornbusch, Sanford. "The Military Academy as an Assimilating Institution," *Social Forces* 33, no. 3 (May 1955).

Duncan, Hugh Dalziel. *Communication and Social Order*. New York: Oxford University Press, 1962.

———. *Symbols in Society*. New York: Oxford University Press, 1968.

Dunlop, Richard. *Donovan: America's Master Spy*. New York: Rand-McNally, 1982.

Durant, Henry, and Ruth Durant. "Lord Haw-Haw of Hamburg: 2, His British Audience," *Public Opinion Quarterly* 4 (September 1940).

Easton, David. *The Political System*. New York: Alfred A. Knopf, 1953.

Edelman, Martin. *The Symbolic Uses of Politics*. Urbana: University of Illinois Press, 1964.

Edgley, Charles, and Ralph Turner. "Mask and Social Relations: An Essay on the Sources and Assumptions of Dramaturgical Social Psychology," *Humboldt Journal of Social Relations* 3, no. 1 (Winter 1975).

Editors of Time-Life Books. *Shadow of the Dictators–Time Frame AD 1925–1950*. Alexandria, VA: Time-Life Books, 1989.

Ehrman, John. *History of the Second World War*. London: Her Majesty's Stationery Office, 1956.

Eilenberg, Lawrence I. "Dramaturgy and Spectacle: A Sense of Proportion", *Journal of Aesthetic Education* 9, no. 4 (October 1975).

Eisenhower Foundation. *D-Day: The Normandy Invasion in Retrospect*. Lawrence: University of Kansas Press, 1971.

Ellul, Jacques. *Propaganda: The Formation of Men's Attitudes*. New York: Vintage Books, 1972.

Elson, Robert T. *Prelude to War*. Alexandria, VA: Time-Life Books, 1977.

Esslin, Martin. *Bertolt Brecht*. New York: Columbia University Press, 1969.

———. *An Anatomy of Drama*. London: Temple Smith, 1976.

———. *The Field of Drama*. London, New York: Methuen, 1987.

Evreinhoff, Nikolai Nikolaevich. *The Theater in Life*. New York: Benjamin Blom, 1927.

Farberman, Harvey. "A Criminogenic Market Structure: The Automobile Industry," *Sociological Quarterly* 17, no. 4 (Autumn 1975).

Felson, Richard B. "Impression Management and Escalation of Aggression Violence," *Social Psychology Quarterly* 45, no. 4 (December 1982).

Ferguson, Francis. *The Idea of Theater*. New York: George Braziller, 1975.

Ferraro, Kathleen, and John M. Ferraro. "The New Underground Railroad," *Studies in Symbolic Interaction*. Edited by Norman K. Denzin. Greenwich, CT: Jai Press, 1984.

Fitch, James M. "The Future of Architecture," *Journal of Aesthetic Education* 4, no. 1 (January 2, 1980).

Ford, Corey. *Donovan of OSS*. Boston: Little, Brown & Company, 1970.

Fox, Frank W. *Madison Avenue Goes to War: The Strange Military Career of American Advertising 1941–45*. Provo, UT: Brigham Young University, 1975.

Frye, Northrop. *Anatomy of Criticism*. Princeton, NJ: Princeton University, 1957.

Fussell, Paul. *Wartime*. New York: Oxford University Press, 1989.

Gamson, William A. "Frame Analysis: An Essay on the Organization of Experience," *Contemporary Sociology* 4, no. 6 (November 1975).

Geertz, Clifford. "Blurred Genres: The Refiguration of Social Thought," *Local Knowledge: Further Essays in Interpretive Anthropology*. New York: Basic Books, 1983.

Gillespie, Joanna B. "The Phenomenon of the Public Wife: An Exercise in Goffman's Impression Management," *Life as Theater: A Dramaturgical Sourcebook*. Edited by Dennis Brissett and Charles Edgley. New York: Aldine de Gruyter, 1990.

Glass, Fiona, and Philip Marsden-Smedley, eds. *Articles of War – The Spectator Book of World War II*. London: Grafton Books, 1989.

Glatzer, Richard, and John Raeburn, eds. *Frank Capra: The Man and His Films*. Ann Arbor: University of Michigan Press, 1975.

Goffman, Erving. *The Presentation of Self in Everyday Life*. New York: Doubleday & Company, 1959.

———. *Relations in Public*. New York: Basic Books, 1971.

———. *Frame Analysis: An Essay on the Organization of Experience*. New York: Harper and Row, 1974.

Gouldner, Alvin Ward. *The Coming Crisis of Western Sociology*. London: Heinemann, 1970.

Graves, Harold N. "Lord Haw-Haw of Hamburg: 1, The Campaign Against Britain," *Public Opinion Quarterly* 4 (September 1940).

———. "Propaganda by Short Wave: Berlin Calling America," *Public Opinion Quarterly* 45, no. 4 (Fall 1978).

Gronbeck, Bruce E. "The Functions of Presidential Campaigning", *Communication Monographs* 4, no. 4 (Fall 1978).

———. "Dramaturgical Theory and Criticism. The State of the Art (or Sciences)," *Western Journal of Speech Communication* 44, no. 4 (Fall 1980).

Grose, B. Donald, and Franklin O. Kenworthy. *A Mirror to Life: A History of Western Theater.* New York: Holt, Rinehart & Winston, 1985.

Gunther, John. *D-Day.* New York: Harper & Brothers, 1944.

Gusfield, Joseph. *Symbolic Crusade.* Chicago: University of Illinois Press, 1963.

————. "A Dramatic Theory of Status Politics," *Life as Theater.* Edited by Dennis Brisset and Charles Edgley. Chicago: Aldine, 1975.

————. *The Culture of Public Problems.* Chicago: University of Chicago, 1981.

Haas, Jack. "Learning Real Feelings: A Study of High Steel Ironworkers' Reactions to Fear and Danger," *Shaping Identity in Canadian Society.* Scarborough, Ontario: Prentice Hall, 1978.

Haining, Peter. *The Day War Broke Out: 3 September 1939.* New York. W.H. Allen, 1989.

Hall, Peter M. "A Symbolic Interactionist Analysis of Politics," *Sociological Inquiry* 42, nos. 3-4 (1972).

Hall, Peter M., and John P. Hewitt. "The Quasi-Theory of Communications and the Management of Dissent," *Social Problems* 18, no. 1 (Summer 1970).

Hanin, Eric Michael. *War on Our Minds: The American Mass Media in World War II.* Thesis, University of Rochester, 1976.

Hare, A. Paul. "A Dramaturgical Analysis of Street Demonstrations: Washington, D.C., 1971 and Cape Town, 1976," *Group Psychotherapy, Psychodrama and Sociometry* 33, no. 1 (January 1980).

————. *Social Interaction as Drama: Applications from Conflict Resolution.* Beverly Hills, CA: Sage Publications, 1985.

Hare, A. Paul, and Herbert J. Blumberg. *Dramaturgical Analysis of Social Interaction.* New York: Praeger Scientific, 1988.

Harlan, Veit. *Records of the Reichspropagandaleitung-Hauptant Film*, World War II Records Division of the National Archives, Alexandria, Virginia.

Harre, Romano. *Social Being: A Theory for Social Psychology.* Oxford: Basil Blackwell, 1979.

Harre, Romano, and J.P. DeWaele. "The Ritual Incorporation of the Stranger," *Life Sentences.* Edited by Romano Harre. London: John Wiley, 1976.

Harrison, Gordon A. *United States Army in World War II—European Theater of Operations: Cross-Channel Attack*. Washington, DC: US Government Printing Office, 1984.

Harrison, Tom. "Living Through the Blitz." More Books, *Horizon 4*, no. 74 (December 1941).

Harwood, Ronald. *All the World's a Stage*. London: Secker & Warburg, 1984.

Hastings, Max. *Overlord: D-Day and the Battle for Normandy*. New York: Simon & Schuster, 1984.

Haswell, Jock. *The Intelligence and Deception of the D-Day Landings*. London: B.T. Batsford, 1979.

Hayes, Michael T. "Incrementalism as Dramaturgy: The Case Study of the Nuclear Freeze," *Polity* 19, no. 3 (Spring 1987).

Hayman, Ronald. *Bertolt Brecht—The Plays*. London: Heinemann, 1984.

Hays, William H. *Self-Regulation in the Motion Picture Industry*. New York: Motion Picture Producers & Distributors of America, 1938.

Heilman, Samuel C. *Synagogue Life: A Study of Symbolic Interaction*. Chicago: University of Chicago, 1976.

Heiss, Jerold. *The Psychology of Social Interaction*. Englewood Cliffs, NJ: Prentice-Hall, 1981.

Hewison, Robert. *Under Siege: Literary Life in London 1939–45*. London: Methuen, 1988.

Hindson, Paul, and Tim Gray. *Burke's Dramatic Theory of Politics*. Avebury Series in Philosophy. Brookville, VT: Gower Publishing Company, 1988.

Hitler, Adolph. *Mein Kampf,* translated by Ralph Manheim. Boston: Houghton Mifflin, 1943.

Hopper, Michael. "Five Key Concepts of the Dramaturgical Perspective," *Free Inquiry in Creative Sociology* 11, no. 2 (Spring 1981).

Horan, Don. *War Chronicles*. New York: Richardson & Stierman, 1988.

Horsfield, John Arnold. *The Art of Leadership in War: The Royal Navy from the Age of Nelson to the End of World War II*. Westport, CT: Greenwood Press, 1980.

Howe, Ellie. *The Black Game*. London: Michael Joseph, 1982.

Huber, Joan. "Symbolic Interaction as a Pragmatic Perspective: The Bias of Emergent Theory," *American Sociological Review* 38, no. 2 (April 1973).

Huggett, Frank E. *Goodnight Sweetheart: Songs & Memories of the Second World War*. London: W.H. Allen, 1979.

Huie, William Bradford. *Can Do!* New York: E.P. Dutton & Company, 1945.

———. *The Case Against the Admirals*. New York: E.P. Dutton & Company, 1946.

———. *The Americanization of Emily*. The New American Library, 1960.

Ichheiser, Gustav. "Misunderstanding in Human Relations: A Study in False Perception," *American Journal of Sociology* 55, no. 2 (1949).

———. *Appearances and Realities*. San Francisco: Jossey-Bass, 1970.

Jarrell, Randall. "Ernie Pyle," *The Nation*, May 19, 1945.

Jenkins, H.H. *The Diction of 'Yank': Colloquial Speech of the American Soldier of World War II as Found in* Yank *Magazine*. PhD dissertation, University of Florida, 1957.

Jones, Edmund. *Dramatic Interaction: Reflections and Speculation on the Art of Theater*. New York: Duell, Sloan and Pearce, 1941.

Kanter, Rosabeth Moss. "Symbolic Interactionism and Politics in System Perspective," *Sociological Inquiry* 42, nos. 3-4 (1972).

Kennedy, Emmet. *A Cultural History of the French Revolution*. New Haven, CT: Yale University Press, 1989.

Klapp, Orrin. *Ritual and Cult*. Washington, DC: Public Affairs Press, 1957.

———. *Heroes, Villains and Fools*. Englewood Cliffs, NJ: Prentice-Hall, 1962.

———. *Symbolic Leaders*. Chicago: Aldine, 1964.

Klein, Bolger, ed. *The Second World War in Fiction*. New York: Macmillan, 1984.

Kolb, Deborah. "To Be a Mediator: Expressive Tactics in Mediation," *Life as Theater: A Dramaturgical Sourcebook*. Edited by Dennis Brissett and Charles Edgley. New York: Aldine de Gruyter, 1990.

Le Carré, John. *A Perfect Spy*. New York: Bantam, 1986.

Lahr, John, and Jonathan Price. *Life-Show: How to See Theater in Life and Life in Theater.* New York: Viking Press, 1973.

Lane, Barbara M. *Architecture and Politics in Germany, 1918–1945.* Cambridge, MA: Harvard University Press, 1968.

Lapham, Lewis. "America's Foreign Policy," *Harper Magazine* (March 1979).

Laqueur, Walter Z. *Young Germany: A History of the German Youth Movement.* London: Basic Books, 1962.

Larson, Cedric. "The German Press Chamber," *Public Opinion Quarterly* 1, no. 2(October 1937).

Lessing, Gotthold Ephraim. "Contributions to the History and Reception of German Theater." *Hamburg Dramaturgy.* New York: Dover 1962.

Levine, Robert H. "Why the Ethnogenic Method and the Dramaturgical Perspective Are Incompatible," *Journalism for the Theory of Social Behavior* 72, no. 2 (October 1970).

Library of Congress. *Performing Arts Annual –1987.* Washington, DC: US Government Printing Office, 1987.

Lochner, Louis P. *The Goebbels Diaries.* Garden City, NY: Doubleday, 1948.

Lofland, John. "Open and Concealed Dramaturgic Strategies: The Case of State Execution," *Urban Life* 4, no. 2 (October 1975).

———. "Erving Goffman's Sociological Legacies," *Urban Life* 13, no. 1 (April 1984).

MacLeish, Archibald. "The Psychological Front," *Vital Speeches* 8, no. 14 (May 1942).

Maines, David R. "Mesostructure and Social Process," *Contemporary Sociology* 8, no. 3 (May 1979).

———. "In Search of Mesostructure," *Urban Life* 11, no. 3 (October 1982).

Mangham, Iain L., and Michael Overington. "Performance and Rehearsal: Social Order and Organizational Life," *Symbolic Interaction* 5, no. 2 (Fall 1982).

Manning, Peter K. "Dramatic Aspects of Policing: Selected Propositions," *Sociology and Social Research* 61 (October 1974).

———. "Producing Drama: Symbolic Communication and the Police." *Symbolic Interaction* 5, no. 2 (Fall, 1982).

Mayo, James M. "Propaganda with Design," *Life as Theater: A Dramaturgical Sourcebook*. Edited by Dennis Brissett and Charles Edgley. New York: Aldine de Gruyter, 1990.

McCan, Richard Dyer. *The People's Film: A History of U.S. Government Motion Pictures*. New York: Hastings House, 1973.

McGranahan, Donald V. "U.S. Psychological Warfare Policy," *Public Opinion Quarterly* 10 (Fall 1946).

Meltzer, Bernard, John Petras, and Larry T. Reynolds. *Symbolic Interactionism*. London: Routledge & Kegan Paul, 1975.

Merelman, Richard M. "The Dramaturgy of Politics," *Sociological Quarterly* 10, no. 2. (Spring 1969).

Messinger, Sheldon, Harold Sampson, and Robert D. Towne. "Life as Theater: Some Notes on the Dramaturgical Approaches to Social Reality," *Sociometry* 25, no. 1 (March 1962).

Miller, Clyde. "Radio and Propaganda," *The Annals of the American Academy of Political and Social Sciences* 213 (January 1941).

Miller, Lee G. *The Story of Ernie Pyle*. New York: Viking Press, 1950.

Miller, Nathan. *The U.S. Navy: An Illustrated History*. New York: American Heritage Publishing, 1977.

Mitchell, Jack N. *Social Exchange, Dramaturgy, and Ethnomethodology*. New York: Elsevier Science, 1978.

Mixon, Donald. "Instead of Deception," *Journal for the Theory of Social Behavior* 2, no. 2 (October 1972).

Montagu, Ewen. *The Man Who Never Was*. New York: Scholastic, 1971.

*Moral Obligation and the Military—Collected Essays*. Washington, DC: National Defense University Press. 1988.

Morella, Joe, Edward Z. Epstein, and John Griggs. *The Films of World War II*. Secaucus, NJ: Citadel Press, 1973.

Morgan, Brewster. "Operation Annie," *Saturday Evening Post* 218, no. 36 (March 9, 1946).

Mosley, Leonard. *The Battle of Britain*. Alexandria, VA: Time-Life Books, 1977.

Murray, Kevin. "Life as Fiction," *Journal for the Theory of Social Behavior* 15, no. 2 (July 1985).

Murrow, Edward R. CBS Broadcast, 1939.

Nathan, George Jean. *Encyclopedia of the Theater*. New York: Alfred A. Knopf, 1940.

Needle, Jan, and Peter Thomson. *Brecht*. Chicago: University of Chicago Press, 1981.

O'Brien, Connor Cruise. Address at Trinity College, Dublin, 1990.

Olsen, Elder. *Tragedy and the Theory of Drama*. Detroit: Wayne State University Press, 1961.

Overington, Michael, and Ian L. Mangham. "The Theatrical Perspective in Organizational Analysis," *Symbolic Interaction* 5, no. 2 (Fall 1982); 3, no. 1 (January, 1939).

Overy, Richard, ed. *New York Times Complete World War 2*. New York: Black Dog & Leventhal, 2013.

———. *Britain at War*. London: IWM in association with Carlton Publishing, 2011.

Owen, David. *The Battle of Wits*. London: Leo Cooper, 1978.

Padover, S.K. "The Nazi Cinema," *Public Opinion Quarterly* 3, no. 1 (January 1939).

Palmer, Wayne Francis. *Men and Ships of Steel*. New York: William Morrow & Company, 1935.

Perinbanayagam, Robert S. *Signifying Acts*. Carbondale: Southern Illinois University, 1985.

Pirandello, Luigi. *Six Characters in Search of an Author*. Translated by Frederick May. London: Heinemann, 1954.

Posner, Judith. "Erving Goffman: His Presentation of Self," *Philosophy of the Social Sciences* 8 (1978).

Price, Byron. "Government Censorship in War-Time," *American Political Science Review* 36, no. 5 (October 1942).

Psathas, Gary. "Goffman's Image of Man," *Humanity and Society* 1, no. 1 (January 1977).

Puleston, W.D. "Blunders of World War II," *United States News & World Report*, February 4, 1955.

Pyle, Ernie. *Here Is Your War*. New York: Holt, 1943.

Ramthun, Herta, and John Willett. *Bertolt Brecht: Diaries 1920–1922*. New York: St. Martin's Press, 1979.

Reader's Digest Association. *The World at Arms*. London: Reader's Digest, 1989.

Reich, Wilhelm. *The Mass Psychology of Fascism*. New York: Simon & Schuster, 1970.

Renfro, Robert Bruce. *Three American Novelists at War: The World War II Journalism of Steinbeck, Caldwell and Hemingway*. Dissertation, University of Texas at Austin, 1984.

Ritti, R.R., and J.H. Silver. "Early Processes of Institutionalization: The Dramaturgy of Exchange in Inter-organizational Relations," *Administrative Science Quarterly* 31, no. 1 (Spring 1986).

Robertson, J.G. *Lessing's Dramatic Theory*. New York: Columbia University Press, 1939.

Rock, Paul Elliott. *The Making of Symbolic Interactionism*. Totowa, NJ: Rowman and Littlefield, 1982.

Roelter, Charles. *The Art of Psychological Warfare*. New York: Stein and Day, 1974.

Rogers, Mary G. "Goffman and Power," *American Sociologist* 12, no. 2 (April 1977).

Roosevelt, Franklin D. "State of the Union Address." PPAFDR, January 6, 1941.

Rose, Arnold. *Human Behavior and Social Processes*. Boston: Houghton Mifflin, 1962.

Rosenau, James N. *The Drama of Politics*. Boston: Little, Brown and Company, 1973.

Rosenman, Samuel I. *The Public Papers and Addresses of Franklin Delano Roosevelt* (PPAFDR) 1944–45.

Rosten, Leo C. *Hollywood: The Movie Colony. The Movie Makers*. New York: Harcourt, Brace & Company, 1941.

Rotha, Paul. *Documentary Film*. 3d ed. London: Faber and Faber, 1952.

Ryan, Alan. "Maximizing, Moralizing and Dramatizing," *Action and Interpretation: Studies in the Philosophy of the Social Sciences*. Edited by C. Hookway and P. Petit. Cambridge: Cambridge University Press, 1978.

———. "A Theory for Goffman," *New Society* 51, no. 1 (January 1980).

Sacks, Harvey. "Button, Button, Who's Got the Button," *Sociological Inquiry* 50, nos. 3–4 (June 1980).

Sarbin, Theodore. "Contextualism: A World Psychology," *Nebraska Symposium on Motivation*. Edited by A.W. Lanfield. Lincoln: University of Nebraska, 1977.

Sarris, Andrew. *Interviews with Film Directors*. Indianapolis: Bobbs-Merrill, 1967.

Saunders, Daniel Mark. "Drama and Simulation," *Simulation and Games* 17, no. 1 (March 1986).

Schechner, Richard. *Between Anthropology and Theater*. Philadelphia: Philadelphia Press, 1985.

Schechner, Richard, and Michael Schuman, eds. *Ritual, Play and Performance: Readings in the Social Science/Theater*. New York: Seabury Press, 1976.

Schoeps, Karl H. *Bertolt Brecht*. New York: Frederick Ungar Publishing, 1977.

Schur, Norman W. *British English A to Zed*. New York: Facts on File, 1977.

Sellin, Eric. *The Dramatic Concepts of Antonin Artaud*. Chicago: University of Chicago Press, 1968.

Selznick, Philip. *The Organizational Weapon*. Glencoe, IL: Free Press of Glencoe, 1952.

Shakespeare, William. *Henry V*. New York: Washington Square Press, 1960.

Shirer, William L. *Berlin Diary*. New York: Alfred A. Knopf, 1941.

———. *The Rise and Fall of the Third Reich*. New York: Simon & Schuster, 1960.

Sinclair, Thornton. "The Nazi Party Rally at Nuremberg," *Public Opinion Quarterly* 2, no. 4 (October 1938).

Smith, Godfrey, ed. *How It Was in the War*. London: Pavilion Books, 1989.

Snow, David A., Louis A. Zurcher, and Robert Peters. "Victory Celebrations as Theater: A Dramaturgical Approach to Crowd Behavior," *Symbolic Interaction* IV, no. 1 (Spring 1981).

Soley, Lawrence C. *Radio Warfare—OSS and CIA Subversive Propaganda*. New York: Praeger Publishers, 1989.

Sorokin, Petirim. *Sociological Theories of Today*. New York: Harper and Row, 1965.

*Spandau: The Secret Diaries*. New York: MacMillan, 1975.

Speer, Albert. *Inside the Third Reich*. New York: MacMillan, 1970.

Speier, Hans. "The Future of Psychological Warfare," *Public Opinion Quarterly* 12 (Spring 1948).

———. "War Aims in Political Warfare," *Social Research* 12, no. 2 (May 1945).

Stanislavski, Constantin. *Building a Character*, translated by Elizabeth Reynolds Hapgood. New York: Theater Art Books, 1949.

Stebbins, Robert A. "Putting People On: Deception of Our Fellowman in Everyday Life," *Sociology and Social Research* 59, no. 3 (April 1975).

Steele, Richard. "Preparing the Public for War: Efforts to Establish a National Propaganda Agency, 1940–41," *American Historical Review* 75 (October 1970).

Stoll, Donald Robert. *The Dramaturgy of Propaganda: Charles Rann Kennedy (1871–1950)*. PhD Dissertation. Indiana University, 1983.

Stone, Gregory P., and Harvey E. Farberman. *Social Psychology Through Symbolic Interaction*. New York: MacMillan, 1986.

Strasser, Otto. *Hitler and I*. New York: AMS Press, 1940.

Strauss, Anselm. *Mirrors and Masks*. New York: Free Press, 1959.

———. *Negotiations*. San Francisco: Jossey-Bass, 1978.

Strauss, Anselm, ed. *George Herbert Mead on Social Psychology*. Chicago: University of Chicago, 1964.

Strong, Tracy B. "Dramaturgical Discourse and Political Enactments: Toward an Artistic Foundation for Political Space," *Structure, Consciousness and History*. Edited by Richard Harvey Brown and

Stanford M. Lyman. Cambridge: Cambridge University Press, 1978.

Stryker, Sheldon. *Symbolic Interactionism: A Social Structural Version*. Menlo Park, CA: Benjamin/Cummings, 1980.

———. "The Theatrical Metaphor: Can It Aid Conflict Resolution?" *Contemporary Psychology* 32, no. 7 (July 1987).

Sutherland, Edwin H., and Donald R. Cressey. *Criminology*. Philadelphia: J.B. Lippincott, 1970.

Sweetman, Jack. *American Naval History*. Annapolis, MD: Naval Institute Press, 1984.

Szanto, George H. *Theater & Propaganda*. Austin: University of Texas, 1978.

Tannenbaum, Frank. "Definitions and the Dramatization of Evil," *Deviant Behavior: Reading in the Sociology of Deviance*. Edited by Dolos H. Kelly. New York: St. Martin's Press, 1979.

Taylor, Robert R. *The Word in Stone: The Role of Architecture in National Socialist Ideology*. Berkeley: University of California Press, 1974.

*This Fabulous Century: 1930–1940*. New York: Time-Life Books, 1969.

Tobin, James Edward. *Why We Fight: Versions of the American Purpose in World War II*. PhD Dissertation, University of Michigan, 1986.

Townsend, Colin, and Eileen Townsend. *War Wives*. London: Grafton Books, 1989.

Tregaskis, Richard. *Guadalcanal Diary*. New York: Popular Library, 1959.

Turner, Ralph. "Role-Taking: Process versus Conformity," *Human Behavior and Social Process*. Edited by Arnold Rose. Boston: Houghton Mifflin, 1962.

Turner, Ralph, and Lewis M. Killian. *Collective Behavior*. New York: Prentice-Hall, 1972.

Turner, Victor. *Symbolic Action in Human Society*. Ithaca, NY: Cornell University Press, 1974.

United States Federal Communications Commission, Foreign Broadcast Intelligence Service, Secret Special Report, No. 58, Washington: Federal Communication, 22 March.

United States War Department, Historical Division. *Omaha Beachhead (6 June–13 June 1944)*. Washington, DC: Center of Military History, 1984.

Voskeritchian, Thomas D. *Communication as Drama: The Dramaturgical Idea in the Work of Kenneth Burke, Hugh Duncan and Erving Goffman*. PhD dissertation, University of Iowa, 1981.

Waldmeir, Joseph. *American Novels of the Second World War*. The Hague: Mouton, 1969.

Ward, Geoffrey. *The Roosevelts*. New York: Alfred A. Knopf, 2014.

Waugh, Evelyn. *Men at Arms*. London: Penguin Books, 1988.

Weinberg, Sydney Stahl. *Wartime Propaganda in a Democracy*. PhD dissertation, Columbia University, 1969.

Weiss, Paul R., and Robert R. Faulkner. "Credits and Craft Production: Freelance Social Organization in the Hollywood Film Industry," *Symbolic Interaction* 6, no. 1 (Spring 1983).

Wernick, Robert. *Blitzkrieg*. Alexandria, VA: Time-Life Books, 1977.

Whiting, Charles. *The Home Front: Germany – World War II*. Alexandria, VA: Time-Life Books, 1982.

Willett, John. *Brecht on Theater – The Development of an Aesthetic*. New York: Hill & Wang, 1964.

Willis, Jeffrey Robert. *The Wehrmacht Propaganda Branch: German Military Propaganda and Censorship During WWII*. PhD thesis, University of Virginia, 1964.

Wilshire, Bruce. "Role Playing and Identity: The Limits of the Theatrical Metaphor," *Cultural Hermeneutics* 4, no. 2 (Summer 1977).

———. "The Dramaturgical Model of Behavior: Its Strengths and Weaknesses," *Symbolic Interaction* 5, no. 2 (Fall 1982).

———. *Role-Playing and Identity: The Limits of Theater as Metaphor*. Bloomington: Indiana University Press, 1982.

Wind, Edgar. *Art and Anarchy*. New York: Alfred A. Knopf, 1965.

Winkler, Allan M. *The Politics of Propaganda: The Office of War Information, 1942–1945*. New Haven: Yale University Press, 1978.

Wyman, David S. *The Abandonment of the Jews: America and the Holocaust 1941–1945*. New York: Pantheon, 1984.

Young, Thomas R., and George Massey. "The Dramaturgical Society: A Macro-Analytical Approach to Dramaturgical Analysis," *Qualitative Sociology* 1, no. 1 (Spring 1977).

Young, Thomas R., and John Welsh. *Critical Dimensions in Dramaturgical Analysis*. Lubbock, Texas: Red Feather Press, 1984.

Zortman, Bruce. *Hitler's Theater: Ideological Drama in Nazi Germany*. El Paso, Texas: Firestein Books, 1984.

Zurcher, Louis A. "The Sailor Aboard Ship: A Study of Role Behavior in a Total Institution," *Social Forces* 43, no. 4 (July 1965).

———. "The Naval Recruit Training Center: A Study of Roll Assimilation in a Total Institution," *Sociological Inquiry* 38, no. 1 (Winter 1967).

———. "The Staging of Emotions: A Dramaturgical Analysis," *Symbolic Interaction* 5, no. 1 (Spring 1982).

———. "The War Game: Organizational Scripting and the Expression of Emotion," *Symbolic Interaction* 8, no. 2 (Fall 1985).

# Acknowledgments

⸺⧟⧟⧟⸺

The making of a book is a collaborative effort. I'm indebted to Professor John McCormick of Trinity College Dublin, scholar, dramatist, and historian, who chaired my doctoral committee; the brilliant Karl French, friend and editor who graced the pages of this book, always respectful to its academic underpinnings, guiding the narrative from dissertation to trade readership. Tarah Baiman, whose artful words over the years are indelible; Peter Beren, editorial consultant, who offered up an engaging title, and with comprehensive scholarship, helped craft an editorial blueprint; Rebecca Swift and Aki Schilz of The Literary Consultancy, whose direction is coupled with insightful support; Mark Malatesta, a smart and wise literary counselor; Alexandra Lange, whose archival photographic research at the Library of Congress is effective and essentially perfect; Literary Agent Maryann Karinch, an exceptional literary talent, who complements the publishing experience with ineffable admiration; Olga Greco, who with an easy editorial hand, spirited the narrative home; and to Andrew and Natalya Lande, whose patience and love encourage every book. My appreciation and gratitude to you all for your contribution.

# Index

# Other Books by Nathaniel Lande

---∞∞∞---

Cricket, A Novel

Mindstyles, Lifestyles: A Comprehensive Overview of Today's Life Changing Philosophies

Stages: Understanding How You Make Moral Decisions

Self Health: The Lifelong Fitness Book

The Emotional Maintenance Manual

The Moral Responsibility of the Press

Blueprinting: Rebuilding Your Relationships and Career

The Cigar Connoisseur: An Illustrated History and Guide to the World's Finest Cigars

Dispatches from the Front: A History of the American War Correspondent

The Ten Best of Everything: An Ultimate Guide for Travelers

The Life and Times of Homer Sincere Whose Amazing Adventures Are Documented by his True and Trusted Friend Rigby Canfield: An American Novel